GETTING INDEPENDENT!

GETTING INDEPENDENT!

A Proven Entrepreneur's Guide to Starting Your Own Successful Business

FRED N. GRAYSON

To my parents, who always encouraged me to be my own boss. To Nancy, Scott, Deborah, and Andrew, who made the sacrifices when necessary. To Leo Lipkin and Gordon Felton, who provided my professional education. To David Russell, Jr., partner and friend, who helped bring my vision into focus.

Quotation from *Kramer Versus Kramer*, by Avery Corman, Copyright © Random House, Inc.

Copyright © 1981 by Grayson Russell, Inc.

Cover design copyright © 1981 by New Century Publishers, Inc. a subsidiary of New Century Education Corporation.

Cover and Text Design by Arlene Kosarin

Printing Code: 11 12 13 13 14 15 16

Library of Congress Cataloging in Publication Data

Grayson, Fred N.
  Getting independent.

  "A Grayson-Russell book."
  1. Success.   2. Small business—Management.
3. Self-employed.   I. Title.
HF5386.G68   658.1'141   81-2031
                               AACR2
ISBN 0-8329-0110-5

Printed in United States of America

Table of Contents

GETTING INDEPENDENT!

Introduction

Would you like to get independent? When you finish this book you will have the basic knowledge needed to start on the road to financial and personal independence.

No longer will you be concerned about promotions and raises. No more worries about office competition and politics. Forget about those union rules, regulations, and graded increases. Vacations can be yours, wherever and whenever you choose. Automobiles, summer homes, boats and fancy restaurants, once only a dream, are within your reach.

Do you have to be a genius? Is it necessary to start with a lot of money? Are connections important? What about experience? The answer to these questions is an emphatic, "NO!" You do need two things: an idea of what you *want* to do, and the *desire* to succeed.

Why This Book?

I spent sixteen years of my life taking orders from teachers in school, two years taking orders in the Air Force, and six more years taking orders from a variety of bosses. By the time I turned thirty, I'd had my fill of working for other people, and taking orders. I was also frustrated by the large amount of work I did compared to the small amount of money I brought home. Twice I was fired because the companies I worked for were having financial problems. Enough was enough! I decided to start my own business.

I am now my own boss. I own several different companies, including a publishing company, a mail order business, and a video production company. I teach budding entrepreneurs the art of starting businesses, and I am a business consultant. I realized that more people could benefit from my experience if I wrote a book that everyone could use as a guide to success. This book has been based on my own personal experiences to help you. I have also included stories of others who have succeeded, merely because they really wanted to.

How To Use This Book

The book is divided into two major sections. The first deals with six basic areas of business with specific businesses singled out as examples. Read about each area slowly. Try to match your interests with some of the job requirements I have listed. The final section is a double bonus. It deals with mail order. It can be a business on its own (and truly a field that can create overnight successes) and it can be an effective technique for promoting any other business you may decide to enter.

Part Two contains the business basics—how to start and run a successful business, whatever that business may be. You will receive clear, step-by-step procedures for your business that will help you avoid many of the common mistakes that many new business persons make.

My overall desire, however, is to create a reference source that you can use whenever you have a question or face a problem. Each chapter in Part Two will provide you with information. Use it as your personal resource. At first, this wealth of information may seem overwhelming to you—but don't get discouraged. Put the book on your reference shelf and go back to it at your leisure. Select those chapters that are relevant to you, and see how impressed you are with how much you learn along the way. Eventually, you will find that this book has become the cornerstone of your new career.

Good luck!

PART ONE

Getting Independent

Since you spent your hard-earned money to purchase this book, my guess is that you've had enough of working for others. It's time to say goodbye to the day-to-day routine of nine-to-five. It's time to become your own boss and start on the road to independence and financial security.

Can it still happen? Are the days of the self-made millionaires over? Not at all. If you read any of the business publications you will discover hundreds of new success stories every day. Naturally, many successful people, both men and women, are hesitant to discuss their success and wealth; thus, you don't hear about many of them. Others willingly tell their stories; some of them you will read about in this book.

There are also those people who started part-time businesses, hesitant to give up the security of the regular paycheck. Many of these individuals still are supplementing their regular income with the proceeds of their own "moonlight" businesses. They are able to take extra vacations, buy another car, and generally enjoy the benefits of their own part-time operations.

You can control your future. It is up to you to determine the amount of time you want to devote to *your* business. Remember, it is your effort that will determine the amount of money you earn. Let's look at a very typical success story—one that can be yours.

Robert Whitman was an editor for a well-known publishing company. He had worked in the field for almost eleven years. In his struggle to reach the position of editor-in-chief, he had passed through many of the different departments that make up a publishing company: contracts, rights, marketing assistant, assistant editor, senior editor, and finally, editor-in-chief. He was competent and successful.

The only real problem was that he didn't earn as much money as he felt someone in his position should earn. Also, publishing is a low-profit industry, and thus pays lower salaries. Although he received regular salary increases, they barely kept him ahead of the inflationary spiral.

One day while sorting through some recipes, he thought about publishing a vegetarian cookbook. He proposed his idea at the next editorial board meeting.

"*Another* vegetarian cookbook," the sales manager moaned. "There's no more room on the bookstore shelves for another cookbook."

Everyone, including Robert, agreed. "What about mail order?" he suggested.

"I don't have the budget," said the marketing director.

A few weeks later Robert thought about the project again. He agreed there were too many cookbooks in bookstores, but, perhaps there was another way to produce a "different" cookbook. He finally hit on the idea to combine daily vegetarian meal plans with a calendar. However, when he presented the idea to his company, it was again vetoed. Instead of dropping it he decided to produce it himself.

He designed the calendar and wrote the meal plans in the evenings. Through his contacts in the publishing world he talked to printers who gave him production estimates. His experience in marketing had taught him about mail order advertising and he set up an advertising program.

Three months after receiving rejections from the company he worked for he ran several small ads in women's magazines and cooking magazines. To his delight and surprise he was flooded with orders. His printer, who was ready to print the calendars as soon as he gave the word, was also pleased with the increased printing. The customers' response gave the printer enough confidence in Robert to give him standard payment terms. This meant Robert didn't incur a large up-front expense. The cash that came in with each order quickly added up, and in no time his $500 investment was repaid.

His part-time business continued to grow. Every night when he came home from the office and opened his mailbox there were five to ten orders. On weekends he typed labels and mailed out his calendars. In his first year he sold more than 3,500 calendars, at $3.95. His gross earnings were almost $14,000. The financial pressure was gone. He discovered the ideal way to supplement his income.

Unfortunately, while his little business at home was growing, the company for whom he worked was having financial troubles. To alleviate its problems, the company sold out to a large Fortune 500 conglomerate which already owned a movie studio. The publishing acquisition was a natural move for them.

Their accountants, with sharp pencils, keen eyes for profit, and little knowledge about publishing, recommended wholesale firings. Robert, along with almost 150 other employees, was given notice.

As so often happens Robert's sudden job loss turned into a stroke of luck for him. He decided to expand his part-time business into a full-time operation. With little difficulty he added a dessert calendar, party-time calendar, soup calendar and diet calendar. The response was as profitable as his original vegetarian calendar.

Robert now has a small office and a full-time secretary/assistant. He is earning far more than he made when he was working for the large publishing company. In addition, while his company grows he receives all of the benefits that successful small business owners enjoy—including several domestic and foreign vacations every year, which he describes as "research trips" for new publications. The trips are, of course, tax-deductible.

Is Robert's success an unusual case history? Absolutely not. All over the country more and more people are starting their own full- and part-time businesses to dramatically increase earnings. Those that become very successful may employ dozens of people. Others are content merely to supplement their income for such luxuries as entertainment, travel, or owning a second car.

One winter, Barbara Elliot, a doctor's secretary, her husband Allen, a salesman for a small appliance manufacturer, and their two children were vacationing in Florida with Allen's retired parents. Allen told Barbara that if it wasn't for his parents' hospitality they wouldn't be able to afford a vacation. It was not a new concern of theirs. Each year, when they spent time with Allen's parents, their plight became more visible. Each year it also became more expensive just to go out for dinner in Florida. They explored other possibilities.

One night the Elliots were eating at a well-known Florida restaurant. Allen told Barbara that the key lime pie was the most delicious he had ever eaten. Barbara asked the waiter if it was possible to get the recipe. Since the pie was the specialty of the restaurant, they were pleased to give her the recipe.

Back home Barbara made the pie and served it at a dinner party. Everyone raved, and someone said "you should make these and sell them." At first Barbara laughed, but that evening, after discussing it with Allen, she decided to give it a try.

The next day she made two key lime pies and took them around to several local restaurants. She gave a piece of pie to the manager at each restaurant and told him she would sell her homemade pies for a reasonable price. Every manager who tasted her pie gave her an order. Some places ordered more than one. By the end of the day she had sold nine pies.

Making them was easy and inexpensive. She set up an assembly line and turned them out in no time. Then she loaded up her car and delivered them. Some of the restaurants that sell her pies call them "Barbara's Key Lime Pie." She's something of a local celebrity. She now delivers pies twice a week, has her own boxes in which she packs them, and sells about two or three dozen a week. Since she still has her full-time job it's hard to handle any more orders.

Several of her friends have offered to help her make the pies so she could increase sales, but Barbara prefers the personal aspects of the business and, of course, the additional income.

The only problem is that Allen is sick of key lime pie, and never eats it anymore.

Self-employment is becoming a necessary way of life. It is your protection against an uncertain future in the job market. It is also your road to financial security, independence and the *freedom to do what you want*.

Of course, you can always take a second, or even third, job. You can work nights and weekends to supplement your income. Unfortunately, you will still not be in control of your hours or even your future. Self-employment gives you the control to become independent.

Another advantage of self-employment is that by starting on a part-time basis many people in growth jobs can afford to stay longer for less money, in order to develop necessary skills for the future.

As the job market continues to shrink in certain areas of employment, it is natural that the competition for jobs will increase dramatically. If you are not prepared, either with the appropriate education or with the proper experience, you will be passed over and eventually moved out of your company. You also must consider that, according to the employment experts, more than half the work force in the next decade will be in the 25–45-year-old group. Where will you fit in? In order to keep your current job, will you be forced to take a cut in salary or maintain an income that does not keep pace with inflation and your growing needs?

A recent article in the *Wall Street Journal* discussed how most small business owners fared during inflationary periods. "They merely give themselves an appropriate raise in salary," said the article.

Wouldn't that be a nice way to live? Of course it would. And it is not nearly as difficult as you might think. Read on, and find out how you can have all the advantages of self-employment.

This book will start you on the road toward economic independence.

• You will learn how to start a business, with almost no investment at all, regardless of your experience or education.

• You will learn how to prepare a budget for running a business and how to prepare a business proposal to obtain money.

• You will find out about lawyers, accountants, bankers, and the various other people who will help you succeed in business.

• You will learn how to set up the necessary files and records so you'll always know how much money you are making.

• You'll learn to enjoy all the benefits from your business—and not worry about taxes.

• You'll find out how to travel the world, wherever and whenever you wish, and rarely worry about costs.

• We'll analyze six business areas that may present opportunities for your future. By evaluating your own background against the requirements in these business areas, you'll be able to develop a direction for success, and determine what type of business you should start.

If you find that you want a faster way to get independent, you might consider buying an existing business or even starting a franchise. We'll show you how to evaluate what's available.

Are you now ready to start your own business? If you are reading this book, you must be ready. It is your first step on the road to financial and professional success.

1. Hobbies

What better way to earn a living than to turn your hobby into profits! Most of us have some enjoyable spare-time activity that helps relieve the pressures of regular employment. With a little ingenuity and some effort, it is possible to develop a business that can make you independent.

We'll cover a handful in this section, all of which can be started on a part-time basis, with potential for enormous growth. Each description will give you an overview of the business and suggestions for starting and growing. You will be surprised how easily it really is, if you use your imagination. Most of these businesses could also appear in other chapters in this section (e.g. Photography in the Creative chapter), but those in this section are more likely to be commonly enjoyed hobbies.

As with the other job categories in this section, the nitty-gritty details can be found in Part Two.

Photography

Photography is one of the most popular hobbies in the United States, but very few photographers go beyond family snapshots. Although the glamorous parts of the profession, dealing with fashion and personalities are intensely competitive, there are many other areas that are wide open. Some to consider are:

- Special Events
- Technical
- Interior Design
- Models and Performers
- Family Portraits
- Local Sports
- Graduation and Class Pictures
- Portfolios
- Insurance Claims
- Police Photography

The field is almost unlimited. It takes very little to get into business, once you have made a contact. If you wish to serve special interests, you might advertise in the classified sections of your local newspapers or in trade papers.

One idea came to me through a good friend who is a successful interior designer. She asked me one day if I could recommend a photographer to develop her portfolio. I suggested she contact one of my children's baby-sitters, who was a good photographer. My friend hired the young lady to take pictures. She was so pleased with the photos that she introduced other local designers to her. The photographer now has at least two shooting sessions a week, each one netting her $200–$500 per session. She is now ready to hire an assistant who will handle some of the shootings.

How can *you* get started? All you need is a little photography skill, a camera, and lights, although certain types of work such as food or architecture require specialized equipment. Technology is so advanced that you don't have to do much more than aim the camera and shoot for a perfectly exposed picture. However, unless you are an advanced amateur, I suggest you read several books on some technical aspects—lighting, lenses, exposure—as well as general magazines and books.

If you plan to handle special events—weddings, bar mitzvahs, confirmations—contact local churches and synagogues, and catering halls. A letter and business card mailed to prospective bridal couples (check the newspaper for engagement announcements) or to proud parents (names supplied by religious organization) will attract customers. Mailers to modeling and acting schools for portfolio photos are usually successful, especially if your rates are low. Especially in the beginning, while developing your own portfolio, it is best to keep your charges down.

If you are not skilled in darkroom work, it is best to find a local laboratory that can do your work. A good photo lab can make your pictures look better than they were to begin with. Eventually, as your billings increase, you can hire someone skilled in darkroom work who also can assist you in your shooting.

To get involved in family portraits, you might go to the local parks in the afternoon and photograph children. Keep a record of the frame numbers you take of each child, then tell the parent you'd like to show them the photos when they're developed. It is rare for a parent not to buy a photo of her child—especially if it is in color. Once you've sold the photo, you can suggest family portraits. From there, business will grow by word of mouth and solicited recommendations.

First decide the areas you want to specialize in. Practice a little bit, until you are comfortable with your skills. Then write down lists of potential customers. Next to each of the markets, write a list of how to reach them. Consult Part Two for details and techniques. Then go out and start shooting.

Writing

If you ever thought you had a talent for writing, you'll be surprised how easy it is to get started. Not that you'll get a contract for a book at the start—maybe never. However, those people who churn out material for local newspapers and magazines, as well as national publications, find a steady stream of checks in their mailboxes.

Lewis Frumkes always wanted to write. In fact, he had a file of articles and humorous stories he had written but had never submitted for publication. When he came to me with a book of funny definitions about the stock market, I decided to publish it. It was called *Wall Street Laid Bear*. From the publication of that book, which became a successful holiday gift item, Lewis gained confidence. He developed a technique for writing proposal letters for his articles.

Almost from the beginning, his pieces were accepted. Soon his articles and humor pieces were being published by most of the major magazines like *Punch, Harper's, Cosmopolitan, New York Times*, and others. Now he no longer submits an article to various magazines in hopes that one will publish it; instead, he writes a letter of inquiry to an editor who sends him a contract and advance payment if the idea is accepted. Or, from time to time, because of his reputation, editors will call him with an assignment.

It's not always that easy. Lewis is obviously very talented. However, with a little inventiveness, you should be able to develop your abilities and begin selling.

Start by purchasing copies of *Writers Market* and *Literary Market Place*. You will find a complete breakdown of every type of publication and the different kinds of material they accept. *Writers Market* details the rates paid. It makes sense to start small, writing articles for local or regional publications in order to develop credentials. From there, you move on to bigger publications with a wider audience and higher rates.

There are several basics you should be aware of. First, it is easier to sell nonfiction than fiction. Acceptance of fiction depends more on the personal taste of a specific editor. At the same time, the number and variety of nonfiction topics are so unbelievable that it should not be too difficult to find topics to write about. All it takes is a handy supply of reference materials, i.e., a good library.

Next, it is easier to write a proposal than the entire article. Write a letter to an *individual*, not a title, and suggest why your article will be appropriate for the publication's readers. Make it a sales letter, stressing why the material is timely, unique, and worth a reading. An editor will often judge your ability by the covering letter, so make it count.

All manuscripts should be typed on 8½- by 11-inch paper (not the erasable kind), double- or triple-spaced, with wide margins. Number each page and put your name on the top right hand of each page. On the title page include your name, address, and the approximate number of words. Don't forget to include a stamped, self-addressed envelope (SSE) for rejected material.

Never send copies, since magazines don't want to feel that there are other copies floating around; they want exclusive rights. Before you mail anything, read a copy of the publication to assure that your piece is appropriate for it. And, of course, check your spelling. Style in nonfiction is not as important as in fiction, since it is usual for magazine editors to rewrite and style your piece.

It's important to keep articles flowing in the mail, to increase your odds. Make a list like the following, for each article and the magazines that represent a potential market. Be organized and keep going. Although it's easy to become discouraged, if you keep at it you have a good chance to hit it big.

Title	Publication	Result
Vitamins and Skin Care (Proposal)	*Cosmopolitan*	sent 1/28—Rej. 2/14
	Harper's Bazaar	senf 2/15—Accepted
	Self	
	NY Times Mag.	
	NY Magazine	
Testing Infants for I.Q.	*NY Times*	sent 12/2
	Harper's	
	Ladies Home Journal	
	Psychology Today	
Bathtub Gardening (Proposal)	*Better Homes and Gardens*	sent 11/10—Rej. 12/11
	House Beautiful	sent 12/12—Rej. 1/12
	Apartment Living	sent 1/15—Accepted

Cooking

How many of you who are reading this enjoy cooking as a hobby? Those who derive pleasure from developing new dishes and surprising your family or friends with your culinary creations could consider cooking as a money-making opportunity. There are several ways to approach this high-profit business.

First, you might consider baking pies and desserts for local restaurants. Like Barbara Elliot, mentioned earlier in the book, a few tastes to the right person can result in orders. If you have several food stores nearby—supermarkets or small delis—you can offer them the food to sell. Cakes, cookies, and brownies, well wrapped in plastic, should keep for a few days. A creatively designed package label will help sales.

With this type of business, the name of the company can help sales. "Jane's Home-Baked Doughnuts" or "Carol's Chocolate Brownies" give the products that homemade image to entice customers. Regardless of your eventual success and size, keep that homemade approach.

How many people have very special recipes they bring out for special guests? Perhaps there are foods you've developed. Or maybe you have ethnic recipes that have been passed down through generations. You might start a very special take-out service.

There is a young woman who started a gourmet take-out service in San Francisco. Most people in her neighborhood were used to ordering pizza or Chinese food. "How boring," she thought. She and her friend decided to try something a little different and developed seven basic recipes—two soups, three main courses, and two desserts. After figuring out their costs, including packaging and delivery, they hired four local schoolchildren to hand out flyers about their services.

They were overwhelmed by the response. Very shortly, their home kitchens no longer were big enough to handle the business. The next step was a small store, including professional equipment and a full-time delivery person. The two women still do their own cooking because it's what they enjoy doing most of all. All of their friends want to work for them. After all, isn't it nice to get paid for something you have to do anyway?

One step further, but in a similar vein, is the business of catering parties. It takes much more work and organization than the other areas, but pays off in higher profits. Catering involves not just the cooking but all aspects of a party. If you don't want to be so involved, you might volunteer your services to a catering firm or become partners with someone who can handle the organizational aspects.

Specialty catering is a growing field, and its success is based on the vanity of customers, all of whom want to have a better party than their friends'. Thus, if you can provide a unique concept or theme, you immediately guarantee your customers' image in the eyes of their neighbors. Some specialties might be:

Omelets
Crepes
Health Foods
Barbecue
Desserts
Hearty Soups

Of course, don't overlook ethnic themes or foreign-country meals.

If you have an artistic eye you might become a food stylist for photographers. A stylist prepares food in an esthetic presentation for advertisements and commericals.

Jewelry

Most children, growing up, have tried to make jewelry: earrings, necklaces, bracelets. There is a movement today toward small designers and manufacturers supplying one-of-a-kind boutiques. The market is still wide open, and you can sell in flea markets, department stores, boutiques, or through mail order. You need nothing more than skill and the basic materials. Unfortunately, many jewelry designers are unable to afford gold, which has risen so dramatically in price in the last several years. There are other mediums, however, that you can use, including silver, plastic, shells, papier-mache, string, or the latest craze, semi-precious stones.

In the mid-seventies, Catherine Stein was working for a magazine. She was bored with her job and wanted a way out. She and her husband Harris found several Art Nouveau stickpins in an antique store. They had them copied and brought them around to several stores. Someone suggested showing them to an editor at a local magazine. She loved them and ran a short feature in her weekly shoppers column about the Steins and their pins.

Much to everyone's surprise and pleasure, orders came pouring in. In no time at all, the Steins' dining room table became a workroom, shipping office, packing and designing table. There was barely enough room for Harris and Cathy to work. The initial success gave them the courage to take a chance on getting independent. Cathy quit her job and began designing jewelry and manufacturing new items, while Harris continued at his job to assure them enough income to live on.

From the dining room table to a luxurious office on Manhattan's Fifth Avenue took only a few short, hectic years, with a couple of showroom/workrooms in between. During market weeks their offices were crowded with buyers from all over the country. Major department stores and little boutiques were buying their jewelry. Harris left his job to join Cathy, and eventually they took in another partner.

There is hardly a fashion magazine today that does not feature one of their bracelets, bags, earrings, or necklaces. Cathy and their partner Marsha design and sell all over the world, while Harris runs the administrative side of the company. Their business, Catherine Stein, is now one of the major costume jewelry companies in the world. And it started on the dining room table!

There is no question that it takes some skill and a lot of luck. But you can turn the odds in your favor. Read as many books as you can about the various aspects of jewelry making. There are dozens of techniques that you can become familiar with. If it is your hobby, you are undoubtedly already familiar with the process. Then take your samples around with you, along with photos, preferably in color, to potential customers. At the basic level, you may want to start with stores that carry the type of jewelry you want to make. In this way, you will develop a reputation and a steady clientele. Then you can always sell directly to individuals and ask higher prices for your work, because they are, after all, selling them in the stores.

Although there is more of a markup from your cost to the customer, it is often easier to sell to the dealer. You'll make less money per item but can make it up on volume. Make sure you read carefully the chapter in Part Two concerning pricing. It is important that you establish a reasonable price for your jewelry and make enough money at the same time. Don't be so eager to make a sale that you accept a price too low to make a profit.

Flea markets represent an excellent marketplace for jewelry. Whether in a giant "swap meet" or local street fair, there is an ever-changing market passing by. I'm sure you've seen the displays that others put up on the street. All you need in the way of materials is a sturdy table and showcases in which to display your wares. It is an effective selling tool if the customers passing by see you working on other pieces, even if you are merely twisting wire with pliers. It gives an air of originality to your work and helps to develop a rapport with the customer.

Materials should be purchased wholesale from local suppliers. If you have a company name, stationery, a business card, and a tax identification number (available at the state tax department), you will have no trouble buying materials at wholesale costs. Try to keep abreast of changing styles in clothing and be aware of price changes in raw materials. It's important to update your line constantly, changing styles and approach. Finally, you might consider hiring a representative to show your items to the stores. You can spend your time designing and manufacturing, while the rep, who gets paid only for sales, is out knocking on doors. Eventually, your responsibility should be just design, while someone else follows your specifications for manufacturing.

Tour Leader

For those of you who enjoy travel, foreign or domestic, here is a novel idea that takes very little work to get started, but reaps both financial and personal rewards. The major requirement for a tour leader is dependability. In order for people to pay a large sum for traveling with another person, they must feel confident that the trip will fulfill all of their needs and goals with a minimum of effort or anxiety.

If you've ever taken a tour, you should have a good idea of what is required. You must know where you are going, understand the best way to get there, and get around once you've arrived. Hotel accommodations must be made, drivers paid, meals planned, and everyone coordinated. If you've gone to some country or even city or state that you enjoyed and felt comfortable visiting, try to arrange a tour.

First plan an itinerary. Choose a place and what you would like to do. The trip should offer sightseeing and comfortable accommodations. (The older the group of people, the more comfort they will require. Teenagers can sleep in youth hostels without complaining.)

Next, you must make specific plans. What hotels are available? What types of restaurants are nearby? In the U.S., chambers of commerce will be able to furnish this information. For countries overseas, contact the local tourist bureaus or ministries. Set up a carefully referenced filing system, so you will always have information on hand. You will then need to arrange for transportation. The names of bus companies are easily available, and the major airlines will help you, planning your air flight, if necessary.

If you write letters to the public relations departments of the points of interest you plan to see, they will send you volumes of information. You can write up information about each place, taken directly from the material you have received, or pay a college student a minimal fee to write a brief summary of each place.

Before you even try to get clients, it is important that you are totally organized, or else no one will want to take a chance with you. Determine how much you need to charge; think of *all* of the costs, including your profit. You often will find that if you put together a group with enough people, you will get one or two free seats and free accommodations along the way. Thus, your trip is paid for. All you have to do is make sure you figure in enough profit. Part Two will give you all the details of setting up your business and calculating costs. Don't forget insurance.

To find customers, you must do some directed marketing. In other words, a hike through the Grand Canyon would probably not appeal to older folks, but would to teenagers. A tour through the inns of England would have a separate client list. Direct-mail advertising or local newspaper ads are very effective. When customers respond to your advertising, personal contact is the most effective selling technique. If you can't sell over the phone, go visit them. Bring photos, lists, names of hotels, and any other visual aids. All you really need are the brochures from the cities or countries you plan to visit.

The growth of your business is built by word of mouth and advertising. If your first trips are successful, you will have little trouble attracting more clients. You can then train other tour leaders to work for you. Your profits then come from each trip, and you can still take advantage of the vacation benefits by leading your own tours when you wish to get away.

Flea Markets

I mentioned flea markets briefly before, under Jewelry. However, this area is a major industry today. It doesn't matter what you sell; the number of potential outlets for your product is unlimited. Known in California as "swap meets," on the East Coast they are called flea markets. Bazaars and street fairs are in this category also.

It's easy to get started in this exciting business. First, you must have a product, or a product line. It may be something you have made, like jewelry, stuffed toys, carved items, leathercrafts, or photographs and drawings, or you may decide to distribute merchandise. In the "Business Opportunities" section of most major newspapers, there are usually advertisements for peddlers. (Peddlers are the people who sell at these outdoor markets.) These advertisements are for merchandise offerings for which you pay wholesale prices; the goods may be seconds or irregulars. On the other hand, you may want to search out your own items, and you can go directly to manufacturers, tell them what you wish to do, and make a deal with them.

It may make sense to visit several local fairs and speak to the vendors. Ask what sells, what price ranges are best, what locations are preferable. Try to speak with the organizers of the event. They can often tell you a lot about what goes on at a show, and the kinds of people who come to buy. To make a decision as to the types of merchandise you want to carry, merely keep a record throughout several street fairs of the vendors who keep coming back. If they weren't successful, they wouldn't return. From your observations, you will develop an idea of the products or product areas that appear to be selling.

To get into the flea market business, you need only a way to carry your merchandise and a table on which to display it. The more involved your display is, the more you have to deal with. However, people are usually attracted by interesting items and catchy signs, so you may consider investing a little extra. For street fairs, some cities require that you have a vendor's license, and you must call the city hall for information. The license fee is nominal, and you may want only to invest in a temporary one, in order to get a feel for selling.

Part of the excitement of flea markets is the bargaining. You may or may not mark prices on the items. It is important, though, to know how low you can go, and ask for a higher price. If you get it, you're way ahead. If not, it pays to haggle. As long as you don't go below your bottom price, you can sell your product for anything. And your customer goes away feeling as if he or she has made a good deal too.

Several years ago my wife and I were visiting the Metropolitan Museum of Art in New York, and the area in front of the museum was crowded with street vendors. All were selling art or jewelry or crafts. We liked a small piece of sculpture, but when the woman who was selling it quoted the price, we found we didn't have enough cash. Reaching into her ragged burlap bag, she produced a charge machine. "We take American Express and Master Charge," she exclaimed. At that point, we had to buy. It makes sense to provide charge service if you are selling higher-priced merchandise. Selling is easier, because you make it easier for the customer to make a "painless" purchase. With the increase of antique dealers at the flea markets, more affluent people are being lured to the stands.

To establish a charge service you must contact the individual credit card companies (American Express, Master Charge, Visa, etc.) and they will provide you with applications for their service.

This is an excellent business that costs very little to start, because you have very low overhead costs. Pricing is important, however, as well as buying carefully, so consult Part Two for details.

Inventions

Is there any one of you reading this book who hasn't thought, "I wish I had invented the Pet Rock." What about the Hula-Hoop? Not a bad idea either.

This country has been built by individuals who have come up with timely ideas, whether it was the electric light bulb or the skateboard. The range of ideas and needs is very broad, and there's room in the middle for everyone. The only problem you face here, assuming you have the right idea, is that it takes a lot of work. As Thomas Edison said, "Genius is one percent inspiration and ninety-nine percent perspiration." But despite the work involved, you can get it done.

First, though, you must ask several questions.

1. Is your idea original, or has someone else already come up with it? It would be pointless to pursue an idea already developed. Check with stores, catalogs, and trade associations. Visit trade shows and read magazines. Ask other people if they've heard of similar ideas. Don't, of course, give away too many details. In the end, you may have to do a patent search, but it's better to hold off until you've answered the next questions.

2. How will the invention be produced and distributed? The first thought many inventors have is to take their ideas to a big national company. After all, the company would have the money and production capability to produce the product and the marketing ability to sell it. Unfortunately, it is rare for a big company to purchase ideas from the outside. They employ many people to come up with new products, and those are the people who would first look at your product. Their jobs are threatened if you, an outsider, came up with a better idea. Thus, you get rejected. If you could find a way around the product people, perhaps in the marketing areas, you might create interest.

On the other end of the scale, you may be able to produce some items yourself, working out of your home and selling through distributors and mail order. (See the Mail Order section in Part One.) It's a good way to get started if production costs are not too high. Now you have a product and a direction for your company. Even if a big company rejects your product, it may want to buy your company—for a large profit to you.

Why? Many potential buyers understand company operations and profit-and-loss statements better than they understand the technology of an invention. Once your business is in operation, you have proved it can be done. Even if you're not making money, a large company may foresee a way to turn the business around, incorporate it into their own operation to save expenses, and make money. Also, by the time they have made the purchase, the bugs are out of the technology, and the customers exist.

In between these extremes are the medium- and small-sized companies that are always looking for new products. If you don't want to go through the problems of developing the idea and ironing out the bugs, at large expense, try to work with these middle-sized firms.

3. Will your idea make money? There is no set formula, because without the customers you have nothing. However, there are several guidelines for estimating pricing and costs, for evaluating sales potential and markets. All are presented in the technical section of this book.

4. Can you protect your idea? Up to a point, you can. After you are satisfied with the answers to the above questions, you can take several steps. The first is to file a "disclosure document" with the Patent Office. All you do is write up a description of your idea, including illustrations, pay a nominal fee, and register it. Then you can make a patent search to see whether or not the invention has already been patented. You can hire a patent attorney or, to do it yourself, go to the Patent and Trademark Office in Arlington, Virginia. If you are clear, then you can file the patent, preferably through your lawyer. Patents are not 100 percent protection, but the first one on the market with a new item usually makes a lot of money and captures the lion's share of the marketplace.

Typesetting equipment can be as simple as typing. An IBM Mag Card Composer is attached to a low-profile console which contains the unit's electronics as well as a unit for reading and recording up to fifty magnetic cards with a total capacity of 250,000 characters. The composer offers a built-in memory that will retain and replay automatically up to 8,000 characters of keyboarded copy. Courtesy: IBM Corp.

2. Technical Areas

Technical businesses usually require some type of skill and experience before you start a business. It is not always necessary, however, if your strength is more administrative, and you can employ others with the technical ability. Some of the skills, you will see, can be learned; others are merely adaptations of talents you may have now.

Typesetting

Also known as compositors, typesetters are utilized to prepare copy by all companies that print reports, advertisements, books, magazines, cards, and anything else that has the printed word. You need basic typing skills if you plan to do it yourself, but if you want to hire an experienced typist, you can concentrate on selling—getting clients.

This book has been printed through a process known as offset printing. But first this page was set in type by a typesetter, and after it was proofread, corrected, and pasted down on a cardboard sheet, it was sent to the printer. There, it was photographed by a special camera and a negative was made. The negative was held up against a chemically sensitized printing plate in a vacuum chamber, exposed to a high-intensity light, and then developed. The image on the plate was the same as what now appears on this page. The metal plate was then attached to a roller on a printing press and coated with ink by another set of rollers; then the presses began to roll. The inked image on the plate was transferred to another soft rubber roller (called a blanket), and that image was rolled against the paper to produce this page. The method is called "offset printing" because the inked plate does not come in direct contact with the paper but is offset onto the other roller.

It is important that you have some understanding of the process, in order to understand the role of typesetting. Even a page typed in your typewriter is suitable for this offset printing process. Thus, to start a typesetting business, all you need is a somewhat more sophisticated typewriter, which can give you a selection of different typefaces and sizes. The machine must also have the ability to produce justified type, which means that the right- and left-hand sides of the page are equal: all lines are the same length, despite the number of letter characters in each line. The machine accomplishes this by automatically adding the appropriate spacing to fill out or decrease the line.

The major expense, besides space for the typesetting machines, is the cost of the machine itself. You can, of course, lease it from the manufacturers. When you purchase or lease a machine, the manufacturer normally provides a training course for several weeks. During this period, you will develop the technical knowledge necessary to satisfy most of your customers. From time to time, if there are problems, you can always call the manufacturer's service department, which will send someone to help you.

The machines that are available are varied, and it pays to contact companies that manufacture them. Start with a system that is easy for you to use and gives you flexibility in selecting typefaces. Most typesetters have difficulty in setting mathematics, and I would recommend staying away from this area until you are really skilled.

In one form of machine you type in the text without regard to column width or hyphenation. The machine produces a magnetic or perforated paper tape. This tape is then fed into a small computer that is programmed to do hyphenation and proper spacing to create columns of text. The computer then creates a second tape, containing the text as it will appear when printed. That final tape is inserted into a photo-composition machine, which displays the individual characters on the tape and photographs them. You then develop films of the material to be printed.

There are also very simple word-processing machines, manufactured by the major typewriter companies such as IBM. These look like ordinary typewriters, only a little wider. A series of coded keys on each side of the standard keyboard sets the style, spacing, and column width of the material you will print. You have only to type in the text on the standard typewriter keyboard. When the text is completed, you then insert glossy white reproduction paper into the typewriter, push a button, and sit back while the machine types your text over again, the way it should appear in the final printing.

The newest and most advanced method of typesetting uses electronic phototypesetting equipment. An operator uses a keyboard to select the size and style of type as well as the column width, to provide spacing instructions, and to store each character in the computer. The computer then displays columns of type on a screen that is similar to a television, so that you can visually check the text to make any required corrections. Then the material is photographed, and you obtain a film of it. The copy can also be stored for reuse. A machine with storage capabilities is suitable for preparing directories, since a good portion of the material stays the same from year to year, and you can update with additions and deletions while watching it on the screen.

To find machines for purchase, you can consult the yellow pages, under "Word Processing" or "Typesetting." Your newspaper may have a section called "Business Equipment," which may list new or used machines for sale.

Before you go out to sell your service, assuming you already have the machine and have learned to use it, you must prepare a type listing. This is a page or booklet that lists all of the different type styles and sizes you can offer. From this, an artist will design a book or page for you to follow, using type within the capabilities of your machinery. It also makes sense to price the market by making some calls to competitors in surrounding areas to find out what they charge.

Typesetters charge by the page, by the hour, or by the entire job. There is an additional charge for any corrections, deletions, or additions that are not the typesetter's fault. It is important to make sure everything that goes out is well proofread. As the business grows, you may want to hire another typist, to increase your capabilities to two shifts; another machine may be called for. Eventually, a graphic artist can be induced to join your staff to design type or pasteup type into ads or book pages for your clients. By giving the artist free working space, you get to use his talents free when you need them, and the artist can develop his own client list.

It is important that you understand about budgeting for cash flow. (Advice appears in Part Two.) Many clients of small typesetters may be other small businesses, and they often take their time paying bills. The cash flow projection will help you plan your financial future, so you will always have enough money to keep going.

Carpentry

This is one of my favorite areas, especially since it is how I got my start in business. As a child, I always lived in a house and knew that, whatever I brought home, there was room for it in the basement or a garage. Old habits die hard, and even today, though I live in an apartment, I pick up odds and ends I don't have room for. As my wife and I had more children, there was just never enough room, even though we kept moving to bigger apartments. In self-defense, I taught myself carpentry — merely by doing it.

I had always been handy around the house. I bought a lot of do-it-yourself books and went to work building bookcases, cabinets, shelves, etc. I learned through my mistakes. Throughout the years I acquired the tools necessary for carpentry. (Of course, I had to build more storage space for them.)

During this time, my friends asked for my help in their building projects. Either I drew plans for them or I actually helped them do the building. It was my hobby, and I enjoyed the physical effort, since I spent a good part of my days sitting at a desk, talking on the telephone.

At one point, not too many years ago, I found myself out of work, just starting a new company. Scott and Deborah, my children, were in school, and little Andrew had not yet been born. My wife, Nancy, volunteered to go back to work to help me through the next year of start-up. Even with her help, we still weren't making enough money. That's when I thought about becoming a carpenter.

I immediately called all of my friends for whom I had already done some building. I also called other friends and put up notices in the neighborhood apartment houses. Then I went to all the local unfinished furniture stores and developed a price list. Whatever they charged, I would charge 25 percent less. My prices would cover everything, including the materials.

Within a week I was building my first bookcases. More sophisticated furniture followed. Some good friends had moved into a new apartment and suddenly found they were expecting a baby, with nowhere to put her. I divided their dining room and built an entirely new room after reading about how to put up walls from plasterboard. Much of my work, unknown to my customers, was on-the-job training. I soon had more work than I could handle.

The best part about the carpentry business is that I could totally control my hours. If I had business meetings or other work to do, I just didn't do my building. Because most of my first customers were friends and understood my situation, they never pressured me to come to work. Within fourteen months, my other business had grown sufficiently that I could stop my carpentry. I did so with much regret. However, my friends still call for help, and now I can afford to build for them without charging.

Of course, before you get into the business, you should have some basic skill and the right tools. In fact, the right tools will solve most of the technical problems you encounter. Assuming you have some ability, and have had experience building bookcases or even furniture, the first step is to let out the word that you're in business. Notify your friends and neighbors. Ask them to spread the word. Go to local stores to inquire whether they have work for you. Interview other carpenters to establish their rates. You might even consider apprenticing for a while with another carpenter. If you can afford to, offer your services at a very low cost, so the master carpenter will take you on.

In the beginning, you probably won't need too much space. A garage may be the ideal spot to put your equipment. As the need develops, you may consider opening a small workshop. It will give you the space to store extra wood and large electric tools and may also attract customers off the street. If you start doing larger jobs that involve more than one pair of hands, you can hire someone inexpensively, offering the opportunity of apprenticing for you.

If your carpentry skills run to the more exotic, and you can build furniture and other highly crafted items, you might want to look for outlets for your material. You can work on assignment, which eliminates the risk. If, however, you want to produce items for future sale, you should try to find stores that will either display your work on consignment or purchase it from you on a wholesale basis. When you have finished reading the section about Mail Order, you may consider combining the sales potential of mail order with the value of the items you produce, to start a new business.

Cleaning Contractor

This may not start off sounding like an exciting business—after all, who wants to work at cleaning—but it has an exciting potential. In fact, the potential is great enough that you can own a major business without doing any of the physical work yourself. It is a business that utilizes two main abilities: hiring and selling.

Susan Kellman had always wanted to be an actress. She was lucky enough to receive a few bit parts in off-Broadway productions. From time to time she went on the road with stock companies. The theater, however, is one of the most frustrating, highly competitive businesses you can enter. Naturally, her earnings were not steady. So she supplemented her earnings with part-time jobs until she could land the next part. Even then, she would work during the day, with some time off for rehearsals, and then perform at night. She was not only tired from her long schedules but bored with the never-ending job search. She had been a typist, waitress, gal Friday, secretary, messenger, and many more things she could scarcely remember.

One evening, she was working as a waitress for a caterer at a private party. The hostess asked her if she knew anyone who could come in the next day to clean. Susan volunteered for the job. It was a lot of work for her, but the pay was good. When she was asked to come back, she said yes. The following week, however, instead of tackling the work alone, she brought two of her friends, an unemployed actor and actress. The three of them got the work done quickly and efficiently, and they had fun spending the day together. They became a cleaning team, as the word spread through Susan's original satisfied customer. Whenever one of them had an audition, there was always an unemployed performer ready for the work.

Suddenly Susan found she was to go on tour for the first time since she had begun cleaning. She didn't want to give up the business she had developed, but she didn't want to forego the tour. She realized then that she had accumulated a large number of people who had already done stand-in duty when needed and who would welcome another job. Several phone calls to customers guaranteed that there was plenty of work coming up, and she asked each customer to commit to that work in advance. Then she contacted all her workers and determined their availability. Several letters and prepared schedules later, she had organized four separate work forces to cover all of the upcoming jobs.

Upon Susan's return from the tour, she found that business was booming, and she had made enough money to cover all of her employees' costs and still leave her a handsome profit. A call to her lawyer helped her get her new business officially under way.

It has been three years since she started, and her company provides more than cleaning services. If you need a bartender or a waitress for a party, call Susan. Do you need furniture moved? She'll rent a truck and provide several strong actors to do it for you. She's sorry that she had to give up acting to run her business full-time, but the financial rewards were worth it to her.

There is also another area to consider. That is commercial cleaning. Many small offices need some minor cleaning once a week. Office buildings usually provide standard service in the evenings, which involves emptying ashtrays and wastebaskets. But they rarely do such things as vacuuming and dusting of furniture.

If you can find the people to work, and the customers to use them, you too can start a business. Living near a city will usually provide you with an overflow of out-of-work performers, waiting for their big break. Since those breaks come only rarely, you will probably have a large staff of available people. Your workers can be students, also. If you live near a university, you can place a notice on the bulletin board.

The only costs to worry about will be telephone and travel, and some advertising for your service. You can place ads in local newspapers or shoppers with good results, or you can hire some high-school student to stuff flyers under doors in offices or apartments.

Have your customers sign a guarantee that they will not try to hire your workers away from you and insist that your workers sign a similar document preventing them from stealing your customers. You should determine your pricing and your percentage before you start. In essence, you receive a commission on every job, and that is your profit.

Bicycles

If the weather is warm where you are now, when you go outside today you will see half the population jogging and the other half riding bicycles. It is one of the large growth areas in business. If you have any technical knowledge about putting together and repairing bicycles, this may bring you a world of pleasure—and profits.

The focus here is on the community bicycle shop, which provides both sales and service. It is open six days a week throughout the year, and maybe even seven, during the warm months. It is an easy business to run, since customers are not difficult to deal with. However, repairs will begin to take up much of your time. You can't sell bikes without providing service, since customers want to know you'll stand behind your sales. Most purchasers are not mechanically adept and will need constant help from you, tightening brakes, repairing flats, adjusting gears, etc. But repairs are fast to do and involve a high profit margin.

Your actual business will probably be divided into 75 percent sales of bicycles and accessories and 25 percent services and repair. Gross margin of profit can be as high as 30–40 percent. Your biggest expense will undoubtedly be inventory, which can create as much as 75 percent of total operating expense. Although bicycle and equipment selection and starting costs are arbitrary, in a small city store you might need about 200 bicycles. The big sales months are traditionally December, for Christmas bike buying, and May through August, because of summer cycling. If you make enough money during the good months, you will be able to get by during the other months. If you have been able to develop some loyal mechanically minded employees, you might even take more time off during the slow periods.

Hiring is not too difficult in the bicycle business. Most high school students who own bicycles are adept at working on their bikes. A help-wanted sign in your shop window will bring a flood of youthful workers. The large availability can give you additional flexibility during the busy periods, where you can put on a half-dozen workers at minimum wage, offering them discounts on accessories as an incentive.

The ten-speed lightweight bicycle with turned-down handlebars appears to be the biggest seller. The three-speed touring bike and the brightly colored, souped-up juvenile bikes are also popular. Accessory sales and repair services have become an increasingly important aspect of the business due to new safety legislation. Federal officials have proposed bikeways and traffic ordinances for bicycles, with safety education for children. Awareness of laws and requirements will increase your popularity in the area, and purchases of safety equipment will increase your profits. Information is available to you through manufacturers, a variety of bicycle magazines, and associations such as the American Youth Hostels (AYH).

During the past seven years, the bicycle has outsold the car in the United States. More than 75 million bikes have been sold, compared with 72 million passenger automobiles. The outlook for the industry is bright, and getting even brighter, as the upcoming trend in energy conservation increases. The Bicycle Manufacturers Association feels that there are at least 75 million more potential customers. Wouldn't you like to get a piece of that market?

Computer Programmer

Here is a highly technical field that does not require a highly technical background. Employment of programmers is expected to grow faster than the average for all occupations through the 1980s as computer usage expands, particularly in firms providing accounting and business management services and in organizations involved in research and development. In addition to the large number of new people required by the industry, many companies will hire free-lancers and small companies to do the work for them, in order to keep their costs down. Also, the demand for programmers will increase as many processes once done by hand are automated. As technology improves, more small firms will install their own computers rather than rely on large data-processing firms, and this will create a need for these small companies.

Computers can process vast quantities of information rapidly and accurately, but only if they are given step-by-step instructions to follow. Because the machines cannot think for themselves, computer programmers must write detailed instructions called "programs." These programs list in a logical order the steps the machine must follow to organize data, solve a problem, or do some other task.

The programmer usually works from problem descriptions prepared by someone called a "systems analyst" who has carefully studied the task that the computer system is going to perform. These descriptions contain a list of the steps the computer must follow, such as retrieving data stored in another computer, organizing it in a certain way, and performing the necessary calculations. The programmer then writes the specific program for the problem by breaking down each step into a series of coded instructions using one of the languages developed especially for computers. Some small companies cannot afford analysts, and the programmer is responsible for both parts of the process.

As a programmer writes a program, he then tests it in the computer itself, to assure that each of the instructions is correct. Actual data are used, and if they are correct, everything is coded for that computer. A simple program can be written in a few hours. However, programs that use complex mathematical formulas or many data files may require more than a year. As a free-lance programmer, you can pick and choose the types of programs you wish to work with. You also have the flexibility of choosing your hours, since you can work on part of a program at home and other times, when necessary, work with the computer. These programs become part of your portfolio. In fact, if you develop a new program (rather than adapt an existing one) you may be able to sell it to a variety of similar companies, or companies with similar needs. All you do is adapt it for their needs, and make large profits, since the original work was already paid for the first time through.

Although there are no universal training requirements for programmers, they are usually oriented toward business, engineering, or science. Again, these are not hard-and-fast rules. Some firms that employ programmers prefer college graduates with degrees in computer or information science, or other degrees directly related to the project. Some firms do not care if you have a college degree. Most employers would prefer you to have some courses in data processing, accounting, and business administration. However, if you have your own firm (if you read Part Two, What Form of Business, you will see how easy it is to start a company), potential clients care more about performance than about your qualifications. If this becomes a problem, you can easily overcome it. Find someone with impeccable credentials and ask if you can use his or her name as being associated with your company. You might offer the person a piece of the business or a commission. Companies are used to hiring people who may be working for others and free-lancing. Thus, you talk to the client and refer all questions back to your "expert."

It is advisable, however, to take some basic courses. There are many courses taught throughout the United States, in colleges, community colleges, vocational training schools, and other private institutions. Further information about training can be obtained from the American Federation of Information Processing Societies, 1815 North Lynn Street, Arlington, Virginia 22209.

As you increase your experience, you may wish to receive a Certificate in Computer Programming (CCP). This is conferred by the Institute for Certification of Computer Professionals upon candidates who have passed a five-part examination. The institute is located at 35 East Wacker Drive, Chicago, Illinois 60601. As a senior programmer, your income will increase dramatically.

Earnings in this field are extremely high and growing annually as the need increases. Don't be put off by the training, since it is truly a gateway to your future. As you develop, you may want to consider a partnership with more experienced people. You can spend your efforts training and selling, to increase the size and profits of your business.

3. Service Businesses

A service business, in this case, is one in which you fulfill the needs of others. To perform this service you need not have a product to sell—merely your own ability to solve problems. A major advantage of a service business is that you can start without great expense. Your office, at least in the beginning, can be in your home.

Some of the services we'll cover here may involve specific skills, such as bookkeeping. Others, however, require only organizational ability, such as a shoppers service. But the major requirement for any service business is reliability. If you own a store or sell a product, customers are concerned with quality and price. People are willing to accept low-quality items for equally low prices. A low-quality service, however, is unacceptable, and you will lose customers.

Since you are dealing on a personal level, you must also be flexible in order to meet the continually changing needs of your clients. Each person requires and expects individual attention, which will keep you on your toes. If you are successful in your business, your earnings are based on the number of clients you have and how much you can charge for your service.

Bookkeeping

This business requires some specific skills in both accounting and organization. Free-lance bookkeepers charge for their services by the hour, and if you wish to have your own business, you can slowly develop a list of companies for whom you can perform your services. If you are not already a bookkeeper, you can probably take some basic courses at a local adult education center.

Simple bookkeeping involves paying and posting bills, balancing the checkbook, and maintaining the journals and ledgers. These are very simple functions that don't demand a C.P.A. degree but take up enough time that small businessmen don't want to do them themselves.

Also, if the bookkeeping is entrusted to an accounting firm, it will cost almost ten times more.

Soliciting clients is not too difficult. You can start by approaching people you know who own or work for small- to medium-sized companies. Then ask local storekeepers; stationery stores, delicatessens, florists, and other small, often family-owned, businesses are good prospects. Too often they employ their accounting firm for the basic bookkeeping; so stress to the owner how inexpensive it will be if you do the work.

When you get an account, ask the client to have his accountant explain the current systems. As long as a system is being used, your job is not much more work than putting numbers in the right spaces. Only you will know how easy it is.

Expenses are minimal—business cards, stationery, calculator with paper tape, accounting pads and pencils. Not too bad. As the number of your clients increases, you can raise prices and hire people to do the work. Because most of the work is done in the client's office, you can save money on overhead. Employees can be paid either on a percentage basis or with a salary.

A new type of bookkeeping service might appeal to some of you: personal bookkeeping. There are many disorganized people and busy executives who would welcome some assistance in setting up records, balancing checkbooks, and paying bills. You can charge a regular monthly service fee, instead of an hourly charge. You can probably handle ten clients at $50–$100 a month, in no more than two or three days.

Travel Agency

Despite inflation and the increased cost of fuel, there has been an enormous growth in the travel business. Both vacation traveler and business traveler need a large variety of services, including transportation and accommodations. Most people turn to travel agents to take care of these needs and assure them that they are receiving the best service and the lowest costs.

There are currently more than fifteen thousand independent travel businesses in the United States and Canada, and they devote all or most of their time to travel and related arrangements. Because of the enormous growth of this business, it has become more specialized and much more efficient. However, there are very few educational requirements necessary, although it might be helpful for you to work in a travel agency for six months before going out on your own. There are courses offered to give you basic training, and you can contact the American Society of Travel Agents (ASTA), 711 Fifth Avenue, New York, New York 10022, for additional information.

The amount of capital required to open a travel agency varies with the type of services you will offer. Basically, you will need office space, decorated attractively in order to make your clients feel comfortable. You will need a variety of reference books, schedules, timetables, and other forms of information. You may eventually need a computer. When I travel, I call my travel agent, Martin. While I'm describing where I want to go and when, he's punching buttons on his computer console. The machine instantly gives him availabilities on the airlines, and my reservations are made and confirmed before I've hung up. It's that type of service that keeps me coming back to him.

There are ways to get started, however, without a large investment. If you have worked part-time with travel agents, they may let you have desk space in return for a percentage of your business. Thus, you still have your own business and develop your own clientele while making full use of the existing materials and overhead of the agency. When you have developed a large-enough selection of clients with a mix of personal and business travel, you are ready to consider your own office.

As a travel agent in some states you will need a license, you are an official agent of airlines, shipping lines, railroads, hotels, etc. You must deal directly with these companies to receive their approval for you to function as their representative. Your income is derived from the company that received payment for the service; the client does not pay you. You receive a percentage of the billings for the trip, a percentage that varies with the types of accommodations you have made.

To increase your clients, it is important to be familiar with many different places, so you can often recommend places to your clients that you yourself have been to. Very often the airlines, shipping lines, and hotels will give you free trips in order for you to recommend them. These trips are just one of the side benefits of this business.

Interior Decorating

There are two similar businesses that are often confused: decorating and design. To become a designer, you must pass an extremely difficult examination and have a sufficient amount of education and experience. Designers are usually fully qualified to work along with architects, with the construction in building. A less rigid profession is that of interior decorator.

There is a considerable amount of overlapping within the two fields. The decorator, though, does not usually make structural changes; he is primarily responsible for the decorating of the interior design. This may be in the residential market, for home and apartment dwellers, or in the commercial and office market, which represents a large and growing area.

To get started, you must have good taste and some sense of design and color. Your function at the beginning level is to help people select colors, match fabrics, and purchase furniture. (There are courses available in most cities to give you an understanding of these areas.) Thus, your first responsibility is to establish sources of supply. If you live in a major city, you will usually have supply sources and showrooms nearby. If you are in a smaller town, it may be a bigger problem; you will have to locate suppliers for every area and develop a listing of catalogs.

You will need stationery, business cards, order forms, and other business paraphernalia (details in Part Two). You will probably not need an office, which will surely keep down your costs. By presenting your business card (or writing on your stationery), suppliers will normally grant you a discount of 20–50 percent off list prices. Thus, when you purchase paint, fabric, or a new couch for your customer, your customer is billed at list price, and you merely pay the discounted price. That difference is your profit.

Your first clients will very likely come from recommendations from friends, or your friends themselves may hire you. Once you establish a reputation, it gets easier to create new business. You might also consider catering to commercial space and contact small businesses. A unique approach might be to concentrate on specific types of jobs, such as law offices. In this way, you can contact lawyers either by telephone or by mail and offer your services.

The initial consultation should be free. After determining the client's needs, you must draw up a written plan of action, including suggested steps you will take. At that point, if the client accepts your proposal, you begin shopping for furnishings. When you are totally familiar with your resources, you will know exactly where to go for each item. You present drawings, photos, color and fabric swatches, and paint chips to the client for selection. Business persons usually do not have the time to follow you around looking at items, so you will have to present everything at once. Others may want to go with you, and that is also acceptable. The suppliers will quote your client retail prices. Since you can get everything at discount prices, you don't have to worry about making your profit. Thus, you don't have to charge for your effort. On the other hand, you can charge for your time; then you can offer your client the advantages of the discounts you receive.

One further note: you should make sure that you have photographs of every job you do. These pictures make up your portfolio and will be used to get additional work. You can also ask satisfied clients if you can give their names for reference. In this way, you build a reputation.

Day Care Center/Nursery School

Gloria and Irena are two young women who had grown tired of teaching in the New York City school system. They felt pressured and stymied at every turn by the local board of education and the academic bureaucracy. They decided to open a day-care center or nursery school in their neighborhood.

The first step was renting a suitable location, and they were fortunate to find a basement apartment in a brownstone building. The neighborhood was acceptable, they felt, for mothers to bring their children to the school. Since they were financing the school from their own savings, they wanted to make careful purchases. They ran several small classified advertisements in shopper newspapers, looking to buy used children's furniture and toys. The response to their request was so overwhelming that they almost considered getting into the used-toy business—but that's another story.

Judicious purchasing furnished their school, and with some repairs, fresh coats of paint, and pictures on the walls, they were ready to start.

Again, they returned to the local shopper newspapers. They began with small space ads, while also placing attractively designed posters around town. Local storekeepers were willing to put their signs in the windows, which lent an air of legitimacy to them. What Gloria and Irena offered were half-day programs for the children. Since there were two of them, they felt they could each handle a class. Thus, they had two morning classes and two afternoon classes.

When mothers came to sign up their children, they were asked if they could volunteer one to two days a month to help out in class. Most mothers were able to do so. With the help of the mothers, Gloria and Irena were able to offer many more services, including trips to local points of amusement, or even to the park.

By calling several other nursery schools and day-care centers, they were able to determine the pricing structure of the competition and had no trouble undercutting the others. As their reputation and popularity increased, they hired a friend who taught science in the school they had both once worked in. Every Saturday, Frank did scientific experiments with older children. Since there was no homework involved and it was essentially pure play, the class was crowded. Frank received a portion of the proceeds from the students and the school received the balance.

The women are now considering moving so they can expand their operation. The only thing holding them back is that they don't know if they want to work that hard. They will soon be able to replace themselves with other teachers and be free to develop other ideas.

Their story is almost a complete, textbook type of development for a nursery or day-care center. They were, of course, extremely lucky to have found an ideal location for their school. That is a consideration you should not overlook if you decide to pursue this lucrative field. Those of you who have raised your own children or organized playgroups for them should have little trouble organizing a school. If you merely want to develop a school and be an administrator, it is advisable to hire a former teacher. As incentive, you might consider offering the teacher a share of the profits. It will save you from having to pay a salary.

Supplies are not a problem if you can build, beg, borrow or repair. Bright-colored paint is fun for the children, as well. A visit to several other nurseries under the pretense of wanting to enroll your child, whether you have one or not, will give you an insight into rates, schedules, facilities, and personalities. Because of the potential liability with children, you should incorporate; also be sure to discuss the proper insurance with your agent.

To attract children, advertise in local papers and put up posters. If you have a child in the local schools, you might ask to put up a notice in the school or send home a note through the PTA. An attractive sign will also bring inquiries from passersby. In the beginning, it is best to limit the number of children you take in, in order to gain experience. Once you have it, you can take as many children as you can handle and, naturally, fit into the classroom.

Shopping Service

As inflation continues to erode our own spending power, wouldn't it be marvelous to buy wonderful items without spending your own money? A shopping service is just that—buying gifts for others, with someone else's money. The success of this type of business rests on two different types of people, both of whom can afford it. The first is the busy working person. The second is the individual who is insecure with his or her own taste. Both of these classes of people will welcome this personalized service.

Let's look at one type of service—the shopper. Customers are attracted by advertising, primarily by mail order or direct mail. The service you offer should be unique and personal. The customer describes the people for whom gifts are required. Find out everything you can about the people. Prepare preprinted size charts, one for each gift recipient. It looks very professional but also makes your shopping easier. At the bottom of each form, you should have separate categories to fill in: clothing, accessories, toiletries, household items, hobbies and crafts, etc. Your customer should try to help you fill in various items that are possibilities, as well as other interests.

Then your job is to go into the stores and try to find the appropriate items. The best thing to do is make lists and work within the price range you have been assigned. When you are shopping for holiday gifts, you can buy in volume, as long as the items are for different customers.

Part of the service should include not only holiday buying but also special events. Each customer should have a calendar that you fill in with the names and birthdays, anniversaries, or other occasions of the people you have to purchase for. When working for busy business-person, don't forget their office help.

Fees charged, are normally a percentage over the retail price, such as 15 percent or 25 percent. At 25 percent, for every $100, you make $25. Your major cost is for advertising, to solicit customers. Once you have customers, ask them to recommend other friends to you. Your business will grow by word of mouth and through advertising.

There is another service, similar to personal shopping. A gift service is often successful during holiday seasons. You contact a large variety of manufacturers for sample items, designed, let's say, for the business-man. These items would normally be jewelry, perfumes, leather goods, and high-fashion items. You can rent a showroom, or hotel room, where you can display the items. Customers come and order from you, and you thus have no risk in purchasing merchandise, until you sell it.

Another novel form of shopping service was started recently by Carmen Giusto. From a toy distributor she knew, she received com-puterized printouts of the distributor's inventory, plus the catalogs of all the brands in stock. Along with several other women who went to work for her on a commission basis, Carmen set up buying parties (much the same as Tupperware), where people came to read the catalogs and purchase toys at discounts. When the local schools, religious or-ganizations, and other clubs heard about her service, they asked if the women could present the items at various organization fairs.

The secret to success in this type of business is to find the right timing, product, price, and market. Of course, that's one of the very basics of most businesses. But in Carmen's case, she had the perfect item (toys) at the right time (Christmas) for the right market (primarily mothers) at the right prices (discounted). Everyone was pleased with the results, and most of the organizations have already requested the service for next year, which assures Carmen of a ready-made market.

You too can start a similar service business. What you need is the product, or selection of items. Ask yourself what people look for at specific times of the year. Then approach manufacturers or distributors for the right to sell the merchandise at discounts, if that is part of your plan. You will get the lowest prices from the manufacturer, since the distributor makes a markup on what it sells to you.

Study the success of such shop-at-home services as Tupperware and Avon, and you will see that the market is always eager to buy products in the comfort of home or office, or to take advantage of lower prices.

Party Service

Unlike catering, this area deals with special events: anniversaries, birthday parties, theme parties. It takes not much more than creative thought and a knowledge of where to obtain other services.

Have you ever been to a child's party where a clown performed? Or a pony ride was offered? Or been to a restaurant that had a special party room? Couldn't you do the same thing for someone else? You may not believe it, but when you advertise yourself as an "expert" at arranging parties, most people will hire you, because they feel insecure.

Before you start soliciting business and designing stationery and business cards, you must put together a file of services. Some of these might be:

Food Services	Cake Designers
Magicians	Balloons
Bartenders	Waitresses
Rental Equipment	Florists
Liquor	Cleanup Service
Invitations	Caterers

If your client is giving the party at home, it saves a major part of your effort. However, if the party is outside the home, it is your responsibility to locate the restaurant or hall. In a service business such as this, you can either charge a flat fee or a percentage above the total cost. Your major expense is your time, and when you have a large, easy-to-use file of services and people to contact, you don't have to spend a lot of time organizing. You will, however, have to make sure that everything gets delivered and set up and that the party flows, while standing in the background.

Try to obtain letters of commendation from satisfied clients; photographs will also help. These will go into a photo album that becomes your portfolio.

As you grow, it is important to read "shelter magazines," which are those publications that deal with home cooking and entertaining. From there you will develop ideas for themes and sources. You may eventually have to hire an assistant to coordinate the business and make telephone calls. Thus, you will probably need an office. When you plan your overhead budget, you should project those future expenses somewhere down the road.

Creative Representative

If you have a flair for meeting people and can sell yourself, an exciting way to make money is in the field of creative representation. What does that mean? It means that you become an agent, or personal representative, for creative talent: photographers, artists, singers, musicians, craftsmen.

One advantage of this type of work is the freedom of time you will have, as well as the almost unlimited ability to control your earnings, once you've developed a clientele. Specifically, your responsibility is to find work or shows or outlets for people with marketable talents.

Another advantage is the type of people with whom you associate. If you enjoy show business or the arts, you will be able to work and socialize with this interesting, creative group of people.

To start yourself in this business, you must first develop a list of clients. Even one, of course, will do. Show business is extremely competitive and may be worth passing up for the time being until you are truly familiar with the business and work involved. The way you find clients, whatever their field, is to go to shows—art shows, photography exhibits, nightclubs, theater. Perhaps you know people who are considered talents but don't have the ability to turn themselves into a marketable product. Naturally, most creative people are capable of stretching their abilities to the limit to produce their works. But unfortunately, very few of these people are able to deal in business situations, especially those starting out.

When you find someone you like—and it's important to like both the person and the work—you try to find work. Let's take a craftsman, say a ceramist. The first step in the process is to develop a portfolio. You will need a biography of the artist, including where he went to school, teachers of note, shows that his work appeared in, and a statement, possibly by the artist, of his own appraisal of his work. This philosophical statement can be used by you to describe to others the work you represent.

There must be photos or drawings to enhance the value of the portfolio. In addition, if the artist has won any prizes or had any positive reviews from previous showings, these should be in the portfolio.

Step two is selling. Make a list of all the local galleries that might handle this person's work. Don't feel limited only by your area's galleries. Contact owners and discuss the work with them, playing up the potential sales capability and the aesthetics of the work. Most galleries will take merchandise on consignment. It means that they get a percentage of whatever is sold. Whatever is not sold is returned to you. Frequently, people who represent artists or craftsmen eventually open their own galleries. What better way to show off your client's work!

If you get a showing, make sure the gallery will do some sort of advertising. It may be an expense you will share with the gallery. It is important to invite all of your friends and the artist's friends to a special opening, where you will serve wine and cheese. Very often, friends and acquaintances will be the first buyers.

In a city with a reasonable number of advertising agencies, publishing companies, magazine publishers, corporate headquarters, and retail stores, you might want to consider representing photographers. Most photographers specialize. You should find an assortment of photographers who can cover a wide range of job assignments. You might expect 15–35 percent commission for jobs brought in to the photographer.

Again, you must develop a portfolio, including any published works. If you are presenting slides, show the pictures in a plastic slipcase, or carry around a viewer, or even a projector. Visit the art directors in agencies and publishing companies. In large corporations, there is a thriving business in annual reports. Find out who is in charge and contact the person. If your photographer is especially skilled in product and fashion, the local retail stores always need pictures for advertisements, statement stuffers, or catalogs. Starting photographers with few credits will welcome your help, so they'll have time to devote to their creative activities.

The business techniques for creative representation are fairly simple when you start. You can be a sole proprietor, but you will need a lawyer you can call upon to draw up contracts with your clients. Eventually, you may consider setting up a corporation, if business truly warrants it. You can then have all payments from customers made directly to your corporation and pay the artists the share they are to receive from that corporation. To begin, however, you won't need much more than an ample supply of business cards, stationery, and a winning personality.

Typing Service

If you don't know how to type now, it may pay for you to enroll in a typing course given by a secretarial school. To this day, I truly believe typing was the most valuable course I ever took throughout my years of schooling. It carries me through my daily work with ease, not to mention the term papers I have to type for my children. I will always be able to make a living as long as I have my typing skills.

Most companies need the help of typists. There are thousands of college and high-school students who write papers and do not have the ability to type them. Publishing companies always need people to type manuscripts in either rough or edited form. Typing is an ideal service for part-time work as well as full-time work. And it lends itself quickly to expanding and hiring employees. Best of all, you don't even need an office.

The major item you must have, naturally, is a typewriter. It is a major investment, but when you are beginning, you can rent or lease a good machine. With the advent of the self-correcting typewriters, anyone can be a professional. If your skills are presently a little rough, go back for a brush-up course. It shouldn't take very long for your fingers to start working again.

One of the first steps in starting your business is to contact other typing services. Interview them as if you had something for them to type. Ask the types of clients they service, what their rates are, what kind of delivery of finished typing you can expect. From this information you can set up your own rates and schedules. Many typists charge by the page; others work on an hourly basis. If you can type ten pages an hour, at $1.25 per page, you would be better off that way, rather than charging $7.50 per hour. It depends on the level of your skills.

Step two is developing a list of customers. Start by placing ads in local newspapers or shoppers. Make telephone calls to local businesses. In larger companies, there may be an office manager that you can speak to. Don't overlook publishing companies and periodicals such as newspapers and magazines. Also, there are a lot of small companies, such as market-research firms or business consultants, who always need reports typed for their clients. A notice on bulletin boards or in dormitories of local high schools or universities will surely bring you business. If prospective clients ask for experience, be prepared by getting a list of your friends who will verify that you have worked for them. Eventually, you will have real credits.

One great pleasure you will derive from this type of business, as well as other service businesses, is that you can project and control your earnings. For example, let us assume that your costs for operating the business are $1,500 per month. That means it will cost $18,000 for the entire year. If you want to have an income of $30,000 per year, you must then earn $48,000 a year ($18,000 expenses + $30,000 income).

At some point in your growth, you may have far too much work to handle. Very often you may get several jobs all at once, and there is just no way to get them done. To be prepared for that problem, you should hire your own free-lancers, preferably on an hourly basis, so you end up making a profit on every page you do. The difference between what you charge your client and what you pay your typist is your profit. In this way, not only can you do your own typing but your business will increase by having the ability to take on as much work as possible. Also, by having the free-lancers, you can make more time to solicit business. The more business you have, the more money you can make.

Public Relations

If you have an outgoing personality, self-confidence, and an understanding of human psychology, you might consider getting into the field of public relations. The major function of someone in this area is to help present the best image possible for a business, government, university, or individual. It is a career that brings you in contact with interesting, intelligent people on both sides of the table: your employers and the media.

One of the best things about this area is that the earnings are extremely high. In addition, there are no major requirements to get into the field. You are called upon to perform many different functions, and if you are able to present the story in the best light, you've done your job. Let's explore, for a moment, what this entails.

Public relations experts may work with the press, community- or consumer-related groups, political campaigns, fund raising, or employee recruitment. In some ways, the work entails "telling the employer's story." Most companies have in-house and outside public relations consultants. Their job is to put together information that keeps the public aware of the company's policies, activities, and accomplishments, and at the same time, keeep management aware of public attitudes. After preparing the information, they may contact people in the media (radio, television, press) who might be interested in publicizing their material. Many radio or television announcements, special reports, newspaper items, and magazine articles start at a consultant's desk. Most of the guests you have seen on television shows such as "Today," "Tonight," "Donahue," and others have come to promote their books, records, or movies. The guest's publisher or producer has employed public relations consultants to get them on the show to publicize their new work—and sell more copies or bring more people into the theater. Without those in public relations, you would find television talk shows very dull.

Public relations experts also arrange and conduct programs in which company representatives will have direct contact with the public. Such work includes setting up speaking engagements and helping prepare speeches for company officials and politicians. They may also be in charge of producing and showing films to the public to make them more aware of their clients' abilities.

Often, public relations consultants work together with advertising agencies to assure that the advertising prepared by an agency presents the company or individual in the best light.

Sometimes, consultants specialize in fields with which they are most familiar or those areas they most enjoy. If you enjoy travel, you can try to land hotel or airline accounts. Restaurant accounts provide you with good food. Entertainers and those companies in the entertainment business bring you into contact with a world of continuous excitement.

There are two sides of the business with which you must first become familiar. The first is the media and other individuals who provide you with access to large groups (convention directors, educators, or consumer-affairs leaders). Your responsibility is to establish a relationship with these people, in order to assure a broad audience to whatever message you may bring to them from your client.

On the other side is the client. It may be anyone, or any company. Because this is a business that deals with ideas, you should develop concepts and programs *before* you solicit business. There are many small businesses that have no idea about public relations. Your job is to convince them that, for a reasonable fee, you will get their names mentioned.

In order to understand the nature of this business, if you open the travel section of your local newspaper, you may see an item about a well-known performer appearing at a local club or hotel. The client is probably the club or hotel. Normally, there would be nothing of note to encourage the journalist to write about. However, if a well-known star is coming to town, that may be news. The public relations consultant working for the hotel prepares a news release announcing the performer's arrival. When the paper reports the star's appearance it also happens to mention where he or she is performing. In essence, it is like free advertising.

When you pick up a newspaper and find that Broken Drill Oil Company has discovered oil that will make everyone rich, who do you think has advised the newspaper? The public relations representative. If the item appears in enough papers and enough people read it, perhaps they will rush out to buy stock. If they buy stock, the price rises and the company is happy. The PR representative has earned his fee.

On the other hand, if you bought a new toaster, and it continued to burn your toast, you might write a nasty note to the manufacturer. The person who responds to you will often be the public relations director, whose job it is to assure that the company maintains adequate relations with its consumers.

If you wish to enter this lucrative field, it may be wise to consider working for a short while with another public relations consultant or firm. In this way, you begin to understand the nature of the business, and most important, develop contacts. As you start meeting media people, you will take them to lunch or dinner and begin to know them personally. At some time in the future, you may call them for a favor to help one of your clients get a notice in the paper or on television.

You will also begin to learn about the various functions of the PR rep and develop your own interests within the field. The world of public relations is a sometimes glamorous world, combined with creative and competitive work.

4. Creative Areas

Creativity, imagination, and talent are prerequisites for a career in creative areas. People in art, design, music, and communications are involved in expressing ideas and emotions, often in a very personal manner. These areas of work give you the unique ability to combine self-expression with an opportunity to make money.

Performing artists express themselves through music, drama, or dance. They may use their talent to say something serious or profound about the human condition, or they may simply provide entertainment. People in design occupations use visual means, such as light, space, color, and texture to convey feelings or create a particular effect. Fine artists might create a painting to express an emotion. Applied artists create or design objects that serve a practical purpose as well as make our surroundings more pleasant to look at.

Those people who are in communications occupations deal with mental images created by words. They use the written or spoken word to inform, persuade, or entertain others, and they need to be able to express themselves clearly, accurately, and in an interesting manner.

In order to succeed in a creative area, what counts more than educational background is ability or talent and practical experience.

Technical Writer

This is the computer age, and technological innovations are being introduced faster than ever. By putting scientific and technical information into language that can be readily understood, technical writers play an important role in our society. The job entails writing, researching, and editing technical materials. Some writers may even increase their scope and produce publications or audiovisual materials.

Robert Hanratty worked for a publishing company in Chicago, but always wanted to work for himself. He was tired of being on salary and worrying about pleasing his boss all the time. He finally quit when a new opportunity arose for him, enabling him to take the chance.

At a party he met a video producer. She and her husband produced medical films for doctors. They were lecture-type presentations narrated by doctors in specific fields such as psychiatry, neurology, and pathology. The producers turned out three films a month and were desperate for writers. Bob took their number and called the following day. He told them a little about his experience (which wasn't great, but he exaggerated), and they decided to try him. "The worst that can happen," he told himself, "is that they won't use me again."

He was given the doctor's report and a set of slides used to illustrate the lecture. All he had to do was transpose the report into dialogue. It was the easiest money he had ever earned. The producers approved his first few pages, and he took it from there. Within two months he was able to give notice at his job and write the scripts full-time, doing two a month. Each script took him only a week or less, so he had a lot of free time.

Bob used the free time to obtain other business. Again, a chance meeting in an office brought him in contact with a man who wrote product information for a major drug company. He asked Bob to help him, since he had more work than he could handle on his own. Bob accepted and was soon earning three times the money he had earned while employed and was able to pick and choose his assignments.

Eventually the two men formed a partnership, sharing all the work, and they hired an artist to increase their capabilities. Now they are able to produce entire booklets for the drug companies, instead of merely writing them. They are considered a medical production company and work for drug firms, journals, and laboratories.

Technical writers set out to instruct or to inform, and often they do both. They prepare manuals, catalogs, parts lists, and instructional materials needed by sales representatives who sell machinery or scientific equipment, as well as by the technicians who install, maintain, and service the equipment. These are the people who write the instruction sheet for your new washing machine and prepare the parts listing for the bicycle you have to assemble. They also write the instructions for new games that come on the market.

The bulk of the writing involves manuals, reports, and proposals. Technical writers may write specifications or prepare speeches and news releases. They may edit or write technical books if they have the skills and knowledge or may prepare articles for magazines. Their responsibilities are varied, depending upon their abilities and knowledge.

Technical writers usually begin an assignment by learning as much as they can about the subject. They study reports, blueprints, sketches, drawings, parts lists, specifications, mock-ups and product samples, to become familiar with product technologies and production methods. They must read technical journals, if necessary, consult with engineers, scientists, and technicians.

Free-lance writers set their own hours and often work at home.

Those who become well established can earn extremely high incomes. They may rent offices and employ typists and researchers. Part of the pleasure of writing may be the travel that is sometimes necessary when researching material.

There is no specific type of education required to become a technical writer. Very often, if you have the skills, you can get the work. There are some institutes and seminars that can enhance your skills. You may have to take specific courses from time to time, just to stay on top of your specialty, if you have one. When you begin, you might wish to consider working as an assistant to another writer until you have gained the techniques and some contacts. But once you have the contacts, it's time to start your own company.

To find potential clients, solicit those companies that produce products with which you are familiar or in which you have some interest. Eventually, you should approach any company with technical and scientific materials. Don't overlook the government, both local and federal. It is the single biggest employer of technical writers.

Display Specialist

If you remember watching the television show "Rhoda," you will know what a display specialist does. That was Rhoda's career. The job involves designing and installing exhibits of clothing, accessories, and furniture in store windows and showcases and on the store sales floor. The designer's aim is to develop attractive, eye-catching ways of showing merchandise to the best advantage. Within the field there are different categories. Model dressers specialize in dressing mannequins for use in displays. Others may be considered showcase trimmers. Some may specialize as window dressers.

To create a setting that enhances the merchandise, display workers need imagination as well as knowledge of color harmony, composition, and other fundamentals of art. They may, for example, choose a theme— say, a beach setting to advertise bathing suits or surfing equipment— and design a colorful display around it. Or perhaps a winter scene would feature a mannequin in ski clothing, on skis, surrounded by other snow-related items sold by the store. Once a design idea has been approved by the store's management, the display specialist obtains the clothing and props and other necessary accessories. Then craft skill comes into play.

Many display workers, as well as having a strong artistic sense, are able to construct many of the props themselves. They may be assisted in these tasks by a helper, or by a maintenance worker assigned to them by the store. Part of the design idea includes a budget, and they must be able to purchase those items that are not available from the store, such as background settings and lighting equipment.

Displays change on a regular basis, depending upon the type of store. Many stores change monthly, others seasonally. The busy seasons for retail establishments are usually Christmas and Easter, and you may find yourself working overtime, and taking on part-time helpers.

There are no educational requirements for display work. You can learn the skills by working for a store, or you can make some sample sketches and a budget and try to put yourself in business.

How do you go about doing that? Begin by walking around your neighborhood. Look at all the store windows. Make notes about each one—good and bad points. Then spend some time looking at those stores with a reputation for outstanding displays. Walk through the store to see if the windows are somehow related to the showcase displays. Then go home and start working.

Step one begins with selecting those stores you plan to solicit as clients. Pick a variety—pharmacy, clothing, food, etc. Start planning your design. Make notes about what would be important to the store because of the season, political event, or other current point of interest, in order to attract people. Remember that if people stop to look in the window because it's interesting, there's a good chance that these people will become customers. Then draw some pictures, rough sketches of how you would see the window. When you have come up with the idea that you feel is best, start to color it in, to make sure it all works. In addition, prepare a parts listing.

What items will you need in the window? Will you need a mannequin or two? What clothing will they wear? Unless it's a department or clothing store, you will have to obtain the clothing somewhere. Try to get a store to lend you the clothing—in fact, try to borrow everything, if you can—for a mention in the window of the contributing store's name. Those items that you must purchase you can usually keep after dismantling the display, so buy things you like. Put together a construction list also, including all the wood, electrical items, nails, wire, plugs, or other items you will need. Then prepare an estimate of what everything will cost. Mark up those costs to include an adequate profit, and that is your plan.

The second phase is selling. It pays to go after customers you know, who would be the easiest to approach. Old stores with older owners are often poor customers. Their attitude is, "We've been doing it this way for twenty-five years, and we don't think we should change." Once you have established some credentials and a portfolio, it becomes easier to convince them it's time for that change.

Any store with a window, and any shop with an inside display area represents a potential customer. It may be very simple to develop your list of clients, and it also may take some knocking on doors. It is an ideal business to begin with little or no start-up expense. All you really need are some creative ideas.

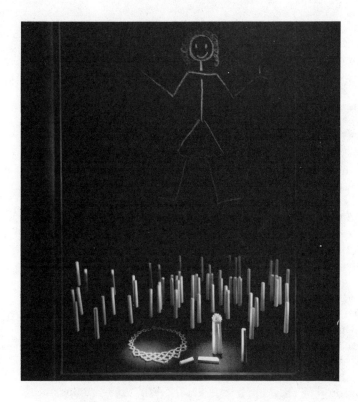

A Tiffany & Co., N.Y. window designed by display artist Gene Moore shows a whimsically drawn stick figure peering down at sticks of chalk and a diamond necklace and ring. Courtesy: Tiffany & Co.

Commercial Artist

This area is for those of you who are already working in the field of commercial art and want to find a way out of the day-in day-out drudgery. It is your chance to say good-bye to nine-to-five, to develop your own business, and to make more money than you could ever hope to earn working for someone else.

Your first step is to prepare a portfolio and a resume *before* you leave your current job. If you ask around, you will find that everyone is free-lancing on the side, and that is how you should start too. The resume should include any pertinent work experience and studio course. You should also indicate any grants or fellowships received and exhibitions participated in, noting the name of the gallery or museum. If you have won any awards, be sure to highlight them.

After the resume is the portfolio, gear the portfolio to the client. If you are planning to solicit book or magazine publishers, feature any covers or text designs you have done. If you plan to enter the advertising field, select the best ads you've produced. At the end of the portfolio, include photographs of displays and samples of items you have designed: stationery, logos, etc. All these materials should be carried by you in some convenient form—either in a zippered loose-leaf binder made for this, attache case, or accordion file. If you work from slides, you should have a portable slide viewer with you. Unfortunately, artwork may lose its effectiveness when reduced to the size of a slide and viewed through a small hand viewer, since the quality of the work may be difficult to judge.

You must constantly revise and update your portfolio and try to keep it looking presentable. Often, the art director may ask you to leave it for a few days, and after considerable handling, it may get worn. Also, if you do encounter enough people who ask you to leave the portfolio, you may have to have duplicates. Be sure everything is labeled, so the viewer will know what he's looking at, even when you're not around.

The field of visual art offers the greatest number of jobs in the commercial art world. The printing, publishing, and packaging industries taken together form the graphic arts industry, one of the nation's largest industry groups. According to the Education and Technical Foundation of the Graphic Arts Industry, Inc., the amount of business done each year by the industry is growing at a higher rate than the nation's total production. Art-related jobs in these industries run from technical production jobs through art directors. Whether you are doing simple paste-ups or designing complete publications, including text, illustrations, and covers, the field still offers many possibilities.

Thus, you have to determine where your skills lie and what types of accounts you want to handle. You can find interviews through word of mouth, or you can prepare an interesting promotion. If you are currently employed, it is better to go on interviews through recommendations or through people you know. In this way, any sales literature you prepare won't fall into the hands of the company for whom you work. However, it is usually accepted that most people in the graphic arts industry supplement their income by moonlighting. Wouldn't it be more satisfying to earn enough money from the business you know and enjoy best, without working for a boss?

To establish a price, you should have some idea as to your own abilities, and how long a job should take. Inquire first what the company's budget may be. Some companies pay on an hourly basis, others by the job. If you get paid by the hour, you should establish a competitive rate scale by asking several others what they charge. If you would rather get paid on a per-job basis, have some idea how long it will take, so you won't make less than the hourly wages. Unless you wish merely to gain experience, you shouldn't take jobs for which you will not make an adequate amount of money. You probably won't lose a customer. You will gain respect, and the next time a job comes up in your price range, you may get the call. You have established yourself as a professional who gets professional wages. Otherwise you will get a reputation for low prices, and although you may get lots of work, you won't be making any profit.

Try a wide variety of clients at first, and don't be put off by the line, "I'm sorry, you just don't have any experience doing this type of work." Insist that you are a talented designer and can translate the ideas into the appropriate medium. Typical assignments would be record albums, magazine, book, or publication design; package design or exhibits. You might work for advertising and public relations agencies, or department stores doing promotional artwork. You might design corporate logos or stationery and business cards for a small business.

There are also numerous free-lance groups you might consider joining. You pay an annual fee to be put on a list of people to be distributed to various companies who hire designers and artists. If there is a specific job, the client calls the group, who in turn may give your name. Printers may also be a good source of clients for you, since they do work for the people you will work with. Ask that they give out your name.

As you increase your skills and develop a regular clientele, it becomes easier to plan your income. At some point, you will be able to leave your job and set up your own studio. Eventually, you will be able to bring in another artist. Or, if you find that you would rather do that work, you might hire a rep—a person who will go out to do the selling and represent you with the companies. The representative is a marketing person who will get paid only when you get paid. The rep's best interests are your best interests. This saves you from the hours of traipsing around with your portfolio, and you will be able to concentrate on doing more creative work and having more time in which to do it.

Modeling

This section is not just for women. Not any longer. Today there is a growing field for men as well as women—and children too. Look in the newspapers and magazines. There's a growing trend toward older models also.

You don't necessarily need experience for modeling. What it really takes is having the right look at the right time. There is no way to know that in advance, so you must prepare yourself for that eventuality.

As you know, modeling can be a glamorous and exciting career. Very successful models enjoy fame, travel, and the opportunity to meet famous personalities. It is hard work, however, and not always glamorous. The hours for some models are irregular, and it takes a while to build a reputation. There are many kinds of modeling you should know about.

Fashion models generally work for clothing manufacturers, dress designers, department stores, or dress salons. They may model clothing in fashion shows or private showings or model informally—in store restaurants or on the sales floor, for example. In fashion shows, these models display clothing on a platform or runway. While the announcer describes what they are wearing, they stand, turn, and walk past customers and photographers, and point out special features of the design. They may stop to tell individual customers a garment's price and style number.

Some fashion models specialize in showroom work. They are known as showroom or fitting models and are employed by clothing manufacturers to model clothes and accessories for the fashion buyers who visit manufacturers' showrooms on their regular buying trips. Many of these models work in New York's garment district. The major requirement of a showroom model is to have standard measurements. Perfect size is more important here than a pretty face.

Photographic models are hired by advertising agencies and freelance photographers, usually for a particular assignment. These models are seen on magazine covers and billboards in advertisements of all kinds. Artists' models pose for painters, sculptors, photographers, or art students. They must be able to hold a pose for long periods of time, and often they are asked to pose without clothes or in skimpy costumes.

Some models work in films and television doing commercials. They may demonstrate cosmetics, shampoos, deodorants, clothing, soaps, or other products. Often, acting experience will give you a head start in this field.

There are also models who are hired to demonstrate new products and services at exhibits, trade shows, and sales meetings. They are also hired to appear at conventions, benefits, and political rallies. These models may also find jobs as beauty consultants, fashion consultants, personal store shoppers, or tour guides.

Modeling jobs are available in nearly all urban areas, but most jobs are in the biggest cities. The overwhelming majority of models work on a free-lance basis, often through agencies that arrange assignments for them. They are, essentially, employment agencies, working on a commission basis. For every job the agency arranges, the model usually pays 10 to 20 percent of the modeling fee. The agencies may also help train you, select your clothing, and help you develop a style. Once you are listed with an agency (and they don't take just anyone), they will make an effort to help you find steady work. They'll help you prepare a portfolio of photographs of yourself in a variety of poses and kinds of clothing. That portfolio is sent around to prospective clients.

A word about the portfolio here is necessary. Most models, male or female, should have one. It is your calling card. If you can afford it, find a photographer who specializes in this type of work (locate one in the Yellow Pages). If you don't have the money, try to find a photographer who is looking for the experience. There are hundreds of young photographers, very often at a local university, who would be pleased to prepare a portfolio of pictures for you. Bring a variety of clothing, makeup, and other accessories with you to the session and try to present yourself in a variety of poses, hairstyles, and clothing. For the beginner, posing for these pictures will give you excellent experience in front of the camera.

Not all models get their jobs through modeling agencies. Some department stores hold auditions that give aspiring models a chance to model at store fashion shows. Fashion shows sponsored by local community organizations offer another opportunity for prospective models. Still, you will need the portfolio.

Finding a job as a model takes a lot of stamina and the ability to accept rejection. Often there will be hundreds of other men or women looking for the same few jobs. Your chance for success rests on the way you carry yourself, the way you look, and, very often, on pure luck. As you progress in the field, though, clients will know your name and ask for you. This will eliminate much of the competition you will have to face. And also with that, your earnings will grow.

Female models usually command higher salaries than male models. In 1979, salaries for models working through agencies ranged between $20,000 and $50,000 a year. However, the more successful models can earn $150,000 to $250,000 a year and more. If you appear in a television commercial, you may be entitled to residual payments every time the commercial appears. In this way, you will have a steady source of income, even if you aren't working at the time.

One word of warning—there is a difference between modeling schools and modeling agencies. The modeling schools teach students how to style their hair, walk and stand gracefully, pose in front of a camera, and apply makeup. Students also learn about skin care, diet and nutrition, exercise, speech, and etiquette. the main business of these schools is conducting classes—not finding you work.

This is a good time to get into the field, if you are interested and think you are qualified. With rising advertising expenditures and sales of clothing and accessories, there will be an increased demand for both photographic and fashion models. Start making the rounds of the agencies, but don't overlook the department stores, convention centers, and manufacturers. Leave your name and portfolio, and check back from time to time. One or two good breaks can skyrocket you to fame and fortune.

5. Sales Opportunities

Sales work offers a wide range of career opportunities and an excellent chance to start out on your own. The educational requirements for most types of selling careers are not particularly stringent. Even if you are selling technical equipment, you will normally be trained by the manufacturer or distributor. If you wish them, technical courses are always available at local schools, especially community colleges. There you can get a background of business administration, marketing, and even selling. In addition, you can learn the technical aspects of the equipment you wish to sell.

Within the field of selling, there are different approaches. You can sell services or products, work for several companies as a sales representative, or be a broker, buying from one to sell to another. This section also will include information about retail selling—owning a bookstore. In many companies, the salesmen make more money than the president of the company.

One of the most lucrative types of selling careers is being a *broker*. Let's look at what a broker does. The dictionary defines it as one who negotiates contracts of purchase or sale for a fee or commissions. At its simplest form, you pick up a telephone to solicit a customer. Then you call someone else to locate the product or service requested by your customer. By putting the two of them together in a deal, you make a commission. You may even make the commission from both sides of the deal.

Insurance Agent and Broker

Insurance agents and brokers sell policies that protect individuals and businesses against future losses and financial pressures. They may help plan financial protection to meet the special needs of a customer's family; advise about insurance protection for an automobile, home, business, or other property; or help a policyholder obtain settlement of an insurance claim.

Agents and brokers usually sell one or more of the three basic types of insurance: life, property-liability (casualty), and health. Life insurance agents, sometimes called life underwriters, offer policies that pay survivors when a policyholder dies. Depending on the policyholder's circumstances, a life policy can be designed to provide retirement income, funds for the education of children, or other benefits.

Casualty insurance agents sell policies that protect individual policyholders from financial losses as a result of automobile accidents, fire or theft, or other losses. They also sell industrial or commercial types of insurance, such as workers' compensation, product liability, or medical malpractice insurance.

Health insurance policies offer protection against the costs of hospital and medical care, or loss of income due to illness or injury. Often, this type of insurance is offered by the life insurance agent as well.

Do you have to work for another company in order to be an agent or a broker? Not at all! It is usual for agents or brokers to have their own offices or share space with others in the same field. In this way, you have the use of services offered by others in your field, and if you offer life insurance and someone else in your office offers health insurance, you can now offer your client full service.

All agents and most brokers must obtain a license in the state in which they plan to sell insurance. In most states, licenses are issued only to applicants who pass written examinations covering insurance fundamentals and the state insurance laws. Agents who plan to sell mutual fund shares and other securities also must be licensed for that by the state. Many colleges and universities offer courses in insurance subjects. Other courses you may have taken in school—business law, economics, business administration—can also help an aggressive salesman. There are special review courses that prospective agents and brokers can take, in order to prepare for the examination.

Actual training will be provided, usually, by the company for whom you plan to sell. Or, if you wish to start by training in an insurance office, you will get your "trial by fire." Six months of experience in a small office can help learn the basics of the business and understand many of the potential needs of your clients.

In 1967 Kenneth Arlen went to work at a friend's agency. He had plans to go into his own business but wanted first to learn the business. His friend Bob had taken over the agency when his father had died and was still not experienced enough to handle the large number of clients already dealing with the agency. He welcomed Ken and immediately turned over a large number of accounts to him.

One of the major requirements for any salesman is enthusiasm and self-confidence. Ken had plenty of both. In a short while—six months— he had developed a strong understanding of the business, studied for the agents' examination, and passed it with flying colors. At that point, his career took off. Ninety percent of the customers who had once called Bob's father now would speak only with Ken. In addition to maintaining and increasing the old accounts, with license in hand, Ken increased his working hours. A lot of appointments to sell life insurance take place in the evening, and Ken rarely missed an evening appointment.

One year later, after passing his exam, Ken had made so much money that he offered to buy out Bob's share of the agency. Bob realized he was no match for Ken's drive and felt that it might be a good opportunity to make some money and still not have to work so hard. So Ken purchased his friend's company and found himself the owner of his own agency. During this growth period, he also acquired a new home with a swimming pool, and two new cars. He and his wife now travel to another country every year. In addition, they always attend the different conventions for agents and brokers throughout the United States.

Most successful agents and brokers enjoy an excellent life-style. Once they've begun, their earnings are based on commissions. The more they sell, the more they earn, and the more aggressive salesmen can earn hundreds of thousands of dollars a year, plus all of the fringe benefits. As your business grows and you plan to open an office, you can then think about hiring agents to work for you. You will train them and pay them, but you get a portion of whatever they sell. In this way, you can increase your earnings again, without working any harder. The advantage in this business is that once you've sold a policy to a customer, it will normally be renewed every year, without too much additional selling. Also, it is likely that you will get additional business—health or casualty—from the client, and hopefully he will recommend other friends to you, to make your selling job easier.

If you are interested, it pays to contact different companies about available training programs. Remember that an agent usually represents one company, while a broker can represent many different companies.

Real Estate Agent or Broker

Here is a field that requires many of the same skills as an insurance agent or broker. Best of all, advancement in the field of real estate is expected to rise faster than the average for all occupations through the 1980s, in order to satisfy a growing demand for housing and other properties. The area within the field that offers the most potential will probably be home purchases and rental units. Shifts in the age distribution of the population over the next decade will result in a larger number of adults with careers and family responsibilities. They are the group that makes most of the home purchases. As their incomes rise, they can also be expected to purchase large homes and even vacation homes.

Real estate is an excellent field for anyone beginning in business or transferring from one field into another. Also, because a major requirement is ambition, anyone wishing to go into his own business can succeed with flying colors in real estate, if you have that drive. One of the new areas in real estate sales is the franchised brokerage that is part of a national or regional real estate organization. This is an excellent way to get training and a head start in the business.

Real estate agents and brokers must be licensed in every state and in the District of Columbia. All states require prospective agents to be a high school graduate, be at least eighteen years old, and pass a written test. The examination—more comprehensive for brokers than for agents—includes questions on basic real estate transactions and on laws affecting the sale of property. Most states also require candidates for the general sales license to complete thirty hours of classroom instruction. Those seeking a broker's license must complete ninety hours of formal training. In addition, there is usually a requirement for experience in selling real estate—generally one to three years. If you have a degree in real estate, that requirement may be waived.

Once you've passed the requirements, you are ready to be on your own. Your prospect list for clients and properties can be unlimited. It's important that you advertise your services, so prospective sellers and buyers can contact you. You may also walk around town knocking on doors—not homeowners' properties, naturally, but commercial properties. Most business properties post the names of the managing agents, and you should contact them, ask for permission to represent them and ask if there are any current vacancies. It's important to follow up these calls continually by mail and telephone.

In residential real estate, you may be part of a multiple listing service that gives you, and all other brokers in the area, all of the available listings. The advantage for the seller is that he gets enormous exposure. For you, it merely means you'll have to work a little harder to beat the competition. However, direct mail or advertising can help you stand out from the competition.

In large urban areas, commercial or industrial properties are at the top of the list. The earning potential is much greater in this area, since the overall rental or selling price for commercial space is much higher than for residential space. In order to specialize in these areas, you must have a strong knowledge of leasing practices, business trends, and location needs. You must also know about transportation, utilities, and labor supply.

On the other hand, if you plan to sell residential properties or apartment rentals, you must be familiar with the location of schools, churches, shopping facilities, hospitals, and public transportation. In selling or renting residential real estate, agents generally meet first with potential buyers to get a feeling for the type of home they would like and what they can afford. Then they may take the client to see a number of homes that appear to meet his needs and income. Because real estate is so expensive, agents may have to meet several times with a prospective buyer to discuss properties.

It's important to stress those points that may be important to the prospective client. For example, to an older family you may emphasize the compactness of a house to eliminate a lot of walking. To a young family you may stress the nearby schools and shopping facilities and the spacious floor plan to permit expansion, if necessary.

Because you are also working for the seller, you must follow the seller's requests and bargain over prices, even presenting counteroffers to the purchaser. You might even be involved in the closing stages of a sale and help arrange for a loan, title search, and even assist in the final meetings.

As important as selling is the locating of properties. A good part of an agent's time is spent on the telephone, obtaining listings. You may spend half your day on the telephone, exploring leads gathered from advertisements and personal contacts. You can determine how much a property is worth by evaluating it in comparison with similar properties on the market.

Earnings in this business are primarily by commission. The rates differ according to the type of property and its value. The percentage paid on the sale of farm and commercial properties or unimproved land usually is higher than that paid for selling a home. Sometimes you may have to divide the commission among several agents in a firm. If it is your own, you are the broker, and get the lion's share. Many experienced real estate agents earn well over $50,000 a year, and brokers can earn more than that. In addition to the income, you will also benefit nicely from many of the extras, such as new cars, insurance coverage, and other tax-deductible items that you will be entitled to. You should also consider joining clubs or various local organizations in order to increase your contacts.

Although there are some basic requirements to enter this field in a way that you will be able to make more money, the overall advantages of this type of self-employment are well worth the effort.

Sales Representative

Practically all manufacturers, whether they make computers or can openers, use some type of sales representative. Many of the companies employ their own salesmen. Other companies find it beneficial to hire a representative. A sales representative may carry many different product lines, as long as they can be bought by the same customer. You may sell copying machines to businesses and represent three, four, five, or more different companies. If you sell to bookstores, you may carry five different publishers' lines, as well as greeting cards. The advantage of being a representative (or "rep") is that you have a bigger choice of products to offer your customer. If you work in the fashion business, you may carry several different lines of clothing, all of which can be purchased by a department store or boutique. Or you may carry different price levels, to suit the needs of particular stores or departments.

Your income comes primarily from commissions, and there is no limit to the amount you can earn. John Franklin was at a party one evening in 1978 and met a young man who was visiting from France. He mentioned to John that he managed a children's clothing manufacturing company in Paris and was in the United States looking to sell the line to the department stores.

At that time, John had been working for one of the major television networks, selling time. He liked selling, but wasn't moving ahead fast enough. Besides, he didn't like the man he worked for, who was always checking up on him. It was one of those split-second decisions that can change the course of a person's life. John volunteered to be the United States representative of the clothing line.

The man was thrilled at the offer. It saved him the job of visiting stores, and he was able to report back to his company in Paris that he had "discovered" a representative. They even agreed to give John exclusive rights to sell in this country.

"Now what?" was all he could think of for the next few weeks. He had never done anything like this before. He didn't even know to whom he could sell the clothing. He was used to selling something entirely different, an intangible item. Finally, at the library he came across a book that listed every buyer's name and department in all of the department stores and buying offices. It was worth spending a few weeks trying to sell. Without quitting his job, John began to use his spare time to make phone calls. He was able to make appointments with the buyers in the New York stores, since he worked in that city. His friend, Armand, had sent him samples, brochures, and photographs, and John carried them with him to his meetings. Perhaps his timing was right, or perhaps John was just a good salesman, but with his first call he wrote an order. He continued to do so on every call thereafter, much to his surprise, since this was high-priced merchandise. One month into the selling season, there was no way John could conduct both businesses, his own and the network's. He started his own business.

With the earnings he had made in the first month of sales, he was able to open a small office and hire a secretary to type orders and answer telephones. At one meeting, a buyer suggested that John contact a friend of his, someone in the children's clothing business who was looking for additional representation.

John met with the friend and soon had his second line of merchandise. When the spring market season opened, John had four lines of merchandise, two from America, one from France, and one from Spain. Then came the road trip across the country, visiting the major department stores from New York to Los Angeles. It took three weeks, and when he returned, he had to hire another person to help with the orders. Business continues to grow, and John is now considering forming a partnership with another manufacturer's rep who carries only European men's sportswear. In this way they can save money by merging operating expenses and split even higher profits than they make individually.

Indeed, all things are possible, and you too can enjoy the benefits of being a representative. Your earnings are limited only by the amount of sales you make and the type of merchandise you carry. A good part of the work may involve travel, and you can deduct expenses such as transportation, meals, hotels, and any entertainment you enjoy. Your vacations can be taken almost whenever you wish, unless they interfere with market periods. In most industries, there are certain periods where orders are written, and these are known as market time. In fact, if you do not live in the area where market meetings will take place, you can enjoy your trip to that location as a vacation and take a few extra days enjoying the sights and restaurants.

Look around you today. Determine, if you can, what areas would interest you most. Where would you like to travel? What kind of people would you like to deal with? What is your own expertise? Make a list of types of items that would interest you and make some telephone calls. Often in the "Business Opportunities" section of major newspapers, there's a section called "Merchandise Offerings." You can always find items or lines to carry. You may also find a section called "Representation Wanted." These ads are ideal.

Call the company and make an appointment. Find out what it's offering. Determine later how much you have to sell in order to make a sufficient income, based on the offered commission. Avoid buying merchandise to sell, since you will be stuck with it if you cannot sell it. As a rep, you have little risk, except for the expenses of your sales calls. Also inquire if the company has other reps, and how many. If it doesn't, ask if it has ever used reps and what kind of business they have done. Does the company have its own sales staff? In essence, you must determine with whom you will be competing to sell the goods and whether the merchandise has any potential. It doesn't pay to carry a line that won't sell.

If you carry several lines of merchandise, you will quickly be able to determine which lines are best. It is with those lines you will spend the largest amount of time. The other goods become filler and additional business. The manufacturers know this happens, but it is worth it to them, since they don't have to pay you any salary or benefits. Any sales are extra for them also.

You will need business cards and stationery and probably order forms and statements. Depending on the type of sales and the area, you may even need a car. As your business develops, you will also need office space and someone to answer phones and do the typing. Try to hire someone who can also sell over the telephone to give you additional impact with your merchandise. If you need catalogs, photographs, and samples, the manufacturer will usually supply them. It is his responsibility to give you sales-support materials. It is your inventiveness and ability, however, that will sell the products.

The advantage of this type of business is that you can begin with a very small investment. For much less than $1000 you can begin an operation from your home. Once you have your basic selling supplies, your major investment is your time.

Printing Broker

If you're looking for a business that involves very low start-up costs and can bring you high profits with little risk, this may be the area for you. In fact, the primary advantage of being a broker—almost any kind of broker—is that if you have strong selling ability, you can earn a great deal of money and have very few real expenses.

A printing broker sells printing services. However, unlike a salesman who works for one company, you represent many companies. Each of the companies should have a variety of specialties, so you can offer your clients the widest possible range of services. To get started, you will need both clients and printers. You will also need some technical knowledge, and may have to work with a printer or a salesman for six months to learn the basics.

Normally, printing companies specialize in particular aspects of the business, primarily to suit the capabilities of their printing presses. There are, of course, full-service printers who do everything. But usually, you will find them in different categories: newspapers, magazines, advertising brochures, books, business forms, stationery, etc. Since many printed items such as books and magazines must be folded, sewed, stapled, or bound after they are printed, you must also look for binding services. Many printers do their own work; however, there are those that do not have the appropriate binding facilities, and you must also arrange to have that done, if requested.

After you have filed the proper forms to start your business, the first step is to locate as many printers as possible. Go through the Yellow Pages to find the printers in your area, or contact the Printing Industries of America, Inc., 1730 N. Lynn Street, Arlington, Virginia 22209, for additional information and lists of companies. On your stationery, request from the printers the right to act as a broker. They will tell you what services they offer and give you written quotes when asked. Some printers may give you a percentage of the printing price as your fee. Others may merely permit you to mark up the price to make your fee.

When you have enough names, set them up in a book, categorized by services. Each section should contain the names, contact people, and the types of equipment each printer or binder has.

The second phase of the business is to develop customers. This is a little more difficult and involves knocking on doors. Start with the people in business that you know. If you have left a company, you might ask them to give you some work. Send out some direct mail advertising. Make calls to set up appointments. When you leave a customer's office, give him something to remember you by—a business card or a pen with your company name imprinted on it. Offer to quote for jobs. Explain that you offer a variety of services and can guarantee top-quality work, as well as personal service.

When a client asks you about a job, you should have a "spec" sheet on which to write the specifications of the job. Each printer has his own form, and you can develop your own from the samples. Ask the printers to give you some training, so you can understand what they can and canot do and why. Because you represent potential business to them, at virtually no expense, they will be glad to cooperate with you. Once you've seen the operations, you will be able to talk to your customers with much more confidence.

After you've received a complete quote for the printing (and binding, if necessary), retype the quote on your own stationery, detailing all of the specifications and a final price. That price should include your commission or fee. If the printer is willing to give you a percentage of the job, say 5 percent, that is your commission. If the price is not too affected by another increase, you can tack on an additional 5 percent to the customer. Thus, you make more money. On a job, for example, that is quoted at $25,000, the printer will give you $1,250. If you add on another 5 percent to the $25,000, you will also receive $1,250 from the customer, after the bill is paid. Thus, when the customer sends you a check, you merely deduct both fees.

The customer will be dealing with you, either as an individual or as a company, and will pay you directly. Remember that all of your selling expenses are tax deductible, and there is virtually no end to the number of deductions you can develop to maximize your income.

While searching for business, start with the standard sources. Go to advertising and public relations agencies. Don't forget the magazine and book publishing firms, if you can provide that type of service. All businesses, large and small, use forms, stationery, labels, and other related products. If you have one or two good but inexpensive printers of these items, you can prepare a mailing or handout. Go through office buildings (or hire someone to do it for you) and leave a brochure at the front desk, marked for the production manager or office manager. Each of them is a potential customer.

Make sure you don't overlook nontraditional sources of business. What about the local organizations that put out monthly newsletters or bulletins for their members? Restaurants may be looking to have menus printed. PTA groups publish newspapers. Are there local political clubs you can contact to print their candidates' handouts? The list of potential customers is endless.

Part of the selling job involves entertaining. The people who are in the position to make purchasing decisions in larger companies always enjoy going to nice restaurants for lunch or dinner or to theater or sporting events. Many of the brokers I have met in the publishing business own several seats at the local stadiums and hand out tickets from time to time to their customers. You may have to make that investment at some time, as your clientele develops.

There are two main reasons for this type of activity. First, when you eat with a client, you both get to know a little about each other. It's important that you try to find out about the customer's personal life, so you can refer to it once in a while. Keep a file on the customer that includes the names of his spouse, children, etc. When you call, you can always ask, "How's Sally feeling?" The customer tends to think of you as a warm family-oriented person, one who can be trusted.

The second reason for providing such things as tickets to shows or sporting events, or an occasional bottle of liquor or wine, is that it develops a feeling of obligation toward the giver—you. In other words, when you give a present to a customer, however small, he feels that it should be repaid at some time. Hopefully, it will be repaid by giving you a job to print. Once you've gotten you first job, unless it turns out to be a total disaster, it is highly likely that you will continue to get work. After enough time dealing with the customer, you will probably have him call you for quotes, rather than the other way around.

As your business grows, you may need an office and eventually someone to answer telephones and type orders, quotes, requests for prices, etc. If someone is taking care of the administrative functions in the office, you will have more time to solicit business. Also, it gives you the opportunity to get away from time to time, knowing that someone is there to look after the business.

Direct Selling

Regardless of your professional or educational background, if you are involved in direct selling you have an opportunity to earn more money than others in professional careers. It is really up to you how much you can earn, and all it takes is drive and adequate research into the appropriate products you can sell.

Basically, direct selling involves distributing a product from a manufacturer or a distributor directly to a customer. The customer can be a home consumer or a business person.

The beauty of this type of selling is that you can sell almost anything to anybody. For the home consumer, any type of household articles have strong potential: vacuum cleaners, cleaning utensils, car-care kits, encyclopedias, beauty items, cooking utensils, and small and major appliances. You can also sell jewelry, watches, books, magazine subscriptions, and food. The list is limitless. For the price of business cards, some mailing pieces, and postage, you can begin to earn thousands of dollars.

What are you going to sell? The first thing to do is start reading a variety of different newspapers and magazines to see what products are coming onto the market. Subscribe to the magazines designed for those looking for new products and for salesmen. Go to trade shows to see what's on display. Talk to your friends about what they would be interested in purchasing. Finally, ask yourself what kinds of products you would enjoy selling and demonstrating.

Most of the products are obtained directly from the manufacturer, and you will receive a discount or commission on whatever you sell. If you deal through a distributor, you will receive less money, since he is marking up the price already to get his commission. When you have determined what you would like to sell, go to the library and consult *Thomas's Register*. This book lists all categories of products manufactured in the United States and gives a complete listing of those companies who produce the merchandise. On your business stationery, write to these companies requesting permission to distribute. Determine the following from them:

1. Can you distribute merchandise?
2. Will they provide you with samples (on small items)?
3. Will they give you sales literature?
4. What are the list prices and your discounts?
5. Can you sell their merchandise at discounts?
6. What are the extra delivery charges?
7. How long does it take to ship?
8. What styles, colors, sizes, etc., are available?
9. What about service, damaged goods, returns?
10. Are there volume discounts? This means the more you buy, the bigger discount you receive.

It is possible, in direct selling, to earn from 10 percent to 100 percent profit on the selling price of your products. In addition, since you have very little overhead and do not have to pay costs for stores, you can afford to discount merchandise to make it more enticing for the customer to buy from you.

Selling is an art that can be developed as you go along. Determining the needs of your customer is the first step, and once you've done that, you can tailor the sales pitch of your product to him. The most popular and successful approach is the door-to-door technique. Find a neighborhood or large apartment building and begin ringing doorbells. Step one is to get in the door. You can do that easily if you offer a free item or a sample of the product. Once inside, begin to describe the product. If you have samples, show them or demonstrate to the customer how they work.

Some items, especially more expensive ones, can be presented at first over the telephone, or through catalogs and brochures. This is known as developing leads. If people answer direct-mail pieces, or if they invite you to visit them through a phone call, you have an ideal customer lead, someone who is probably interested enough in the product to buy.

Customers are worth money to you in more than one way. Not only are they valuable when they purchase merchandise from you but they are also important for future sales. If a customer is satisfied with your product and you, you have the potential to sell him again and again. Also, satisfied customers are willing to give you referrals, and you will be introduced in some way to the customer's friends. That saves you the cost involved in soliciting new customers.

If your business grows sufficiently and you would like to add additional income without having to work harder, you might consider hiring salespeople to work for you. They will work on commission, and you will have to split your profits on each sale with them. However, it is more money than you would have made had you not had the salesperson working for you. After all, you would probably not have made that sale. Many housewives, looking to supplement their husbands' incomes, have the time and desire to work their own hours.

You must train your salespeople, and you can do that by taking them around with you on your own sales calls. Let them do most of the talking after a few calls, so you can critique them later. Have the salesperson introduce you as the supervisor, checking up on the district. The customer will feel protective of the new salesperson and often buy, just to demonstrate support *against* the supervisor and for the salesperson. Always pay your salesperson a commission, even if you did the selling, since it is a good incentive.

When you have developed a sales force, you can consider selling through the party plan. Like the famous Tupperware parties, the idea is to gather a dozen people into one room where the salesperson can present the products to all the customers at once. In this way, you cut down on sales calls. The person holding the party is given a free gift or additional discounts on anything purchased, and she or he invites friends. Each person at a party also can act as a referral service or throw their own parties for you.

Fortunately, as your own boss, you can sell whatever you want. You may consider changing items from time to time, or adding new products to your current list. Once a neighborhood of customers has been established, they begin to look forward to your return visits with regular and new products. If you sell disposable items (vacuum bags, perfume, toiletries), they will call you for reorders.

In addition to home selling, sales to businesses are booming. As technology improves, there is a growing need for support items and paper products. Your approach to a business is essentially the same as to a home. Send out catalogs or brochures or walk through office buildings ringing bells. If nothing is needed, always leave a business card and a brochure or flyer. You never know when a need suddenly develops, and your flyer pops up at the right time. It is very likely that you will get continuing business from corporate accounts, once they've made their first purchase from you.

Direct selling is a gateway to success and wealth, if you have the ambition. In the beginning, you must develop your product line. It may also take some time to develop the skill for this type of selling. But once you've made your first few sales, you'll feel as confident as if you've been doing it all your life.

Owning a Bookstore

Bookselling can provide a profitable business for those interested in retail selling, and being involved with the world of literature, ideas, and art, as well as the managerial aspects of this type of business. As ordering techniques become more automated, the rate of success for bookstores increases.

Sales volume and good management are essential to bookstore profits. Most successful bookstore owners do the lion's share of the work themselves, hire a minimum of outside help, buy and control inventory wisely, and manage all other costs closely. It involves a large amount of time and requires courteous personal attention to the individual customer's needs. Also, you must reach a total sales volume of $100,000 to $150,000 per year, in order to succeed in the business. With wise purchasing and innovative selling techniques, it should not be too difficult to achieve.

The American Booksellers Association, the organization that serves bookstore owners, recommends that you have at least six months' experience working in a bookstore before opening your own. The experience will lead to knowledge about small business management and accounting, understanding and locating source materials, and helping you to make your final decision.

It is important that you select your location with an eye to the surrounding community. You should try to locate in areas where the people are well educated with high incomes. Preferably there should be schools or professional offices nearby. Another desirable location would be in a downtown business district or shopping center with heavy pedestrian traffic, close to ample parking. You will need 1,500 to 2,000 square feet to start a small store. Most of that area should be for display and selling space.

Much to the advantage of the bookseller is the way books are purchased from publishers. Books are sold on a returnable basis. If you order books from a jobber, distributor, or directly from the publisher, you are permitted to return them within a reasonable period of time. Thus, with close, accurate inventory control, you can keep the stock turning over at a rate that will insure an adequate profit for your business.

Along with the common bookstore items, hard- and soft-cover books, you may also consider carrying magazines, stationery, diaries, calendars, gifts, games, and greeting cards. A new, highly profitable area for bookstores has been *remaindered* books. When a publishing company finds that certain titles aren't selling well or are overpriced, it sells its inventory to a remainder house, which buys the books for a fraction of the list price. These books are sold to booksellers at large discounts that enable them to make higher profits, even when the titles are sold to the customer at more than 50 percent discount. Many of these items are "coffee table" books, large, oversized gift books that may normally cost $25–$50 and now may sell for $5–$10 discounted.

If you are located in an area serviced by a book distributing company, you should contact someone there for assistance in starting your store. Based on the distributor's experience, he can advise you about fixtures (even giving you free display racks) and recommend starting inventory. That will help in planning your start-up costs.

Because retailing is a six-day-a-week business, you should consider having some help, even if it is merely part-time. In small neighborhood stores, you can set up personal monthly charge accounts for local residents. If you are near an elementary school, you should have a good selection of books for young children. You might have a special children's reading session on Saturday mornings, to entice the parents into the store. Publishers will advise you about authors' tours, and you may be lucky enough to have the author make a personal appearance to sign books—and sell them. Periodic mailings about specials and new titles to your regular customers can increase business.

Most important, however, is effective inventory control. Your distributor can help you, but it is important to set up an easy-to-control system that can easily be taught to employees. In this way, you will never be out of stock for important titles and best-sellers. Also, you won't find yourself sitting with fifty copies of a book that won't sell more than two copies a year. You can always special-order books if the customer is willing to wait.

Before you begin, make sure you have done adequate planning for finances and future growth. Subscribe to *Publishers Weekly*, the trade magazine for the publishing industry. It is published by the R. R. Bowker Co., 1180 Avenue of the Americas, New York, New York 10036. It will keep you informed of forthcoming new titles from the publishers, as well as special deals you can take advantage of to increase your profits.

You must also plan on advertising on a continual basis. Publishers often offer special cooperative advertising plans, whereby you and the publisher can share the cost of an ad. By advertising several books from different publishers, you can dramatically reduce the costs of your advertising.

Obviously there are hundreds of other retail selling opportunities. I've only presented one, here. However, a bookstore operation illustrates most of the skills required for retail sales: ordering, pricing, customer contact, inventory control, advertising, display, etc.

6. Mail Order

When people talk about mail order, they immediately think about Sears, Roebuck or Montgomery Ward. What about all the thousands of others who have made their fortunes in the mail-order business? Every day you probably receive several mail-order pieces. If you've received several mailings from the same company, there's a reason—it's successful.

Today, the mail-order business is a way to increase your earnings enormously and *quickly*. Unlike almost any other business, you can test a product and find out within a few weeks whether you will be successful. If you are, you can parlay your earnings into a small fortune. All you do is copy your initial success, increasing first the number of ads and then the products you can sell.

In Part Two the subject of mail order is presented as an advertising technique, or method, rather than as a business unto itself. That chapter merely demonstrates how direct mail is used to supplement other types of sales. However, in this chapter you will learn how to create an entire business, including developing a product and an advertising program and determining your success.

One of the major advantages of the mail-order business is that you can start the business on a part-time basis, reinvesting the income to expand your business to the point where you can leave your current employment and get independent. There are thousands of small mail-order businesses throughout the United States that started with very little money—and one good idea. As the sales grew, they used their earnings to buy more and more ads, until they were making hundreds of thousands of dollars. Others increased the physical size of their businesses, investing in warehouse space, dozens of employees, and enormous monthly mailings. Although there are very few Sears, Roebucks, there are thousands of success stories.

What is Mail Order?

Primarily, mail-order selling means dealing with customers without meeting them in person. Orders come in to the company through the mail or by telephone. The telephone sales business is considered a part of mail-order advertising and is highly specialized, using techniques similar to mail-order. Very often you will see ads that implore you to call a special number to place your order. "Special operators are standing by to take your call." Sound familiar? Many of those ads appear on television or are broadcast on the radio. They, too, are considered mail-order advertising.

There are a variety of techniques used, and we will discuss most of them briefly, while concentrating on three major areas: display advertising, classified advertising, and catalogs and brochures.

Each type of advertising uses different methods, with one common goal: to entice people to send in their money and order to you. Almost everyone is a potential customer, but to be successful in the mail-order business you must determine which products will appeal to what specific groups of people. In large urban areas, sophisticated shoppers can buy anything they want at discounts. Thus, city dwellers will be less prone to buying mail-order merchandise merely because of price. There must be something else to encourage them to buy from you. They may be interested in a novelty item or something that appeals to one's specialized interests, business, or hobby. Those who live in more rural areas may buy because certain items are not immediately available or because you offer a price discount. Another reason people enjoy shopping by mail is that many people are thrilled to receive presents in the mail. It is a habit left over from childhood, when you may have sent away for a Captain Midnight decoder signal ring or returned the liner from a bottle of Ovaltine for a Little Orphan Annie secret message pin.

Types of Mail Order

Display advertising utilizes advertising space in newspapers and magazines. The ads may be small, one-inch "shopper ads" or expensive full-page offers. Any mail-order display ad that is big enough should contain a coupon. In order to attract the largest number of customers, you must do everything possible to make ordering easy. A coupon implores the reader to take action immediately, and all they should have to do is fill in their name and address and include a check, if that is part of your ad.

Classified advertising is a technique that uses the small classified sections in thousands of magazines and newspapers that reach both general and specialized markets. Unless you have already ventured into the classified-advertising business, you will be greatly surprised at the enormous number of different magazines published in this country. We'll explore those later. Generally, these ads sell low-priced items or offer free information, in an effort to develop a mailing list of potential customers. Because the type of advertising you select often reflects the quality of the product you are selling, it is more difficult to sell higher-priced items through classified.

Catalogs and brochures are a specialized form of mail-order advertising and involve sending advertising pieces to a carefully selected list of potential customers.

Often, people find shopping through catalogs a convenience. At Christmas time, hundreds of different catalogs are sent to millions of prospective customers offering every type of merchandise imaginable. They can buy Wisconsin cheese, Harry & David's foods, Fruits of the Month, steaks from Chicago, thousands of little items from Sunset House, and anything else in the world they might think of. Without leaving the comfort of their homes, except to mail in the orders, they can take care of all of their holiday shopping by merely checking off lists of items and filling in the forms. Enclose a check, drop it in a mailbox, and await the orders. Although it is an expensive form of advertising, it is excellent if you can target your audience and reach them in a more personal way than display or classified advertising. You can sell one item with a brochure or mailer; you can sell hundreds through a catalog.

There are other forms of mail-order advertising that we will discuss later on in this chapter. These three methods, however, are the most successful, and you can sell virtually anything through mail order. Furthermore, it offers you the opportunity to keep tight controls on your costs, by enabling you to test each product or method of selling. If you owned a store, for example, you might be in business for six months before you found out that you weren't going to succeed. In mail order, you can tell within a week or two after an ad breaks. If it makes it, you increase your advertising. If it doesn't, you stop, without any additional continuing expenses.

What to Sell

Before you start your mail-order business, you've got to have something to sell. It could be one or more products, or it could be a booklet or other informational publication. One of the most popular mail-order pieces we all receive is for magazine subscriptions.

How do you find a product? In earlier chapters I suggested exploring the "Merchandise Offerings" section in your local newspaper or contacting manufacturers. When you find a product, you must make a determination as to whether mail order is truly the best way to sell it. You can also find ways to develop your hobbies into marketable items. For example, one of the most successful ads that appears in classified-advertising sections is "How to Raise Bees in Your Spare Time." This is a hobby that someone has turned into a profit-making idea. If you have some specialized hobby that can offer either information or a service, you might want to try to sell by mail order.

The major advantage when developing a product into a mail-order item is that you can test to determine whether it will sell or not. I have been in a variety of mail-order businesses in the last fifteen years, and some of my experiences should serve as a lesson. The major problem in developing a new product for sales is that there is no formula for success. If there were, we would all immediately adopt the formula and go out and make a million dollars. However, there is no sure way to determine what people's needs and desires are at any one time.

In 1970 I found two products that I thought were going to make me rich. The first was a unique little bottle cutter. I saw the tool at a trade show in Vermont, contacted the manufacturer on the west coast, and received permission to be the seller on the east coast. I tested several different ads, both classified and display, and found both types to be immediately successful. I bought the bottle cutters for $4.50 and sold them for $10. Shortly after I began selling them, other ads began to appear, offering different models of bottle cutters. (This illustrates a basic technique in the mail-order business we will discuss shortly, called "follow the leader.") My sales slipped slightly from the competition, but after an article appeared in the *New York Times* about bottle cutters and their popularity, business picked up again. The success of my sales encouraged the manufacturer to go after bigger game, and within eight months, he had received a big contract from one of the major chain stores.

The original packaging was ideal, a corrugated cardboard box; all I had to do was affix a label to it with the postage and send it out to our customers. Once the big contract came through, the packaging changed into a beautifully designed thin box that I had to wrap before mailing. The boxes frequently broke in the mail, and finally I was forced to stop selling them. But in less than a year I had made several thousand dollars and considered that venture successful.

At the same time, I had been to a national merchandise show, where thousands of manufacturers take booths in order to display their merchandise and look for distributors. There I discovered a unique plastic camera. Essentially it was a plastic box and metal lens that clipped onto an Instamatic film cartridge. I received permission from the manufacturer to sell it through mail order.

I ran several classified ads, two display ads in local newspapers, and even printed up several thousand handout brochures. I hired my wife and son Scott to hand them out in front of Yankee Stadium before a baseball game. At the end of a month I had sold three. I have always felt that that campaign should appear in the *Guinness Book of World Records* as the most spectacularly unsuccessful mail-order campaign. Fortunately, though, it didn't cost me more than a few hundred dollars—and a lot of damaged pride.

On the other hand, while I was running ads for the camera and bottle cutters, I was also doing free-lance direct mail for several publishing companies. From one mail-order campaign that included two brochures sent to elementary schools, I sold three titles for a total of 240,000 copies within four months. That was an average of 80,000 copies of each workbook, for a gross sale of almost $500,000.

What, then, is the answer? Do you merely flip a coin to determine yes or no on an item? Sometimes you may have no choice. Your advantage in mail order is that if it doesn't work after testing, you don't have to spend any more money. On the other hand, there is another method, which I mentioned briefly while describing my bottle-cutter sales: "Follow the leader."

Open a magazine and look for a dozen different display mail-order ads. Then look at last month's issue. How many of the same ads appeared? Go back to earlier issues and see if the same ads are there. Once a successful item and ad is found, the advertiser sticks to it, week after week, month after month, year after year. Why work hard developing a new product when someone else has already done the work for you? The initiator has borne the brunt of the testing costs and has found a formula. As long as your ad is sufficiently different from his, in order not to violate business ethics, you can sell the same type of product.

The idea is to research hundreds of different publications, going through all the back issues and determining what products continue to be sold. If the ads weren't successful, they wouldn't keep appearing. And if you look closely, you will find that other, similar ads, from different companies, appear in the same publications. They sell similar products, in a similar way, whether it's in the classified section or in a larger display ad.

Finding the products should be no problem either. Consult the *Thomas's Register* at your library for a listing of all major manufacturers by category. Contact the manufacturers and ask for permission to sell their products and their discount to you. Tell them that you plan to sell through mail order. They may have already tried and can give you their success rates, or failures, and save you the effort.

There are variations of the follow-the-leader method, of course. If you become successful with this technique, you may want to alter it somewhat. Take a classified ad and expand it into a display ad. Take a product originally sold to one market and develop a new one, with a little twist. Upgrade a product by changing the packaging. Rewrite a successful booklet, without plagiarizing. Adapt foreign products to American markets.

I know already, however, what you are going to do. You think you have a great idea that will make you a million dollars. Of course, all entrepreneurs have million-dollar ideas. That's what gets us started in the first place. So if you plan to go ahead on your own, instead of taking one step at a time and playing follow the leader, you had best read on and discover the technical methods and procedures for successful mail-order advertising.

Display Advertising

Once you have determined *what* you are going to sell, you have to decide *how* to sell it. Step one is to decide what type of mail order to use. Step two, determine the best way to present it, and finally, step three, write the advertisement.

When selecting display advertising, you should first determine what magazines and newspapers will be read by your potential customers. Some products appeal only to specific groups of readers; others have more general interest. Remember that the ad will reflect the quality of the product. And again, even though you have developed your own product, if you play the follow-the-leader game, you will determine where similar products have been advertised.

It is difficult to teach you here how to write a display ad. There are volumes written on the subject, and I suggest you go to the library and read a few. Also, study what others have done. Some of the basics, though, are as follows:

1. Write a headline that's a "grabber." Some of the more famous are, "They all laughed when I sat down to play the piano," and "The Lazy Man's Way to Riches." Both of those get the reader involved immediately and encourage him to read on.
2. More copy is better than less copy. The more you say, the easier it will be to overcome the natural skepticism of the reader. Be specific and write very simply.
3. Offer money-back guarantees. Only a very small percentage of customers ever return merchandise, but it gives you credibility and an image of trustworthiness. Some people give a year's guarantee on a product.
4. Use testimonials. If people write in to tell you how pleased they are with your product or service, inquire if they will permit you to use their testimonials. Publications are stricter today about them and want assurances that they are legitimate claims.
5. Encourage immediate action. Time limits for ordering at special prices or limited availability will encourage readers to order right away. Free incentives help also, or an offer of "postage free if you order within 10 days" might encourage immediate action.
6. Simplify ordering. I mentioned it earlier, but give clear ordering instructions, either providing a simple toll-free telephone number or a coupon to be clipped and sent.

7. Demonstrate, if possible. If your advertisement is big enough and there's enough room, try to illustrate the product with a simple photograph or line drawing.

California Millionaire Wants To Share The Wealth

And He Wants to Share It With Everyone In New York

You think you've got problems?

Well, I remember when a bank turned me down for a $200 loan. Now I lend money to the bank — Certificates of Deposit at $100,000 a crack.

I remember the day a car dealer got a little nervous because I was a couple of months behind in my payments — and repossessed my car. Now I own a Rolls Royce. I paid $43,000 for it — cash.

I remember the day my wife phoned me, crying, because the landlord had shown up at the house, demanding his rent — and we didn't have the money to pay it.

Now we own five homes. Two are on the oceanfront in California (I use one as my office). One is a lakefront "cabin" in Washington, (that's where we spend the whole summer — loafing, fishing, swimming, and sailing.) One is a condominium on a sunny beach in Mexico. And one is snuggled right on the best beach of the best island in Hawaii — Maui.

Right now I could sell all this property, pay off the mortgages, — and — without touching any of my other investments — walk away with over $750,000 in cash. But I don't want to sell, because I don't think of my homes as "investments." I've got other real estate — and stocks, bonds, and cash in the bank — for that.

I remember when I lost my job. Because I was head over heels in debt, my lawyer told me the only thing I could do was declare bankruptcy. He was wrong. I paid off every dime.

Now, I have a million dollar line of credit; but I still don't have a job. Instead, I get up every weekday morning and decide whether I want to go to work or not. Sometimes I do — for 5 or 6 hours. But about half the time, I decide to read, go for a walk, sail my boat, swim, or ride my bike.

I know what it's like to be broke. And I know what it's like to have everything you want. And I know that you — like me — can *decide* which one it's going to be. It's really as easy as that. That's why I call it "The Lazy Man's Way to Riches."

So I'm going to ask you to send me something I don't need: money. Ten dollars to be exact. Why? Because I want you to pay attention. And I figure that if you've got $10 invested, you'll look over what I send you and decide whether to send it back...or keep it. And I don't *want* you to keep it unless you agree that it's worth at least a hundred times what you invested.

Is the material "worth" $10? No — if you think of it as paper and ink. But that's not what I'm selling. What I am selling is information. *More* information than I give when I'm paid $1000 as a guest speaker. *More* information than I give in a one-hour consultation for $300.

But you're really not risking *anything*. Because I won't cash your check or money order for 31 days *after* I've sent you my material. That's the deal. Return it in 31 days — and I'll send back your check or money order — uncashed.

How do you know I'll do it? Well, if you really want to be on the safe side, post-date your check for a month from today — *plus 2 additional weeks.* That'll give you plenty of time to receive it, look it over, try it out.

I know what you're thinking: "He got rich telling people how to get rich." The truth is — and this is very important — the year before I shared "The Lazy Man's Way to Riches," my income was $216,646. And what I'll send you tells just how I made that kind of money... working a few hours a day...about 8 months out of the year.

It doesn't require "education." I'm a high school graduate.

It doesn't require "capital." Remember I was up to my neck in debt when I started.

It doesn't require "luck." I've had more than my share. But I'm not promising you that you'll make as much money as I have. And you may do better. I personally know one man who used these principles, worked hard, and made 11 million dollars in 8 years. But money isn't everything.

It doesn't require "talent." Just enough brains to know what to look for. And I'll tell you that.

It doesn't require "youth." One woman I worked with is over 70. She's travelled the world over, making all the money she needs, doing only what I taught her.

It doesn't require "experience." A widow in Chicago has been averaging $25,000 a year for the past 5 years, using my methods.

What does it require? Belief. Enough to take a chance. Enough to absorb what I'll send you. Enough to put the principles into *action*. If you do just that — nothing more, nothing less — the results will be hard to believe. Remember — I guarantee it.

You don't have to give up your job. But you may soon be making so much money that you'll be able to. Once again — I guarantee it.

I know you're skeptical. Well, here are some comments from other people. (Initials have been used to protect the writer's privacy. The originals are in my files.) I'm sure that, like you, these people didn't believe me either when they clipped the coupon. Guess they figured that, since I wasn't going to deposit their check for at least 31 days, they had nothing to lose.

They were right.

And here's what they gained:

'Made $50,000 just fooling around'
"In February 1974 you sent me (for ten bucks) your Lazy Man's Way to Riches. Since then I have made approximately 50 grand ($50,000) just fooling around on the basis of your advice. You see, I really am lazy — otherwise I could have made 50 million! Thank you!"
Mr. R. McK., Atlanta, GA

'$24,000 in 45 days'
"...received $24,000.00 in the mail the last 45 days.
"Thanks again."
Mr. E.G.N., Matewan, W.VA

Made enough to retire at 41
"If it hadn't happened to me, I wouldn't have believed it...A few years ago, I had nothing to lose. I was unemployed and broke. I didn't even own a car and I lived in a cheap apartment. My total assets were half of a Ducati Motorcycle, and my liabilities could be read on my BankAmericard statement."
"Now, thanks to you and the 'Lazy Man's' program, I have made enough money (at age 41) to retire in style. Let me assure you that I have not 'come into' any money by inheritance or marriage or by any other means except through the practicing of your program..."
R.A., Huntington Beach, Calif.

From $50 to $565 per week
"...when I sent for your (Lazy Man's Way to Riches), I was delivering the L.A. Times for $50 per week...Now...I earn an average of $565 per week, have $7,000 in the bank and a condominium that's worth $85,000..."
J.N. Culver City, CA

Takes in $587,000 in 2 years
"Everything you say is true. I'm a lawyer. I ordered your material two years ago. I received it within a few days and put your method to work immediately. Since then I have taken in $587,000 by following your system. Needless to say, I have given up my law practice — it just wasn't worth working anymore."
C.F.A. Provo, UT

'Wow, it does work!'
"Oddly enough, I purchased Lazy Man's Way to Riches some six months ago, or so, read it..and really did nothing about it. Then, about three weeks ago, when I was really getting desperate about my financial situation, I remembered it, re-read it, studied it, and this time, put it to work and WOW, it does work! Doesn't take much time, either...I guess some of us just have to be at a severe point of desperation before we overcome the ultimate laziness, procrastination."
Mr. J.K., Anaheim, CA

Made $70,000
"A $70,000 thanks to you for writing The Lazy Man's Way to Riches. That's how much I've made...
"I use this extra income for all of the good things in life, exotic vacations, classic automobiles, etc. Soon I hope to make enough to quit my regular job and devote full time to making money the easy way..."
Mr. D.R., Newport Beach, CA

$260,000 in eleven months
"Two years ago, I mailed you ten dollars in sheer desperation for a better life...One year ago, just out of the blue sky, a man called and offered me a partnership...I grossed over $260,000 cash business in eleven months. You are a God sent miracle to me."
B.F., Pascagoula, Miss.

'Steadily upward ever since'
"I ordered Lazy Man's Way to Riches in June...by September, my career was launched and has gone steadily upward ever since."
Mrs. B.A., Walnut Creek, CA

$7,000 in five days
"Last Monday I used what I learned on page 83 to make $7,000. It took me all week to do it, but that's not bad for five day's work."
M.D., Topeka, Kansas

What I'm saying is probably contrary to what you've heard from your friends, your family, your teachers, and maybe everyone else you know.

I can only ask you one question.

How many of them are millionaires?

So it's up to you.

A month from today, you can be nothing more than 30 days older — or you can be on your way to getting rich. You decide.

The wisest man I ever knew told me something I never forgot: "Most people are too busy earning a living to make any money."

Don't take as long as I did to find out he was right.

I'll prove it to you, if you'll send in the coupon now. I'm not asking you to "believe" me. Just try it. If I'm wrong, all you've lost is a couple of minutes and a postage stamp. But what if I'm right?

©Joe Karbo - 1979
17105 South Pacific
Sunset Beach, Calif. 90742

PROOF!

Don't take my word for it. These are excerpts from articles in newspapers and magazines:

me:
He only works half the year in his stunning office on California's Sunset Beach, and even when he's there he puts in short hours... In other words, Joe Karbo, 48, is the prototype for... "The Lazy Man's Way to Riches."

Seattle Times:
Is it all honest? A man who has done business with him says Karbo's reputation is excellent, and that he has managed to conduct mutually beneficial deals with him with nothing but a handshake and an oral agreement.
Want to be rich? Take my advice and follow his.

Boston Herald-American:
The book has drawn hundreds of letters from persons who have profited by it.

Los Angeles Herald-Examiner:
An unpretentious millionaire, Joe Karbo of Huntington Harbor is a vibrant, living testimonial to his intellectual, pragmatic conviction.

Forbes:
After bouncing around show biz, advertising, and real estate, he made his fortune. Last year (1972) he made $250,000.

Money Making Opportunities:
Maybe Joe Karbo has the secret. Don't you think you owe it to yourself to find out what it is all about? ...I just finished it — and I'm off on a vacation myself. Get the idea?

Singles Register:
Many people have tried to duplicate Joe but they aren't even carbon copies. There's only one "JOE"!

The Boston Globe:
Jay Haws of Chico, Cal. said the pep talk in "The Lazy Man's Way to Riches" has "changed my life," and upped his freelance graphic designer income from $2000 to $30,000 annually.
"I'm not rich yet," said Haws, "but I see the light at the end of the tunnel... It gave me the swift kick in the pants that I needed."

Long Beach Independent:
He's programmed the path to riches for the lazy man.

The Kansas City Star:
He prints statements like "Most people are too busy earning a living to make any money." He should have added that too many people these days are too busy earning a living to do any living.
He also sincerely believes that a person can be lazy and make the manna. "If you're working hard, you're probably in the wrong job," he said.

Sworn Statement:

"On the basis of my professional relationship as his accountant, I certify that Mr. Karbo's net worth is more than one million dollars."
Stuart A. Cogan

Bank Reference:
Bank of Westminster
8251 Westminster Avenue
Westminster,
California 92683

Joe Karbo
17105 South Pacific,
Dept. 180 - P
Sunset Beach,
California 90742

Joe, you may be full of beans, but what have I got to lose? Send me the Lazy Man's Way to Riches. *But don't deposit my check or money order for at least 31 days after it's in the mail.*

if I return your material — for *any* reason — within that time, return my *uncashed* check or money order to me. On that basis, here's my ten dollars.

Name ______________
(PLEASE PRINT CLEARLY)
Address ______________
City ______________
State ______ Zip ______

SORRY — NO COD'S

Joe Karbo's mail order advertisement is famous for its unique approach. The headline is a "grabber" and the copy is persuasive. Dozens of similar ads from other companies have imitated this one.

Because copywriting is an art, it is impossible to go into more detail. It may pay for you to hire someone to write and design your ads for you. A classified help-wanted ad in the employment section of your local paper will attract dozens of eager people looking for free-lance advertising work. Most professionals supplement their income with moonlighting, and you can take advantage of their availability. Make sure their work is figured into your advertising budget.

Once you have determined which publications you want your advertisement to appear in, you must write or call each one. On your stationery, request them to send you rate cards. A typical rate card will detail the costs of space for different sized ads, starting with the smallest size possible up to full pages. Also, larger-circulation publications permit you to buy regional editions, which enables you to conduct less expensive tests. You can also consult *Standard Rate & Data*, available in your local library, which details all of the rates for available publications. Rate cards usually duplicate the information in the book.

When you have decided on the size and format of your ad, you can estimate the costs for your test. If you run the ad in more than one publication, you merely calculate the total cost. In order to measure which publications were more successful for your approach, each ad should be keyed. You can add a department listing on the address portion; for instance, Dept. NT, might mean the ad ran in the *New York Times*. It is important to count carefully the number of responses you receive, and from which publications, in order to measure the success of your copy and your media selection. You should also record the number of responses you receive on a daily basis, from the day the ad appeared. By doing so, you will have a timetable against which to measure future ads; it will also tell you whether the ad is still going strong or has died.

Want to save a little money? Here's an inexpensive idea that can benefit any growing mail-order business. When an advertising agency places an ad in a publication for a client, the agency usually receives a 15 percent discount from the publication, its fee for doing the work. You, too, can get that fee if you establish your own "in-house" agency. Pick another name, separate from your company name, and print stationery. When you place an ad, use the in-house company stationery and request the discount. Not all publications will recognize the agency as a legitimate entity, but it is worth the effort. Most publications accept that businesses do this to save the 15 percent, but they are happy to have your advertising dollars and usually do not argue with your request. At the end of a year, the 15 percent saved on your media budget adds up to a substantial benefit.

As soon as your advertisement appears, start keeping records of responses, size of orders, frequency, which publications, etc. As your business continues to grow, you will be able to make qualified judgments as to which ads should run where and the best times to advertise.

Classified Advertising

Here is a business so simple and so obvious that most people tend to overlook its potential. The classified advertising part of mail order is such an inexpensive form of advertising that it is easy to get into and out of, in order to save money.

The major place to advertise for this type of sale is in magazines, rather than newspapers, except for certain specialty publications, such as the *National Enquirer*, the *Star*, the *New York Times*, and a few others. However, hundreds of magazines that accept classified advertising represent a large potential market for you.

The potential of classified advertising versus display advertising is not as strong on a volume basis, since you cannot sell high-priced items successfully through classified ads. But if you have an item, service, or booklet that you can sell for a reasonable amount, say, less than $10 (lower is better), then you should explore this method.

Developing your media sources is the same as for display advertising. Consult *Standard Rate & Data*, research current and back-list publications to find repeat business of products, and request rate cards. You will note that the rates are lower for general publications and higher for more specialized magazines. Normally, classified ads are paid on a per word basis, although some publications permit you to run a display ad within the classified section. Again, ask yourself, "Do the people I want to reach read this type of publication?" If the answer is yes, go with that publication. As you will see when you check rates, you can afford to sell your products to a wider range of people for the same amount of money as one display ad would cost. However, costs should not be your only factor. Some items lend themselves better to one kind of advertising than the other. Sometimes you will find the answer only through trial and error.

The basics of writing a classified ad are the same as those for display ads:

1. Headline. Again, start with the grabber. "Prizewinning Dessert Recipes." "Rejected?" "Make Extra Money at Home."
2. Description. Tell about the product or service. "Detailed guidebook explains how to make millions." "Waterbeds for sale."
3. Market Identification. Usually, in a classified section there will be headings under which your advertisement should appear. If there is no heading specifically for your ad, request that one be inserted. If your ad is to appear only under a general heading, create your own in the ad itself: "Inventors." "Gourmets." "Writers."
4. Price. If you are trying to make a sale, you must give the price. If you are offering free information, make sure that you state that.

5. Action. "Write today." "Call immediately."
6. Address. Don't forget to give your name and address. To save money, you can leave out "street" and other unimportant items, such as "Inc."
7. Code. Although this should be part of the address, don't overlook the code that indicates to you which publication the response is from. It can be a department number, a suite or room number, or a different spelling of your name.

When you run your classifieds, you will have to test continually to determine which publications produce best, which copy draws more responses, etc. There are different categories of magazines that you can try, and you should spread your advertising around enough to give you some qualified indications of success. Too many people have lost money by using the results of one or two ads to project future sales. They were sorely surprised when the bigger expenditures didn't pay off.

It is effective marketing to run your ads on a continuous basis, in order to familiarize your readers with your product. Certain months, however, can be skipped. Sometimes it will be based on seasonal products. Usually, January is an excellent month for advertising; December, the worst. Your concern should be when the magazine is available for purchase, not the cover date of the magazine.

Keep in mind the follow-the-leader principle. When you select the category under which your ad will appear, check the competition. While writing copy, read other ads to see if you're on the right track. Checking a year of back issues will indicate when some items sell better than others. An absence in a magazine of certain types of products will generally indicate that the publication is not appropriate for that item.

Direct Mail

Flyers, catalogs, brochures, and letters are typical direct-mail methods. The most important part of the campaign is your offer, or product. Let us assume that you already have decided what you are going to sell.

Step two is selecting the right mailing list. A mailing list is a compilation of names in specific market categories, such as:

High school principals
Corporation purchasing agents
Subscribers to *Money Magazine*
Stereo equipment dealers
J.L. Hudson store customers
Teenagers

Lists that have been compiled by companies usually have some common characteristic, such as same geographical area, members of an organization, subscribers to specific magazines, employees of similar companies, etc. These lists are put together from a variety of sources, and the largest available selections are usually from list brokers. You will find them in the Yellow Pages under "Mailing List Brokers." Call and request a catalog. The catalogs are free and several of them will provide you with a broad selection of available names.

There are some lists that are compiled by mail-order companies; they are actual customers. To you, they represent a very strong potential for sales. People who normally buy through the mails are apt to make better customers for you.

Finally, the list you compile yourself has tremendous value. Every name that responds to an ad—display, classified, or direct—represents real dollars, for the present order and for the future. Until you grow large enough to have your own computer, type names on multipart labels, available from your local stationery store. It's best to keep them separate by states, as well as by types and categories of products.

Before you purchase or rent a mailing list, you should take the time to find out all of the different types of lists available. In addition to the brokers, you can obtain the Direct Mail List Rates and Data (DMLRD) from Standard Rate & Data Service. This will provide you with information about almost all of the compiled lists, mail-order buyers, and other types of available mailing services. A discussion with your list broker may also aid you in selecting lists you may have overlooked.

Mailing lists rent for prices that range from $25 per thousand to $75 per thousand and up, as of 1981. The quality of the list and its potential are part of what the costs are based on. Where do these lists come from? Here is some insight from an article in the *Wall Street Journal*.

> "The two biggest appeals to mail-order sales are lust and greed." That's the credo of publisher Ralph Ginzburg. Mr. Ginzburg's publication, *American Business*, costs "a mere dollar bill," for one year of issues, and a lifetime subscription is $9.95.
>
> Sound unbelievable? It's for real. Subscribers to this Ginzburg tabloid—and to another called *Moneysworth*, which costs $5 a year—do indeed receive 12 issues a year. But they receive even more than they bargained for—a load of junk mail.
>
> Subscriber names and addresses are sold "to anybody whose offer is legal." Last year, each of the 220,000 subscribers to *American Business* received an average of 110 unsolicited letters. Although his magazines lose money, the sale of the estimated 1.7 million names account for practically all of the $1 million profit his company had last year, based on sales of $7 million.

Not only do magazines sell their subscribers' names but most of the credit-card companies and store charge accounts rent their names to mail-order customers. You can rent small amounts of several different lists in order to determine those with the most pulling power for your product.

After you have made your selection of mailing lists, remember that you are renting the list for one-time use, unless you have purchased additional copies. Mailing lists are seeded with assorted phony names, in order to check up on list users. The company can quickly identify to whom a list was rented and how many times you have used it. If you use it more than the contracted number of times, it is a criminal offense.

However, the names that respond to the ad are yours. This is the most valuable list and may purchase five to ten times more than any other list you might rent. They are your customers and will become used to hearing from you.

Step three, after list selection, is preparing your mailing piece. Although there is no set format, it is important that your mailing contain: a letter, postage-paid reply card or coupon with postage-paid envelope, and an outer envelope.

The letter introduces your product, and, like any other type of advertisement, it must sell the product or service. The coupon is used if you want money returned with the order; the postage-paid reply card is used when an order or response without payment is acceptable. Even brochures or circulars normally have a tear-off reply card so the reader can take action. In catalogs, which are essentially just collections of different mail-order items, there is an order form bound in to facilitate ordering.

Product image is reflected by the style and presentation of the mailing piece. It is important to assure that you do not go overboard on the presentation if it doesn't warrant that type of approach. Bryan Lee spent a small fortune in 1977 trying to establish a newsletter offering information about discount purchases in major cities. The mailing consisted of a letter, a beautiful four-color brochure, an order card, and a reply envelope. The idea for the newsletter was sound, and there appeared to be a need for it. However, Bryan oversold the project. His response rate was disappointing—too small to even cover the costs of his promotion, and not enough to publish the first issue. It seemed that the customers were skeptical about a bargain-hunters newsletter advertised as if it was sold by Gucci or Tiffany. Perhaps, had the mailing gone out typed on two sides of onionskin paper, reeking of budget-cutting measures, it would have had more credibility. Unfortunately, there was no money left after the initial promotion to try another approach.

When your mailing piece has been printed, the next phase is mailing. It is more personal to mail first class, but at 1981 rates of eighteen cents per piece, it is far more economical to mail via bulk mail. Third class bulk mail costs about half the first class rate. Check your post office for all the rates and regulations.

Because you must mail bulk mail in zip code order, it is a tedious job to sort it yourself, especially when you have thousands of pieces. Normally, it makes sense to go to a fulfillment company, which will stuff envelopes, affix postage, gum on mailing labels, and carry it all to the post office. Rates are minimal, compared to the amount of work you would have to do. It is wise to find the company before you prepare your mailing, so you can determine sizes that will fit its machines, number of pieces to be inserted, correct types of labels, etc.

All you can do, once the mail has gone out, is wait. That's the hard part.

The best part is when you open your mailbox, and there it is, stuffed with orders and money. After you have filled the order, deducted your costs for the product and your promotion expenses, the rest of the money is yours. You will, of course, have to pay for your overhead, but if you have been successful, there will be plenty left over—even after paying your taxes.

Miscellaneous Methods

In the chapter about advertising in Part Two, I have covered some other areas that are additional markets for mail order. Television and radio, of course, lend themselves to that kind of advertising. The problem in the beginning is the huge cost of station time.

Michael Velez, an owner of Mid-West Products, Inc., has been selling products successfully for may years through statement stuffers and add-on advertising. When he develops a mail-order product, he first determines who his target audience is. Then he works in conjunction with major credit-card companies to advertise his products in their customer mailings. The advantages are numerous, including enormous markets and an apparent endorsement of the product by the credit-card company. Sales are often in the hundreds of thousands of units for each major campaign.

Calculating Profitability

It is extremely important for you to understand whether or not you are making money whenever you produce a direct-mail promotion. Just because you are not selling directly in person or through a store, don't think that your expenses will be lower. Too often, budding mail-order businesses close because the operator made the mistake of pricing an item too low or getting an insufficient amount of sales from a promotion— and not understanding the profitability of the item.

The only way to assure yourself of adequate profit is to make sure you include all costs involved in the promotion. If you plan to produce your own products, you must include: manufacturing costs, inbound freight costs for all raw materials, assembly costs (per unit, gross, pound, thousand, etc.), and any other related charges.

Then you must include all of the mail-order costs: packaging, shipping, and labor, and the promotion itself. This may include the cost of an advertisement, typing labels and invoices, postage and mailing costs, a percentage for returns, and any other taxes, commissions or royalties you must pay. If you plan to sell via direct mail, you must include the costs of designing, typesetting, and printing a brochure or mailing piece, costs of mailing lists, and postage and handling.

The following is a breakdown of costs for producing and selling sixteen-page booklets through classified advertising. Prices are based on 1,000 copies of the booklet.

Writing	$250.00
Editing	100.00
Typesetting	96.00
Printing	220.00
Shipping	26.40
TOTAL COST 1,000	$692.40

Now you must calculate the costs of processing and shipping the booklets for each order.

Production Costs	$692.40
Packaging	50.00
Packing Labor	75.00
Postage	150.00
Typing Invoice & Label	50.00
Mailing	40.00
TOTAL COST 1,000	$1,057.40

To convert this to a unit price, merely divide by 1,000, and the cost for each booklet is $1.0574, or $1.06. If you plan to sell each booklet for 3.95 + 35¢ for postage, your margin of profit is $3.24 ($4.30 - $1.06), not including advertising costs.

Thus, if you sell 1,000 booklets at $3.95, you will make a gross margin of $3,240.00. Then you must subtract your overhead costs (see Part Two) and your advertising expenses. Whatever is left is your profit.

The profit is really the most important item. After all, for what other reason would you want to be in business, except to make a profit?

You see now why it is important to know whether you are making money or not. If you base your sales campaign on inaccurately calculated prices, you just increase the potential loss of your business. As you expand, you continue to lose more money. If you have calculated carefully, you can keep continual control of your advertising budget, in order to determine where and how you will make the most money. You may buy less expensive ads or even raise the price of the item. It is that balance between making the correct advertising purchase decisions and selling the right item at the appropriate price that makes for success in the mail-order business.

PART TWO

Starting a Business

If you are starting this section, it means that you truly believe you have what it takes to start your own business. It really doesn't matter whether your business is part-time or full-time. The principles are the same, and the dedication to what you want to accomplish is the same. The only difference is in the amount of time that you will be involved. In a full-time business, you will spend all of your working time at the business, and it usually represents your major source of income. In a part-time business, you normally can rely on another income, and the hours are dedicated only by the amount of available time you have.

In this section we will cover:

- What form of business?
- How much money will you need?
- How to raise money?
- Where to find money?
- Management assistance
- Pricing for your market
- Advertising
- Management and record keeping
- Personal pleasures
- Buying a business
- Buying a franchise

As you progress through this section, you will start to get a feel for what is involved in the operation of any business. Most people start their own business with an inadequate amount of knowledge and experience. If you recognize this fact before you begin, you will save yourself many headaches and much money. This is not to say you can't start a business. Rather, be prepared to learn along the way and be aware of your weaknesses. Only in this way can you tip the odds for success in your favor.

Not too long ago, the executive vice-president of a major chemical company left to begin his own business. He had been responsible for a major growth spurt in his company and was considered to be one of the leading executives in his industry. However, the new company, which manufactured and distributed sporting goods, within two years was forced to declare bankruptcy.

How could this disaster happen? There was a very simple answer. The executive had been an expert in his field, chemicals, and a superior manager. He knew very little about sporting goods, except that he was athletic. Also, as a specialist, he had been isolated from the other departments in the larger corporation. The financial area was somewhat unclear to him, and before he recognized his weakness, the company collapsed.

On the other side was Rae Garret. She had worked in the catering business for almost sixteen years. Throughout this time, Rae managed to do everything that was involved in the business. When work was slow, she asked to become involved with different projects. She cooked, served, ordered food, solicited customers. When she and her husband relocated from the east coast to the midwest, she decided to start her own business. The work was harder than she had expected and took up more time than she had planned to give. There were no surprises, however, in running her business. She knew what was required, where to buy supplies, what things cost, how to estimate quantities, and her only real problem was becoming acclimated to an entirely new environment.

Rae tried to keep her business part-time. She worked only two events a month. Her reputation grew, however, and she soon found that she could no longer limit herself. The irony is that although the Garrets moved to be near Mr. Garret's job, he left his employer to come work with his wife. Together they made far more money than they had anticipated. She now has her husband undergoing the training she experienced in the past. They both understand the value of being prepared.

That is what this book should do for you—help you be prepared. Some of the material you will learn for the first time. As you read through other portions, you will begin to evaluate your own knowledge and experience in relation to what the section teaches. Keep notes and try to learn more about those areas in which you are weakest. Use this book as a constant reference. Once you are comfortable with the mechanics of starting a business, you will be ready to explore fields that offer good financial potential. Then merely match your interests and knowledge with the business you want to begin.

1. What Form of Business?

You should know about three basic business forms: single proprietorship, partnership, corporation. Each of these is a legal entity with different purposes, and varying advantages and disadvantages. In most states, establishing single proprietorships or partnerships is very inexpensive. Setting up a corporation is ten to twenty times more expensive.

You might wonder why you should set up any legal entity at all. Why not just go about your business or perform your service without the framework? All the money in or out is yours.

There are several reasons, not the least of which are the psychological benefits of being a "legitimate" business. For a very small amount of money ($25 in New York, $10 in California, $2 in Texas), you can file the necessary papers in order to establish a business that will make you feel good about yourself. This is your business and will grow into an operation that should support you and your family. If it's not fun, if you don't derive pleasure from what you do, you shouldn't do it. Starting and operating your own business is much more difficult than working for someone else, and without continual enthusiasm, your chances of failure are increased.

Thus, step one would be the creation of a legal entity, one that gives you the opportunity to say, "Oh, yes, I'm the owner of Mugwump International." It's not the same as merely saying "I sell tablecloths," is it?

Another reason to have a business entity is the aura of legitimacy you convey to potential customers and suppliers. People are more likely to trust you if you represent a company. After all, your customer or client doesn't have to know you have $11.37 in your account. The customer assumes, merely because you have the credentials of a company name, that you can backup what you're selling.

Each of the business forms has specific pros and cons.

Single or Sole Proprietorship

A single or sole proprietorship means you are operating the business on your own, without any partners. You can operate the business under your own name ("Nancy Jones Designs") or under a separate name ("Designs International").

Setting up a single proprietorship is simple. Your local stationery supply store will probably carry the appropriate forms. The forms might be called "Business Certificate" or "Certificate for Sole Proprietorship" or "Certificate of Conducting Business under an Assumed Name." This doesn't mean an alias. It means that you are using a name other than your own for your company.

Weekend Party Service
Craftworks
We-Fix-It

These are examples of assumed names. You cannot use the abbreviation "Inc." unless you are incorporated.

To set up the single proprietorship, indicate the name of the business and your name and address, have it notarized, and take it to your county clerk's office. Normally you will fill in three copies: one for the state, one for your records, and one for the bank, to enable you to open an account in the name of the business.

Advantages and Disadvantages of Single Proprietorship

Advantages	Disadvantages
Low start-up cost	Unlimited liability
Freedom of operation	Hard to raise money
Complete control of profits and losses	Hard to establish credit
Little working capital needed	Unbalanced management

Advantages
Low Start-Up cost: The fee, in most states, is very low; to file business papers will run from $2 to $50.
Freedom of Operation: Since you are the sole proprietor, no one else can tell you how to run your company or what decisions to make. Very important is the fact that the government requires very little reporting.
Complete Control of Profits and Losses: The money that goes in and out of the business, after expenses, is all yours. No one can tell you how much to take or to spend, except your own common sense.
Little Working Capital Needed: Since a single proprietorship usually starts small, it doesn't require a large investment, either for working capital or partner's equity.

Business Certificate

I HEREBY CERTIFY *that I am conducting or transacting business under the name or designation*

of

at

City or Town of   County of   State of New York.

My full name is*

and I reside at

I FURTHER CERTIFY *that I am the successor in interest to*

the person or persons heretofore using such name or names to carry on or conduct or transact business.

IN WITNESS WHEREOF, *I have this*   day of   /   19   , *made*
and signed this certificate.

....

* Print or type name.
* If under 18 years of age, state "I am..................years of age".

STATE OF NEW YORK
COUNTY OF   } ss.:

On this   day of   19   , *before me personally appeared*

*to me known and known to me to be the individual   described in and who executed the foregoing
certificate, and   he   thereupon   duly acknowledged to me that   he   executed the same.*

Certificate of Conducting Business under an Assumed Name, for Individuals.

Disadvantages
Unlimited Liability: Liability is the amount of responsibility you have to others. If you do something to hurt or damage someone, that person can sue your company. In a single proprietorship, and in a partnership, you are liable above and beyond the holdings of your company.

In a small business, you might not have to worry about liability to any large degree. Of course, in a restaurant, for example, if someone became ill, you could be sued. You could lose your business, your house, car, savings, stocks—even your lawn mower.

You should analyze the operation of your business and talk to your lawyer to determine the amount of risk you run.

Hard to Raise Money: Unless you are well known by the bank as a prospective investor, it is usually easier to obtain or borrow money under the name of a company rather than in your own name. Try it out yourself. Would you sooner lend money to "Peter Brown" or to "Computer Systems Products"?

Hard to Establish Credit: This falls into the same category as raising money.

Unbalanced Management: It is a pretty well-accepted fact that no one person can do everything in a business. Unfortunately, most entrepreneurs find this hard to accept. But if you make a list of all your attributes, you might find yourself lacking in one or two areas. Are you financially oriented? Creative? An administrator?

In a single-person operation, important areas often go neglected. You could, of course, hire the person or persons to fill in the gaps or take on a partner. Because you're the owner and operator, however, you'll have to make the final decisions. Do you trust your decisions in all areas?

Partnership

Those people who would prefer a broader management base and a chance to alleviate some of the ongoing responsibilities of a small business might wish to consider taking in partners.

A partnership is the shared ownership and control of a business. In a general partnership, normally two or more persons share equally in the operations of the company.

It's as easy and as inexpensive as forming a single proprietorship. The form for filing, available at the stationery store, is similar. It is usually called "Certificate of Conducting Business as Partners."

Fill in the name of the partnership and names and addresses of each partner, have it all notarized, and file it in the county clerk's office. Again, one copy is for the state, one for your files, and one for the bank. However, you may also want individual copies for each partner.

X 74—Certificate of Conducting Business as Partners.
Individual — Corporation.

COPYRIGHT 1973 BY JULIUS BLUMBERG, INC., LAW BLANK PUBLISHERS

Business Certificate for Partners

The undersigned do hereby certify that they are conducting or transacting business as members of a partnership under the name or designation of

at

in the County of   , State of New York, and do further certify that the full names of all the persons conducting or transacting such partnership including the full names of all the partners with the residence address of each such person, and the age of any who may be infants, are as follows:

NAME *Specify which are infants and state ages.*   **RESIDENCE**

....

....

....

....

....

....

WE DO FURTHER CERTIFY that we are the successors in interest to

the person or persons heretofore using such name or names to carry on or conduct or transact business.

In Witness Whereof, *We have this   day of   19   made and signed this certificate.*

....

....

....

....

....

State of New York, County of   **ss.:**   INDIVIDUAL ACKNOWLEDGMENT

On this   day of   19   , before me personally appeared

to me known and known to me to be the individual   described in, and who executed the foregoing certificate, and   he   thereupon   duly acknowledged to me that   he   executed the same.

Certificate of Conducting Business as Partners.

Advantages and Disadvantages of Partnerships

Advantages	Disadvantages
Low start-up and filing fees	Unlimited liability
Broader management base	Divided authority
Tax advantages	Lack of good partners
Limited regulation	

Advantages

Low Start-Up and Filing Fees: The rates are similar to single proprietorship fees.

Broader Management Base: As discussed previously under the subject of single proprietorship disadvantages, partners give more input into a business. A banking friend once said that when he looked at a company that was trying to borrow money, he wanted to be assured the company had strong management in operations, sales, financial matters, and production. If you can do it all, that's fine. If not, the additional partner or partners can make the difference between success and failure.

In analyzing my own first business failure, I realized that I was not knowledgeable enough to deal with the financial management of a growing company. The next time around, I made sure I had a partner who could be responsible for finances and business operations, while I handled the creative side, marketing, and production. We have remained partners in many other ventures we have entered into. Our knowledge has expanded to encompass the other partner's areas, but our spheres of responsibilities remain the same.

Tax Advantages: A partnership does not pay a separate tax on its income; each partner is individually responsible for his or her own taxes. However, the partnership must file an *Information Return 1065*, a schedule of which is appended to each partner's individual return.

The profits are shared equally by partners unless you have agreed between yourselves on other percentages. If your company has made a profit of $10,000, each equal partner would declare an equal share of that amount.

However, the losses can be borne only by those contributing capital. Imagine that a company with two partners lost $10,000. If each partner invested an equal amount of money, regardless of the amount, each would be able to write off, or show a loss, of $5,000. (If a spouse is the partner, it doesn't make much difference.) If your partner puts up $5,000 and you put up $3,000, your partner would write off $5,000 and you would write off $3,000; the remaining loss of $2,000 would be borne equally by the two of you. Thus, your partner could show a $6,000 loss and you would declare a loss of $4,000.

This book is not intended, by the way, to be an accounting or business law course, so specific examples for your needs should be discussed with your accountant and lawyer.

Limited Regulation: The government expects you to pay your taxes, and each of the partners is responsible to each other. *You* set up the rules by which you operate.

Disadvantages
Unlimited Liability: The difference between the liability in a single proprietorship and a partnership is that in the event of a losing lawsuit, your partner can also lose his lawn mower. The two of you are equally liable.
Divided Authority: "She says potātō and you say potätō." Who reports to whom? Whose word is final? Who has authority?

The only way to avoid many of these problems is to decide beforehand who does what. In case of a disagreement, no decision can be made.

How many people have you met who have had to sell or abandon a business because the partners couldn't agree? In a good marriage, parents agree to be consistent in the raising of their children. Successful parents don't get caught in the middle of "Mommy says . . . ."

Successful partners agree on certain operational and philosophical criteria. Naturally, they will disagree quite often on other items. An effective decision process must be established in the beginning. Again, if your spouse is your partner, this process can save a marriage.
Lack of Good Partners: Unless you have had a prior working relationship with your partners, it's hard to determine what they will be like when you start your business. Some are just not competent, and when you find out eventually, it can lead to a parting of the ways. Often, the parting is bitter.

Some people don't make good partners. They don't share. They count hours, days, measure their work in relation to yours. Successful partnerships are often the result of each partner's accepting his or her responsibilities. If there's a job to do, you do it. You don't worry that another partner came in at 11:00 A.M. or went home at 4:00 P.M., while you stayed until 8:00 P.M. You measure the success of the operation, function, or department, not the amount of time put in.

You've got to stop thinking of yourself as an employee, a nine-to-fiver. You're an owner or partner, and your work is now measured differently. Survival, money, growth are some of your measures, not time or lunch breaks. And good partners, those who can share and accept responsibilities well, are hard to find.

In a part-time business, these values become even more important. It is likely that if you have a partner, perhaps your spouse, you will both work for the business in spare hours. If your hours don't coincide, you will both be working on your own. Necessarily, then, you set up your relationship and the measurements so you can evaluate them together, when you have time with each other. Once one partner loses confidence in the other, the partnership, as well as the business, is usually doomed.

Corporation

A corporation is a legal entity with individual stockholders, although you can be the sole stockholder. Normally, a lawyer performs the necessary incorporation work, although books can tell you how to do it for very little money. One such book is *How to Form Your Own Corporation Without a Lawyer for Under $50,* by Ted Nichols. But a personal lawyer knows more about you, your family, and your aspirations and can direct you in a much more positive way toward establishing the corporation that suits your needs. Fees can run from a few hundred dollars to over a thousand dollars. It pays to shop around for an affordable price.

The lawyer's fee usually covers several operations. The first is the name search. You are asked to present three proposed corporate names, in your order of preference. Usually a search firm researches the availability of your company name in the capital city of the state in which you are incorporating. If your first choice of name is already in use, they research the second and continue until they find a clear name.

The lawyer also prepares a minute book and a corporate record book. If you so desire, he will even issue you stock certificates. If you are the only shareholder, you will receive all the stock. If you have partners, or shareholders, they will each receive the number of shares equal to their investment.

Advantages and Disadvantages of a Corporation

Advantages	Disadvantages
Limited liability	Regulated by the government
Specialized management	Higher start-up costs
Transferable ownership	Extensive record keeping required
Easier to raise capital	Double taxation
Possible tax advantages	

Advantages
Limited Liability: Unlike a sole proprietorship or partnership, the liability is usually limited by the corporate structure. If someone sued your company, the assets of the corporation could be attacked. You, however, would be unapproachable. In some instances, usually with bank loans, you may be a personal guarantor on a loan, and as such, you are still liable for the payments, either of principal or interest. A few years ago, a gourmet soup company came under attack when several people became ill or died from botulism. The company went out of business, but none of the stockholders was held personally liable. Within two weeks, the company was back in business under a different company name.

When you determine what business you are going to start, you should talk to a lawyer to decide the extent of your liability. In many part-time businesses, liability is minimal and not worth the extra cost of incorporation.

Specialized Management: Like a partnership, additional shareholders can bring to a business, experience, abilities, and money that you may not have.

Transferable Ownership: Because you are issuing stock, all the shares can be sold to remove yourself from the business, or you can sell a portion of the shares to raise additional money, when needed. In small corporations, where only a few shareholders are involved, it is important for the shareholders to have their lawyers draw up a shareholders' agreement. This spells out the legal responsibilities to each other and also makes provision for distribution of money in case of death or dissolution of the business. Normally, shareholders who wish to sell their shares are asked to offer them first to the other shareholders of the corporation.

Easier to Raise Capital: To those individuals or organizations that invest or lend money to small companies, there is more of a feeling of confidence in a business if it is incorporated. Corporations are bound by government regulations, and this, in itself, is enough to inspire confidence. When dealing with other companies or customers, the title, "Inc." at the end of your company name assures them that you are legitimate.

Possible Tax Advantages: Subchapter "S' of the Internal Revenue Code offers those corporations with less than fifteen shareholders the opportunity to be taxed as a partnership. In a partnership, as we discussed earlier, partners may deduct losses from their personal income. In a corporation this process is not possible, except in a "Sub-S Corporation." Thus, if a company is not going to show any positive earnings, this election is an advantage. Many people use this format when attracting high-income investors, since it gives them the opportunity to offset the company's losses against their income and reduce their overall tax liability. Once the corporation begins to show positive results, it can then elect to be taxed as a general corporation.

Disadvantages

Regulated by the Government: The government keeps a close eye on corporations and their financial growth. It is unlikely that a small part-time business has too much to worry about, but a corporation must face a variety of responsibilities, such as franchise taxes, corporate taxes, state, city, and federal taxes. Unemployment tax, Social Security, and a host of other forms must be filled out.

Higher Start-Up Costs: The initial lawyer's fee may be more than many people are willing to risk when starting up a new business. Later we'll talk about how to estimate what those start-up costs should be, but the initial filing fees are much greater for a corporation than for a sole proprietorship or partnership.

Extensive Record Keeping Required: In order to satisfy the requirements of the IRS and any other government agencies, it is important to keep well-organized records. Efficient record-keeping is necessary for any business, but especially important in a corporation.

Double Taxation: The best way to illustrate this problem is to show you the difference between a sole proprietorship and a corporation. In a sole proprietorship, if your company earned $15,000, that money would be taxed as part of your personal earnings. If you were single, and this was your sole income, you might pay about $2,900 in withholding tax.

In a corporation, that $15,000 would first be taxed at a corporate tax rate and then if distributed to you as dividends, it will be taxed as income to you. Because you own the corporation, in essence, you are being taxed twice. If, on the other hand, you instead paid yourself a salary of $15,000, it would be taxable to you but deductible from corporate income and consequently taxed only once.

In a year, five years, or ten years, the little part-time operation you plan to start may resemble nothing like its roots. Thus, instead of starting with the business format that may be far more than you currently need, select the format that suits your current operation. You can start with a sole proprietorship and eventually take in a partner. When that partnership becomes successful, you may need to incorporate. It doesn't make sense to spend the money now, nor to undertake the various expenses and record-keeping chores unless they are necessary. Talk to your lawyer and to your accountant. Ask their advice before you commit yourself.

2. How Much Money Will You Need?

The two biggest problems that most businesses encounter are poor management and insufficient operating capital. In this section, we'll cover all you have to know in order to start in business and keep going for at least six months—even if you do no business at all.

How much is enough money? Every business has different needs. A service business, such as a typing service, needs very little money to start working. However, a manufacturing operation, with inventory, raw materials, machinery, and people to run the operation, is extremely expensive. Due to the wide differences between businesses, I cannot recommend any set amount.

All businesses, though, follow guidelines with appropriate adaptations for their own needs. You must understand the requirements of your business well enough to understand what things cost and what type of sales you can expect. Without this knowledge you will invariably underestimate your financial needs and find yourself out of business before you've really had a chance to start. If you are prepared with the right information and are honest with yourself about your future, you'll have a fighting chance.

Overhead

The first requirement of an estimate is the part that covers your daily operating expenses. It is called "overhead." It is also known as "operating costs" or "general and administrative (G & A)." The overhead has little bearing on sales, nor is it specifically influenced by sales. What this means is that as sales grow, your overhead remains fairly constant, except when you require more personnel, bigger offices, etc. However, your estimate for overhead should be based on your current needs from six months to one year. The good manager will continuously evaluate his business and adjust his overhead if a change is required.

The basic components of overhead are:

Rent
Utilities
Telephone
Salaries
Supplies
Insurance
Postage
Travel and entertainment
Taxes
Professional fees
Advertising

We'll cover others shortly. Also, one major item—advertising—may come under a different heading, cost of sales, depending upon the nature of your business. Let's analyze each component:

Rent: All businesses that use a separate space pay rent. Rent, naturally, varies by location, and no general amount exists. Commercial space usually rents by the square foot. Most people are not familiar with estimating required space by the square foot, since we normally rent or buy a home or apartment by the number of rooms it contains.

The best suggestion is to look at a few different places first, to understand what your requirements may be. For example, 200 square feet might be a room $10' \times 20'$ and may be sufficient for your needs.

Even if you plan to work from your home, you must allocate some of your budget for rent, even if you never actually spend it. Pricing of your service or product must take into account all costs, including overhead. If you were to base your pricing, and the total amount of sales you need in order to make money, on an overhead that did not include rent or utilities, you would be undervaluing your sales.

Suppose your product takes off, and your success causes you to hire additional help. No longer would your kitchen, basement, or garage be adequate; you'd have to rent the necessary space. Your overhead would increase drastically. The selling price, based on a minimal overhead, would no longer be adequate to cover the costs. It would require you to increase the volume of sales to levels that might be unrealistic or impossible, just to pay the additional expense. Or the price of your product or service would have to go up to a point that might not be realistic in the marketplace, and sales would suffer.

Plan for the future of your company and budget a portion of your rent in the overhead.

Utilities: This includes heat, light, power, water, and anything else your rent does not cover. It normally requires you to open an account with your local utility company. To estimate your costs, ask other tenants in the building where you rent. The utility company can also give you that information.

Telephone: Business rates for telephones are usually higher than residential rates. Again, even if you work at home, it is more professional to install a separate telephone, with strict instructions to the children about keeping hands off. Think of the impression a client or supplier gets when a four-year-old answers the phone. You might consider an answering machine, if the telephone is vital to your business.

If you are in a separate office, away from home, you might consider installing two numbers on a push-button phone. In this way, you can make outgoing calls without worrying about missing incoming calls.

Salaries: If you are the only person in the business, you have no other salaries to worry about. However, from time to time you might require additional help, either shipping, typing, bookkeeping or selling. It's important to plan ahead for those times so you have adequate funds. Even if you don't spend the money, you should be prepared.

The amount you take from your business is up to you. When you operate a part-time business, it is preferable to take expense money out of the company, instead of salary. Even if you don't take salary, put it into your budget as a number to aim for. How you take the money you want out of a business is up to you.

Supplies: Everything, from pencils, paper, and stationery to typewriter ribbons, stamp pads, and toilet paper is considered supplies. It does not include material necessary for producing a product.

Insurance: Normal "fire and theft" insurance is usually sufficient, but it depends upon the type of business. Some businesses require liability insurance. Those engaged in food services may need other types of coverage. It's important to check with your attorney about your individual requirements, before you speak to an insurance agent.

Medical and disability insurance is normally not necessary in a part-time business, since often you are otherwise employed, and most businesses have medical and disability coverage. If you are not covered, you may want to adopt a medical plan.

Dental insurance is extremely expensive for small companies. When your business starts to make money, you can initiate an Executive Dental Repayment Plan. In this plan, you pay the dentist personally and then repay yourself from the business account.

If you have a partner in your business, you should be aware of "key-man" insurance. Each partner owns a life insurance policy on the other. If partner A dies, then the proceeds from the policy are paid to partner B or the company. That money is used to hire a person to do the deceased partner's job.

Postage: The expenses for ordinary postage are included here, rather than those costs for sending direct-mail brochures, or the postage for shipping the products. Those costs would be advertising and cost-of-sales, respectively.

Travel and Entertainment (T & E): Any "ordinary and necessary" expenses that pertain to the conduct of business are accounted for here. These include such items as meals, entertaining clients or potential customers, travel to business locations such as sales calls and conventions, certain gifts to people, and a variety of other events. In the section covering "Personal Pleasures" we'll go into greater detail.

Taxes: You may want to consult with an accountant on this subject, but the accompanying worksheet will help you get an idea of what to expect. Your business will be subject to federal, state, and local taxes. These include Social Security, corporate income tax, if a corporation, unemployment, and more.

Worksheet for Meeting Tax Obligations

This worksheet is designed to help the owner-manager to manage his firm's tax obligations. You may want your accountant or bookkeeper to prepare the worksheet so you can use it as a reminder in preparing for and paying the various taxes.

Kind of Tax FEDERAL TAXES	Due Date	Amount Due	Pay to	Date For Writing The Check
Employee Income Tax	_____	_____	_____	_____
and Social Security Tax	_____	_____	_____	_____
	_____	_____	_____	_____
	_____	_____	_____	_____
Excise Tax	_____	_____	_____	_____
Owner-Manager's and/	_____	_____	_____	_____
or corporation's	_____	_____	_____	_____
income tax	_____	_____	_____	_____
	_____	_____	_____	_____
Unemployment Tax	_____	_____	_____	_____
	_____	_____	_____	_____
	_____	_____	_____	_____

STATE TAXES _____ _____ _____ _____

_____ _____ _____ _____

Unemployment Taxes _____ _____ _____ _____

Income Taxes _____ _____ _____ _____

Sales Taxes _____ _____ _____ _____

_____ _____ _____ _____

_____ _____ _____ _____

Franchise Tax _____ _____ _____ _____

Other _____ _____ _____ _____

_____ _____ _____ _____

_____ _____ _____ _____

LOCAL TAXES _____ _____ _____ _____

Sales Tax _____ _____ _____ _____

_____ _____ _____ _____

Real Estate Tax _____ _____ _____ _____

Personal Property Tax _____ _____ _____ _____

Licenses (retail,

vending machine, etc.) _____ _____ _____ _____

Other _____ _____ _____ _____

_____ _____ _____ _____

_____ _____ _____ _____

If you are a sole proprietor or in a partnership, your personal income tax payments must be prepaid or kept current on a quarterly basis. You are allowed certain tax deductions under the Self-Employed Individual Tax Retirement Act. You should ask your local bank about IRA or Keogh plans.

Professional Fees: A lawyer and accountant are required upon occasion. if you are incorporating, you will probably use them. However, this budget allocation is not for business start-up, but rather for ongoing use. If you plan to use an accountant quarterly to prepare tax forms, estimate the annual charge, divide by twelve, and use that number as your monthly estimate. Allocate a portion for legal fees; the more technical your operation, the more you will use a lawyer.

Advertising: I usually prefer to keep this a separate item from the other operating expenses, because it truly can be considered a cost-of-sales. Cost-of-sales varies with the amount of sales, and I normally recommend that new part-time businesses set a fixed advertising budget. Thus, you can project the advertising budget into the overhead. Just skip a line as you list this entry, to set it apart from the others.

Be aware of these other items:

Messenger service
Machine rentals (typewriters, copying machines, computers, postage meter)
Dues and subscriptions
Interest payments (on any outstanding loans)
Maintenance and cleaning service
Miscellaneous (to absorb any unbudgeted items)

Each business has its own peculiarities, and an analysis of your business and others in the same field should give you an indication of the categories required in your operating expense budget.

To make this easier to understand, and to put it into practical form, look at Worksheet No. 1.

WORKSHEET NO. 1

	Estimated Monthly Expenses	Estimated Yearly Expenses
Rent	$	$
Utilities		
Telephone		
Salary: Executive		
Other		
Supplies		
Insurance		
Postage		
Travel & entertainment		
Taxes		
Professional fees		
Advertising		
TOTAL		

Buy yourself several books of accounting paper, transfer the worksheet categories to a page, and begin filling in your estimates. You will eventually need thirteen-column paper. We'll go through a typical estimate, so you will have an idea of what the numbers might look like.

Keep in mind that even though your business may be in your house, you should allocate overhead expenses. The money will not necessarily be spent. These figures are basic business tools and are to be used to recognize and identify important areas of your business. The numbers are not to scare you but to direct you.

Here is the worksheet filled in.

WORKSHEET NO. 1

	Estimated Monthly Expenses	Estimated Yearly Expenses
Rent	$400.00	$4,800.00
Utilities	100.00	1,200.00
Telephone	200.00	2,400.00
Salary: Executive	1,000.00	12,000.00
Other	225.00	2,700.00
Supplies	75.00	900.00
Insurance	75.00	900.00
Postage	150.00	1,800.00
Travel and entertainment	100.00	1,200.00
Taxes	150.00	1,800.00
Professional fees	100.00	1,200.00
Advertising	1,000.00	12,000.00
TOTAL	$3,575.00	$42,900.00

It looks like a lot of money, I'm sure. What this worksheet indicates is that in order to be in business, without selling anything, you will need $3,575 a month, every month. Naturally, you would expect to sell enough products or services to be able to cover those bills. However, most businesses take some time to start, especially those where you do some type of manufacturing. Or, if you open a small shop, it takes a while for the fixtures to be set up and inventory put into stock. On your own worksheet, you should add or delete any items not relevant to your specific business and adjust the numbers to suit your own needs.

If, for example, you work from your home, you probably won't have to pay rent or utilities. You may wish to hold off taking salary for a few months to get your business on its feet. You've already saved $1,500 a month. Advertising can be adjusted according to your business. In a service business it can be held down to the cost of a few hundred letters to potential clients. In a mail-order business, the number may be ten times the budget I've put down. Again, remember that this worksheet is only a tool, and since it is your business, you can do whatever you want.

Start-Up Costs

The next stage of financial planning is to determine your start-up costs, which should be estimated before you start your business.

Normal start-up costs usually include some or all of the following:

- Equipment, fixtures, supplies
- Starting inventory
- Decorating
- Installation of equipment
- Utility deposits
- Legal and professional fees
- Licenses and permits
- Rent deposit

Equipment, Fixtures, Supplies: Any business, when it begins, will need some type of equipment, like a typewriter, adding machine, or calculator, or even a postage meter. Fixtures include furniture such as desks, chairs, and file cabinets, or in a retail outlet, they might consist of showcases, or racks, and lighting. Stationery, paper, pencils, clips, and ribbons for the typewriter are usual opening supplies. This cost is a one-time expense and is not the same as your ongoing operating expenses.

Starting Inventory: If you are selling baskets, cookies, computers, or tropical fish, you will need some inventory before you begin. This is an expense that occurs before you make any sales. On a monthly operating basis, the inventory becomes a cost-of-sales.

Decorating: It could be as minor as a coat of paint, an area rug, and a framed print on your wall. Or, if it's a retail operation, you might wish to invest more money in the ambience.

Installation of Equipment: When you lease equipment such as a copying machine, typewriter, an oven to bake cookies, or a printing press, you normally have an installation charge that is approximately equivalent to a month's leasing fee. Also, the telephone company charges an initial fee to install your telephones.

Utility Deposits: In most cities, the local utility company asks for a nominal deposit before it turns on your electricity or gas. The phone company charges a fee, too, which is not the same as the installation fee.

Legal and Professional Fees: If you are incorporating, you must allocate money for the legal fees. Professional fees include accountants and business consultants, if you use them before you start..

Licenses and Permits: Many small businesses require you to obtain a license, especially in a food-related business. If you plan to sell in flea markets, street fairs, or if you are a peddler, you might need a peddler's license. Contact your local state tax office for information.

Rent Deposit: Most landlords require at least one month's rent as a deposit. It is usually refunded when you leave.

The following Worksheet No. 2 gives an example of setting forth your start-up costs:

WORKSHEET NO. 2

Equipment, fixtures, supplies	$1,000.00
Starting inventory	500.00
Decorating	500.00
Installation of equipment	500.00
Utility deposits	100.00
Rent deposits	400.00
Legal and professional fees	500.00
Licenses and permits	100.00
TOTAL	$3,600.00

The results of Worksheet No. 2 indicate that you need $3,600 to open your new business. Again, like the operating costs, you may have more or fewer items on your own list.

One more item is necessary: your business insurance, so to speak. Starting a new business, even part-time, is very risky. It demands hard work, knowledge, and sufficient capital. Because most businesses don't start earning money from the first day, you have to make sure your expenses are covered. In addition, sales rarely reach your expected level in the first few months, so you have to make up the difference between sales and costs.

In order to do so, and to insure yourself a fighting chance to build your business, I recommend that when you budget your start-up costs, you allow for at least six months of operating costs. Then, if sales don't move to the necessary level fast enough, at least you can pay your rent, telephone bills, and other expenses. The landlord never cares whether your sales were good or bad. He wants to be paid every month.

Thus, based on our projection of $3,575 for monthly overhead, you should allow $21,450 ($3,575 times six months) in addition to your start-up costs. You will need:

Start-up costs	$ 3,600
Six months' operating capital	$21,450
	$25,050

With that amount of money, even if you didn't do any business at all, you would still be able to pay your bills. You could give up parts of your expenses, such as salary, and continue for a few months more. However, if you were at that point, you might be wiser to close down and save money.

Profit and Loss (P & L)

To understand how a business makes or loses money, you should be able to prepare a profit and loss statement. Very simply, the P & L is the difference between what you sold and what it costs you to earn that money. Since all of these accounting forms are necessary to understand your business, a P & L is broken into various components. Here is a very simple P & L using our projected monthly overhead:

Sales	$7,500
Cost of goods sold	− 2,500
Gross margin	$5,000
Operating expenses	− 3,575
Net profit	$1,425

The sales and cost-of-goods-sold figures are hypothetical, of course. Let's look at it in a little less positive way.

Sales		$3,660
Costs of goods sold		− 1,200
Gross margin		$2,460
Operating expenses		-3,575
		($1,115)

The parentheses around the number indicate a loss. Thus, after paying for the cost of goods and your overhead, you'd be $1,115 short. That's the reason for allocating that extra six months' operating capital.

Now we'll prepare a P & L in more detail and move the advertising allocation into the cost of sales.

SAMPLE PROFIT AND LOSS STATEMENT

Sales			$7,500.00
Costs of Sales:			
Cost of goods sold	$2,500.00		
Advertising	1,000.00		
	3,500.00	3,500.00	
		4,000.00	
General and Administrative			
Rent	400.00		
Utilities	100.00		
Telephone	200.00		
Salaries: Executive	1,000.00		
Other	225.00		
Supplies	75.00		
Insurance	75.00		
Postage	150.00		
Travel and entertainment	100.00		
Taxes	150.00		
Professional Fees	100.00		
	2,575.00	2,575.00	
Net Profit		$1,425.00	

This should enable you to have a very clear picture of where your money is going.

Sales Projections

Only from experience, reserch, experimentation, and educated guessing can you make any type of projections of your sales. Though it may take a bit of work, it's important to do. How can you start a business when you have no idea if you are going to make money?

To estimate sales, you must make a list of all the objectives, variables, potential customers, products or services. You plan to sell and start figuring. Here is where you can use your thirteen-column pad. Label the top columns 1–12, and the last column, your total. Start writing down numbers. If you are more comfortable basing you projections on units, start that way. Then calculate unit selling prices.

SALES PROJECTIONS

	Month 1	Month 2	Month 3
No. of units	300	420	500
Unit selling price	$ 25	$ 25	$ 25
Sales $	$7,500	$10,500	$12,500

When you've finished twelve months, add the numbers and you will estimate your total annual sales. If you're selling more than one type of item or service at different dollar amounts, you will have to do individual projections.

Where you offer a variety of merchandise, such as a store setting, you might better estimate the possible number of customers per month times the estimated average sale.

SALES PROJECTIONS

	Month 1	Month 2	Month 3
Average daily customers	40	50	75
Average monthly—24 days	960	1,200	1,800
Average sale	$ 10.00	$ 12.50	$ 14.00
Sales $	$9,600.00	$15,000.00	$25,200.00

Just don't be carried away by the sales figures. Remember that before you have any profit you must account for:

- Cost of goods sold
- Advertising expense
- Overhead

The key to success in any business is two-fold:

1. Increasing sales
2. Managing costs

We'll talk about sales later in this section. Managing costs is made easier by the use of the overhead projections, profit and loss statements, and perhaps the most important projection—cash flow.

Cash Flow

A cash flow is a projection of your cash needs throughout a specified period of time, usually one to three years. It helps you determine when you are going to need additional capital for the business.

To clarify the difference between profit and loss and cash needs, we can look at what happens in a restaurant.

Suppose the sales in a restaurant were $500 for the day. After deducting the costs for the food (cost-of-goods-sold) and the overhead for running the restaurant, you have $100 left over. That means you made a profit!

What would happen, however, if all your customers charged their meals? You'd have much paper guaranteeing your payment at some time in the future, but no cash. Without cash to operate, you are in trouble. The landlord, utility and telephone companies want to be paid. Employees, if any, want payment. Regardless of the amount of sales, you will always need cash in order to operate.

Thus, a cash-flow projection is vital. You can project your sales, and you can estimate your future profits, but without knowing when you will have cash needs, you may be in for painful surprises. The necessity for cash may be a result of some of the following:

1. Longer-than-anticipated start-up time.
2. Fire, theft, or storms
3. Large orders for future delivery that require additional inventory
4. Addition of extra personnel to fill large orders
5. Sickness of sole operator of business
6. Increased costs of inventory
7. Sudden loss of an important customer

The list can go on forever, but you should anticipate anything unusual that may require a sudden need for cash.

A few years ago, a small publishing company, apparently on the road to riches, was forced to sell out to a larger company to avoid bankruptcy. In a few years from its inception, the company had made a name for itself selling educational review books to junior and senior high schools. Their publications were excellent, and their costs easily affordable by the schools.

As the sales grew, additional titles were added to their book list. The problem that arose was in the manner that schools purchased books. In September when most schools opened, teachers began ordering books and continued throughout the school year until May. In June, just before the regular school sessions ended, the schools paid their bills. They had always operated this way. If books were still unsold in the school bookstore, they were returned to the publisher, and then a check was issued for those books that were sold to students.

What was the publishing company going to use to pay its bills for the rest of the year, before it was paid by the schools? The printers, paper mills, and typesetters didn't want to wait nine to twelve months for payment. The staff of the publishing company wanted to be paid on a regular basis. Sales were booming. Cash was bombing. An unfortunate result of poor financial planning.

Small and large companies must prepare a cash flow projection. Part-time and full-time operations both have cash requirements. It's a time-consuming, somewhat involved procedure, but it may mean the difference between survival or failure. Why take shortcuts, when the right way may mean continued success?

Cash-flow projections involve balancing your anticipated cash income from sales or other items such as rent or investments against your expected cash expenses, including cost of goods and overhead.

In order to begin a cash-flow projection, you will need to estimate the following, over the period of time included in the projection:

1. Projected monthly sales
2. Cash in bank at start of month.
3. Expected cash sales
4. Expected collections
5. Any other income expected
6. Cost-of-goods sold
7. Monthly overhead

Projected monthly sales: earlier in this section you prepared this projection. This is an important figure, since most of the other numbers are tied to your sales.

Cash in bank at start of month: This is the amount of money you have when you open your doors for the new month. It's the money used to run your business.

Expected cash sales: Actual sales and cash sales are different, as illustrated by the earlier example of the restaurant with all charge customers. In some businesses, 100 percent of the customers pay with the order. In others, only a percentage pay; many are billed by the company or use charge cards. You need to understand the nature of your business and project realistically the type and percentage of payment you will receive. As business continues, you will develop new information and probably revise these estimates.

Expected collections: Known as accounts receivable, this is the money you expect to collect from what is owed to you from the previous month or months. For example:

January sales $7,500.00
Cash sales (70%)..............$5,250.00
February collections (30%) $2,250.00

In today's economy, more people and companies are extending their payments, and expected collections might look like this, using the above numbers:

	Jan.	Feb.	Mar.	Apr.
Payments:	70%	15%	10%	5%
Actual dollars	$5,250	$1,125	$750	$375

Once you've understood this concept, you can then do a longer projection using Worksheet No. 3. I've filled in sample numbers, using the payment schedule of 70/15/10/5% and hypothetical numbers.

WORKSHEET NO. 3

Estimated Payments: 70/15/10/5%		Jan.	Feb.	Mar.	Apr.	May	June
Est. Sales							
$7,500	Jan.	$5,250	$1,125	$ 750	$ 375		
9,000	Feb.		6,300	1,350	900	450	
10,000	Mar.			7,000	1,500	1,000	500
12,500	Apr.				8,750	1,875	1,250
14,000	May					9,800	2,100
15,500	June						10,850
Total Cash Income		$5,250	$7,425	$9,100	$11,525	$13,125	$14,700
Expected Cash Income		$5,250	6,300	7,000	8,750	9,800	10,850
Expected Collections		—	1,125	2,100	2,775	3,325	3,850

WORKSHEET NO. 4
(Cash-Flow Projection)

	Month 1	Month 2	Month 3	Month 4	Month 5	Month 6	Month 7	Month 8	Month 9	Month 10	Month 11	Month 12	Totals
	1	2	3	4	5	6	7	8	9	10	11	12	13
Estimated sales													
1. Starting cash for month													
2. Expected cash sales													
3. Expected collections													
4. Other anticipated income													
5. Total cash													
(Lines 1 + 2 + 3 + 4)													
6. Cost of sales													
7. Total													
(Lines 5–6)													
8. Overhead													
9. Total													
(Lines 7–8)													
Cash on line 9 is also starting													
cash (line 1) for following													
month													

WORKSHEET NO. 5
(Abbreviated Cash-Flow Projection)

	Month 1	Month 2	Month 3	Month 4	Month 5	Month 6
Estimated sales	7,500	9,000	10,000	12,500	14,000	15,500
1. Starting cash for month	21,450	20,125	20,375	21,900	24,850	28,800
2. Expected cash sales*	5,250	6,300	7,000	8,750	9,800	10,850
3. Expected collections*	—	1,125	2,100	2,775	3,325	3,850
4. Other anticipated income	—	—	—	—	—	—
5. Total cash (Lines 1 + 2 + 3 + 4)	26,700	27,550	29,475	33,425	37,975	43,500
6. Cost of sales (40%)	3,000	3,600	4,000	5,000	5,600	6,200
7. Total (Lines 5–6)	23,700	23,950	25,475	28,425	32,375	37,300
8. Overhead	3,575	3,575	3,575	3,575	3,575	3,575
9. Total (Lines 7–8)	20,125	20,375	21,900	24,850	28,800	33,725

*See Worksheet No. 3

WORKSHEET NO. 6
(Abbreviated Cash-Flow Projection)

		1	2	3	4
		Month 1	Month 2	Month 3	Month 4
1	Estimated sales	—	7,500	9,000	8,000
2					
3					
4	1. Starting cash for month	5,000	1,425	(150)	100
5					
6	2. Expected cash sales	—	5,000	6,300	5,600
7					
8	3. Expected collections	—	—	1,125	2,100
9					
10	4. Other anticipated income	—	—	—	—
11					
12	5. Total cash	5,000	6,425	7,275	7,800
13	(Lines 1 + 2 + 3 + 4)				
14					
15	6. Cost of sales (40%)	—	3,000	3,600	3,200
16					
17	7. Total	5,000	3,425	3,675	4,600
18	(Lines 5–6)				
19					
20	8. Overhead	3,575	3,575	3,575	3,575
21					
22	9. Total	1,425	(150)	100	1,025
23	(Lines 7–8)				

Other income expected: Large companies usually put their money to work in a variety of ways, including real estate, investments in stocks and bonds and in other companies. You may rent one room in your office to help offset costs. This is income derived from services other than company business.

Cost of goods sold: We discussed this earlier when preparing a P & L. Essentially, the costs for producing and selling the goods or services are calculated here. Experience in the business will eventually help you calculate a percentage, and it will be easier to estimate your cost of goods.

Monthly overhead: You can adjust your operating cost projection after obtaining experience with the actual costs. If you project a major increase in sales, expansion, addition of employees, or a partner, don't forget to revise your overhead.

Look at Worksheet No. 4 to see what the format looks like. Copy this onto your own pad and try to estimate your own numbers and put them in place.

Worksheet No. 5 is an abbreviated cash-flow projection using the numbers from Worksheet No. 3. On that worksheet, the numbers within the boxes are the estimated sales. The other amounts are the expected cash sales and expected collections.

One other assumption we've made is the cost-of-sales. We've selected 40 percent as a production cost. As presented in our original projections, advertising expense is figured into the overhead.

If we go back to our original projection of overhead and start-up cost, I suggested starting with six months of operating costs in the bank — $3,575 × 6 = $21,450. That is your first month's starting cash for month.

If all runs smoothly, your cash flow on Worksheet No. 5 will continue to improve. Unfortunately, most businesses don't run smoothly. Any combination of events could reduce your available cash.

Worksheet No. 6 will show you what happens when you start off undercapitalized. Instead of six months' operating capital, start with $5,000. Allowing a month for actual start-up time, sales don't begin until Month 2. To make matters worse, in Month 4, sales fell slightly. Because of a bad storm you were unable to see enough accounts.

As you can see, in Month 2, you are $150 short of cash. In Month 3, you barely break even. Assorted problems may arise, and having extra cash could be the way to survive bad times. In small part-time businesses, especially those that are run from home, you have a better chance of surviving, since you can save on overhead.

Using a cash flow projection properly and revising it on a monthly basis using actual numbers, you can plan for the peaks and valleys in your business. In those seasonal businesses that have slack sales at one period and a boom in another, it is especially important to anticipate your cash needs. The cash flow projection can be presented to your banker, and together you can plan for judicius borrowing and repayment.

Sound management recognizes that occasional borrowing is one of the accepted tools of America's economic system and plans, with the use of the cash-flow projection, to avoid a cash crisis. The amount of cash you will need differs from other operations because all businesses are not alike. Lack of cash can drive a firm, no matter how small or large, into bankruptcy, even though its products or services are first rate and its operations are profitable.

Just don't confuse your profit and loss statement with a cash-flow projection.

3. How to Raise Money

Now that you've figured out how much money you'll need to start your business, how and where do you obtain it?

The first step is to write a business proposal. Not only will you use the proposal to raise money but the preparation of it will enable you to develop a complete understanding of your business far greater than you thought you already had. Each section of the proposal will involve details that only experience or diligent research will bring forth. The knowledge gained will be well worth the effort.

Part I: Introduction

The report begins by introducing the industry, its positive and negative aspects, and a brief description of *your* business. You must emphasize how your business fits into the overall industry and why your business is unique. How will your business compare with others in your field? What is the industry's performance?

Almost all areas of business are represented by some association that will have research and statistical information available for you. You may also consult trade magazines, which are publications that deal primarily with a specific business area. The Department of Labor and other government agencies should also be able to provide you with data you might need.

Your research into these areas may either encourage you to pursue your dream or discourage you from investing additional time or money. Even in a part-time business that may involve less time and money invested, you should be assured that the growth potential is suitable for you to continue.

Part II: The Deal

This part of your proposal is necessary if you are looking for additional investors. Even if you plan to ask a friend or relative to be involved (and more on that later) you should present the deal in a fully professional manner. Money invested by friends or family is usually an emotional move. Unfortunately, the loss of money will also result in an emotion — negative. If the proposal to raise the money was fully professional, your friends and family can make a decision based on facts. They may reject the proposal without feeling guilty. They may also lose their investment and know that they had the opportunity to make up their own minds, rather than be influenced by a personal relationship. No one likes to lose money, but having had a businesslike proposal makes loss easier to accept without any recrimination. In essence, it is your protection.

Description of the deal includes the type of money you are looking for: stock or loan. A loan is repaid, and stock involves equity or ownership in your company. In a partnership, you sell a percentage of the business. In a corporation, that percentage is considered a share, and a stock certificate is issued to cover that percentage.

You must disclose the total amount you wish to raise and what the minimum investment will be. If you want to raise $20,000, you might state that the minimum investment is $5,000. That means that as many as four, or as few as one, may invest. You may sell:

    1 share @ $20,000
    2 shares @ $10,000 each
    3 shares @ $10,000 for one
                  5,000 for two
    4 shares @ $5,000 each

Part of the total capitalization (the total amount of money to be invested on a permanent basis) may come from you. In addition to the $20,000, you may also put up some of your own money. Don't forget, too, that your time is worth money.

Part III: Financials

This is where you attach all the projections you did earlier: cash flow, sales estimates, operating budget, etc.

Part IV: Management

Who is part of the deal? In a small business that operates on a part-time basis, there are rarely more than one or two people involved. Even so, anyone who puts up money wishes to know if you are capable of managing their money and your business.

Description of management is really an expanded form of job resume. Experience in the business or in related fields is important. If you've had prior successes, stress them. When you've written down all of the required information, reread it. Would you invest money in this person?

Part V: Exhibits

Remember the woman who started a key lime pie business? She got her customers by giving them a taste of the actual product.

You can do the same thing. You can show customers photos or drawings of your product; a sample or prototype is even stronger. Testimonials from satisfied customers are also advisable, if available. It's an effective type of marketing.

Part VI: The Overview

Someone once asked Ernest Hemingway how he was able to convey so much information and emotion into his very terse style of writing. He replied that he first went out to learn everything he could about the subject. That accumulation of knowledge would show itself clearly in just a few sentences.

Writing the overview for your business proposal is the same type of procedure. Because professional investors see hundreds of proposals a week, they rarely want to read through an entire report. Instead, an overview gives a brief but enticing description of what the business is. The only correct way to pack all that knowledge into one exciting page is to learn first everything you can about the subject.

Presumably, you will have learned a lot in the process of writing and researching your proposal. The synopsis, or overview, is a result of this work, and although written last, will appear as the first page. If the reader is interested, the balance of your proposal will be read.

Whether or not you plan to raise outside financing, writing a business proposal will be a valuable exercise in business planning. With all the specifics in front of you, it will be easier to make some educated projections about your future success.

4. Where to Find Money

When all of your records are complete and the numbers indicate you have the potential for success, it's time to find the money. Equipped with your business proposal, you must determine who your possible investors will be.

The first place to look is your own savings account. Conventional business wisdom and a host of *How to Make a Million Dollars in Real Estate* books all advise using "OPM," Other People's Money. But in a part-time business where you have another income and are not totally at risk, it is perfectly acceptable to invest your own money.

Also, in a start-up situation that doesn't require much overhead, especially in a personal service business, investing your money in your own business may be better than leaving it in a bank or buying stocks or gold.

One way to determine the advisability of investing your money might be the Return on Investment (ROI) formula. The formula determines what percentage return you will have on your investment. There are several different approaches to the formula. The most simple is:

$$\frac{\text{NET PROFIT}}{\text{TOTAL ASSETS}} = \text{Return on Investment}$$

At the end of a year, for example, if the company had a net profit (after taxes) of $20,000 and total assets (cash on hand, receivables, fixed assets, etc.) of $230,000, the formula would show the following:

$$\frac{\$\ 20,000}{\$230,000} = .087 \text{ or } 8.7\%$$

It also means that you have earned 8.7¢ for every dollar invested. If there are other places to invest your money at that rate of return, you might consider them. However, don't overlook the fact that you also earn a salary and own your own business. An investment in the stock market may give you a greater return, but you still won't be your own boss.

The second place to obtain money may be from friends or relatives. As I mentioned earlier, if your business is successful, you'll be a hero. Just keep in mind that you still have to live with your friends and relatives. A bad investment will create plenty of personal problems.

One of the most available sources for investment is with venture capital investors. These are companies established primarily for investing in new businesses. The people who run a venture capital company are skilled in the financial management aspects of business.

To find venture capital, you must read local or national newspapers and professional and business-oriented magazines. The magazines' articles about venture companies will provide you with a source to contact. In the "Business Opportunities" section of your newspaper's classified ads, you will usually find a section entitled "Capital to Invest." The advertisements may be from venture capital companies or other individuals and companies with money to invest.

You may attract investors by running you own ad under the section called "capital wanted." It may turn out to be the most important ad you ever write, so prepare it carefully.

There are also source books that list companies. One that appears quite complete is *The Guide to Venture Capital Sources* from Capital Publishing Corp., P.O. Box 348, Two Laurel Avenue, Wellesley Hills, Massachusetts 02181. They also publish another valuable book, *The Source Guide For Borrowing Capital*. The books are not inexpensive, but they may be important to you if you have sufficient capital needs. They are also tax deductible, since they are legitimate business expenses.

Another source to explore might be other people in related businesses. Perhaps a potential supplier of yours might find it attractive to finance your venture if it means a new outlet for its product or service.

Following is a listing of types of new ventures that might be financed by different types of suppliers. Look for natural tie-ins, where the new venture can enhance the supplier's business, and the new business can take advantage of the supplier's expertise.

Supplier	New Venture
Printer	Publisher
Publisher	Bookstore
Seed producer	Garden supply store
Jewelry manufacturer	Fashion boutique
Florist	Caterer
Tool manufacturer	Hardware store
Business consultant	Typing service or accounting service
Film processor	Portrait photography

These are just a few types of sources. Use your imagination.

Venture capital is different from borrowed capital. Venture capital does not get paid back; instead, you give up equity, or ownership, in your company. You may resent it, but on the other hand, it might represent the only way you can become your own boss. The more money you require, the more control you will have to give up.

Equity represents three important factors to you. Control of equity (51 percent or more) means control of voting on major company decisions. There may be new locations, additional product lines, acquisitions. A venture capital investment rarely influences your day-to-day operations. As long as the company is successful, the investor does not care about hiring, firing, marketing, sales, salaries or other procedural decisions. Usually the investor will review monthly sales and P & L charts, and unless you are losing money, he will not become involved.

The percentage of equity also represents the amount of profits that are taken from the business. If you make a cash profit of $6,000 and you own 40 percent, you get $2,400 as a bonus. Your partner, assuming his or her ownership is 60 percent, gets $3,600. Normally an investor does not get a salary from the company, so it is only fair to pay back the trust (and investment) in you with bonuses.

The aspect of putting majority equity in another's hands that is least appealing is the possible sale of your company without your approval. In small businesses in which there are partners, it is customary to prepare a partnership agreement. This spells out the terms of your agreement and usually requires that the other partners have "right of first refusal" on the sale of the business. A venture capital investor usually invests to try for the highest and fastest possible return on investment. Often, that means selling the business. Assure yourself that you have the option to have a say in your future.

In very small businesses, especially part-time operations, the immediate potential is not usually large enough to entice an investor. Later, as your company grows and proves itself, you might find willing investors. If you need the infusion of fresh capital, you might then consider selling equity. Your success gives you a strong position from which to negotiate for the larger percentage.

There is another source of equity financing available through a unique program of the Small Business Administration (SBA). These are SBICs, Small Business Investment Companies. The SBIC raises private capital and then leverages that amount with the use of federal funds. There are more than 300 SBICs licensed by the SBA, and there are also more than 100 Minority Enterprise SBICs (MESBICs), whose function is to invest in minority-owned firms. The SBICs invest their money in those businesses that appear to have a high growth potential. Of course, like other venture capital bankers, they will expect equity in your company. You can obtain specifics from the SBA, including a listing of SBICs and MESBICs.

Instead of giving up equity in your business, you might consider borrowing money. You should know how to obtain money, where to find it, and what it will cost you. The best time to borrow money is when you don't need it. That way you can shop around and are not pressed into a quick decision because of immediate need.

The first place to go is the bank. In small businesses, it is often difficult to obtain a loan unless you have a proven track record. Or you must have some type of collateral, which may be inventory, fixtures, machinery, or confirmed customers' orders.

In most cases, the bank will charge you a percentage over the prime rate. The prime rate is that percentage of interest that the bank's prime customers are paying. Prime borrowers are a better risk than you, which is why you pay a few points over the prime rate. Be aware that this is not a fixed percentage of interest; it fluctuates, and so does the amount you pay. If the prime rises, so does your interest rate.

Conversely, if it drops, so does your rate. In 1980, prime rates ranged from 10 percent to 21 percent. Imagine the poor borrower who got a loan for $10,000 at 10 percent. Six months later the interest was over 20 percent. Unless he was prepared for that, his business cash flow would have been severely disrupted.

One of the major sources for borrowing money is the SBA. In 1979, they provided loans to more than 40,000 businesses. Of that number, almost 10,000 were new business ventures that received over $850 million. Those who are eligible for loans are small manufacturers, wholesalers, retailers, service concerns, farmers, and other businesses. The purposes for lending the money are to provide for construction, expansion or conversion of facilities; purchase buildings, equipment, and materials, or obtain working capital.

However, in order to be eligible for a loan, you must first seek financing from a bank or other private source. If you live in a city with a population over 200,000 people, you must apply to at least two banks before applying to the SBA. If the bank rejects your request, it is important to ask if the bank will consider making the loan with a guarantee from SBA. The SBA may guarantee up to 90 percent or $350,000 of a loan made by a commercial bank for start-ups or expansion of an existing business.

To approach the bank and the SBA, you should provide the following items, if available:

1. Your business plan, as discussed earlier. Also explain why you need the money and how it will be used. Include your resume.
2. A written estimate from suppliers if you plan to purchase equipment or make leasehold improvements.
3. A balance sheet and P & L statements for the last three years, if possible.

4. Federal income tax returns for the business and each of the owners for the previous three years.
5. Your business certificate (sole proprietorship or partnership) or corporate seal on the application form.
6. Financial projections, including P & L and cash-flow projections.
7. Miscellaneous materials, including leases, proposed collateral (mortgages, inventory, personal endorsements) and personal financial statements.

If the bank will not make the loan, even with the guarantee from the SBA, you may still be eligible for a direct loan from the agency, if funds are available. You must show an ability to repay the loan. Also, if you are seeking true venture (start-up) capital, the SBA requires you to invest a reasonable amount of your own money.

If you think you would qualify, it makes sense to contact your local SBA office and ask for their pamphlet and applications for a loan.

There are a few other major lenders, in addition to the SBA. The Farmers Home Administration (FmHA) will make direct and guaranteed loans to a wide assortment of businesses. Unlike the SBA, you do not have to be turned down by another lending source to be eligible. If you live in an area with low- to medium-income populations and high unemployment, you may be able to obtain an Economic Development Administration (EDA) loan. The Department of Housing and Urban Development (HUD) also has a specialized lending program, and it may be advisable to contact it.

The National Science Foundation makes money available for research and development. For part-timers with a scientific leaning, their Small Business Innovation Research Program may be for you. The Department of Energy (DOE) and the Interior Department make specific grants also, and if you are interested in energy programs or historic restorations, money may be available.

The number of potential sources for equity funding or company loans is limited only by the imagination. Almost all businesses—from dining-room-table size to IBM—need money. It pays to be aggressive when looking for money. A solid, conservative business proposal can be your biggest asset, and careful preparation of the proposal might convince someone of your responsibility, organization, and financial abilities. Finally, don't take no for an answer. Find out what has to be done to entice the investor or lender—and do it.

5. Management Assistance

This is really just a short word about the people who can help you along the way. Most of the people who will assist you will not be involved with the day-to-day operation of your business. These are people who are part of the support system that all entrepreneurs develop in the course of their careers. They are people who would like to see you succeed and will be glad to lend you a hand.

Partners

Obviously, a partner is very much part of your business. A partner is someone who can share in the business operation and remove certain pressures from your job. It could be your spouse, a business associate, or a friend. As your business grows, the demands of the job increase, and many additional pressures develop. Too often, friendships suffer, and if you can avoid going into business with a friend, do so. Married couples have usually had time to understand each other's strengths and weaknesses. In the business, each is likely to relegate him- or herself to those areas that each is best at handling. Partnerships are like marriages, and the contact with each other on a daily basis is usually more than married couples share. It is thus important to assure yourself that you can work closely with your partner. (The use of the term "partner" does not mean you cannot have a corporation. There may be only two shareholders. It does represent a method of operation, however.)

When large companies look for acquisitions of other businesses, one sign is particularly important. If the age difference between the two partners in a small company is more than fifteen years, they feel the company may be ripe for acquisition. Why? Normally, when there is that difference in ages, there is also a large difference in goals and approaches to the business.

What this really means is that when you form a partnership arrangement with someone else, you must be assured that you both want the same things. The younger person usually wants to make a quick killing, or at least grow as fast as possible. The older partner has more experience and feels, perhaps, that a slow but steady growth is most important. A conflict of the two positions could stall a business and possibly force it into dissolution.

On the other hand, people often search out partners who will put up money for their share. If a partner already has enough money to invest in a business, he or she may wish only to see the money and investment grow. The need for making the big money has already been satisfied. You, however, are still struggling to make your money, and you may find yourself stifled.

Assuming you find the right person or persons with whom you can join forces, there is one other necessity to consider. This is approach. If both partners in a business have exactly the same approach to the business, there really is no need for a partner. You can hire an employee to do the work. Instead, both partners should have different business philosophies—one conservative and the other more adventurous, perhaps. Or one the sales personality; the other, the administrative type. One of the rules that partners make is to agree to disagree with each other. Then, in order to reach a decision about major steps in the company's growth, each partner will have to prove the point to the other. If you then can pass the scrutiny of the other partner, you have done a good job, and the idea probably has more merit than if your partner said "yes" to everything. You've passed a critical judgment.

Although this technique is important for major decisions, it is also necessary to set up rules for the operation of the business. Each partner must be aware of his/her specific duties. That agreement should be drawn up before you enter into business with each other. In the process of spelling out responsibilities, you can also evaluate whether you truly need a partner. Many people feel they can't operate comfortably unless there is someone else to work with. Others can't tolerate another opinion. Having a partner also forces you to look at what you do from another viewpoint, and you learn not to measure your work in anything but qualitative output.

What this means is that you may work twenty-five hours a week and your partner only ten hours, even though you are equal partners. Your concern is what the partner and you accomplish, not how much time was invested. If you are doing what you enjoy and your partner is also, you have no complaints if you succeed. Some people work faster than others. Some responsibilities are more quickly accomplished. If your partner is responsible for the financial aspects of the business, it may take only two hours a week to do the books and ten minutes a month to be in contact with the bank. You may be responsible for running the operation. How can you determine whose job is more important? Without the money, you have no business. Without your operating talents, what good is the money? The amount of time put in is not an indication of quality. If you are the type of person who measures output by the hours at a desk, don't take on a partner.

Lawyer

From time to time in the operation of a business, you may need legal assistance. If you incorporate, you will usually use a lawyer to process the papers. If you negotiate contracts or sign leases, you will need legal help. Hiring a lawyer should not be intimidating.

Obviously, in a small business, you will not need a lawyer on retainer. All you will need is someone you can call upon when necessary. Lawyers usually charge on an hourly basis, although there are many who charge a fee for the assignment. You must be very clear about charges. Those who charge an hourly fee will charge for such things as telephone calls, even if they're with you to discuss the business. That is, after all, a use of their time, for which they should be paid. Only the initial interview is free.

In a large city, there are usually dozens of law firms from which to choose. In smaller cities and suburban areas, you have a smaller selection. It pays to call a larger firm and inquire whether it has a division that handles small start-up businesses. The fees are usually lower. You might ask friends or other lawyers you know to recommend someone. I hesitate to hire close friends, since I think your professional business should be separate from your private life.

Make sure when you interview a lawyer that you know the types of clients he or she represents. Is the attorney familiar with your type of business? It could be very valuable, in time, if your lawyer can advance new ideas or even introduce you to other clients of his who may be of help. A lawyer can also introduce you to a banker or an accountant. Once you have settled on a lawyer, don't be afraid to call for advice whenever you are in doubt as to how to proceed.

Accountant

Unless you have always handled the financial affairs of your family and worked in a business where you did taxes and books, it may be necessary to hire an accountant. The accountant's job is to assure that tax records are filed and kept in an adequate manner. In a corporation it is even more necessary, because those records may come under government scrutiny more often than would personal, sole proprietorship, or partnership records. You may not need the accountant more than a few times a year, but it is important that you have the confidence that the accountant understands the nature of your business and gives you continual input.

Like lawyers, accounting firms and individual CPAs charge by the hour. If you have a regular accounting task that must take place in your business, it is often wiser to hire a bookkeeper to do the work. The bookkeeper can be hired on an hourly basis, but is far less expensive than an accountant. Introduce the bookkeeper to the accountant to learn your systems. Then have the bookkeeper do the regular work, supervised only four or five times a year by the accountant.

Accounting firms may have divisions that deal with small companies. You might find an accountant through personal recommendations from friends or from your lawyer. Establish the fees before you begin using their services.

Banker

What you should concern yourself with is a banker not a bank. This is an individual, usually a corporate loan officer, whose job it is to lend money. Your own personal experience may be that bankers usually say "no." Actually, their job is to say "yes." The bank makes money lending its money at interest and the more money it can lend (with the least amount of risk), the more money it can earn. All you have to do is prove yourself.

That may be easier said than done. Try to find a loan officer on the way up, someone who still wants to make loans with potential, in order to prove himself. Your job is to present your business proposal and cash-flow projections to the banker *before* you need the money, convince him that the loan would be worthwhile and that, as your company grew, your borrowing would increase. However, remember that if you present a reasonable proposal to the banker, you are more likely to receive a loan than if your were unprepared or in desperate need of immediate cash to bail you out.

Keep in mind that bankers deal with many different clients, and a smart banker will try to bring clients together for your mutual gains— and eventually, for the bank's benefit.

If you live in a small town, it may be easier to do business with the local bank that probably handles your personal finances as well. In major cities, where there are hundreds of banks, you have to shop around. Find the bank that offers you the best working conditions and that you feel comfortable with. Some banks may charge a slightly higher rate, but extend your credit to a larger borrowing limit. Others may require you to sign personal guarantees, which you should try to avoid, if possible. Pick what is best for your company.

Suppliers

In a business where you must buy equipment and supplies from other companies, you can often establish a close working relationship with the supplier. The supplier can turn you on to potential clients and customers and might advise you as to better ways to accomplish what you're trying to do. He may have more experience than you, he may know the market better, and he usually knows who has tried something and why others in your field have succeeded or failed. A sympathetic supplier can be one of your greatest assets.

Consultants

Consultants come in all sizes and shapes. There are business consultants who specialize in start-up operations and those who deal only with marketing. Others involve themselves in financial affairs or merchandising. Essentially, business consultants are called upon to give you assistance when you encounter a specific problem that doesn't appear to be within your grasp.

Consultants usually charge an hourly fee, although many charge a fixed amount. It is important that you question the consultant as closely as the consultant questions you. You must know what kinds of companies he has consulted with and what experience he has in your line of business. What do you expect the consultant to accomplish? Don't look for promises of success. A consultant should provide you with a formula or plan of operation that will smooth out your current business problems.

Before you hire a consultant, write down a list of what you hope he will accomplish or solve for you. Before you reject a consultant because of financial factors, determine your priorities. I have been told several times by companies that have called me in for consultations, that they couldn't afford my fee. After they have spoken with me a while, I usually ask them to make a list of the specific problems they are facing. Then I suggest they think about what might happen to their businesses if those problems are not solved. Most people realize that they often can't afford *not* to hire a consultant. One good idea from a consultant can often save thousands of dollars or turn around a failing business.

Some of the major cities have set up consulting services manned by retired business persons, most of whom were successful in their active professional lives and are now donating time for small companies. The Small Business Administration has established SCORE, which you can contact for advice. It might even recommend outside consultants for you.

One final suggestion: you might develop relationships with other entrepreneurs, others in the part-time and full-time self-employment areas, and any other business persons who would be interested in being an advisor. For the price of a dinner, you can consult with outsiders with varied experience. Join associations and attend lectures of management associations. Accumulate material and read the appropriate magazines designed for entrepreneurs. If you learn just one new thing a week, you will keep growing. Each time you discover a new mode of doing business, improve your management capabilities, or upgrade your functions, you move one step closer to financial and professional success.

6. Pricing for Your Market

The approach to pricing is determined by the type of business you will start—service- or product-oriented. Essentially the differences between the two are clear-cut. In a service business, you sell your own technical and creative knowledge. It is your working ability that is being paid for. A product-oriented business sells things, whether it's just one item or thousands of items in a department store.

Regardless of what type of business you start, you must have some knowledge of your potential, in order to determine how you can price your product or service, and then present it to the customer, or marketplace. Your product or service must satisfy the customer's needs or desires. Also, you must make sure you receive an adequate profit for the time, energy, and money invested.

The first step is determining the nature of your business. In the first chapters of this book we presented a variety of businesses and gave you some background in what it takes to get into them and what skills or knowledge must be developed. Perhaps you already have an idea of what you're going to do.

To investigate potential business ideas, you must read, watch, and listen. Read everything you can—newspapers, magazines, advertisements, and books. Watch what other companies are doing. Listen for new trends. This is where the ideas come from.

Social and cultural changes in the world are easy to follow and identify. Most progressive radio and television stations advertise and promote new trends. Self-help and leisure-time activities are among the most popular social and cultural changes taking place in our country. Witness the growth of adult learning centers for continuing education or the growth of the stereo and video markets. Body and psychological awareness movements are at a peak of popularity. Roller skating and bicycling are ideal for people who want something active to do. Who ever heard of jogging until just a few years ago? How many health clubs have opened near your home? Or health food stores? As a country, we are growing more concerned with our well-being. There must be some aspect of this field that would satisfy your need to be your own boss. After all, it doesn't pay to be in business unless you enjoy what you do.

When you have determined what you want to do, it's time to take a critical look. Ask yourself, "Why am I offering this product or service?" Is it something people want that might not be available to them? Or is it something you are in love with? If that is the case, you had better rethink what you're doing. Change it, if it is not oriented toward the consumer. At worst, you may have to discard your idea and start over again.

If you determine that your product or service is on target, you must select the appropriate format. The smart business person sells a product or service based on what appears to be palatable to the consumer. A locksmith doesn't just sell keys and locks; he presents you with the option of security—protect your home and family. Travel ads don't sell trips; they sell romance and adventure. You should judge the best way to present yourself to the public and then create that image. Spend a few hours glancing at newspapers or watching television. Make a list of what is being sold and what the image is that is selling the product. Here are some examples:

Product or Service	Image
Gold	Security
Wood stoves	Economy
Insurance	Fear and security
Men's suits	Sophistication
Liquor	Sex
Diamonds	Love

Ask yourself now, "Who are my customers?" Do you know specifically to whom you are trying to sell? To learn this, you must define your market target. This is determined by market research. It is important to have a clear, accurate, and current knowledge of your market in order to make important business decisions. These involve asking the following questions:

1. Who will buy my product or service?
2. Where are these customers located?
3. How often will they buy?
4. How big or small will orders be?
5. What styles and colors are needed?
6. What sizes are important?
7. How can I reach the market?

Because a small new business usually has limited funds to spend on marketing, you must determine this information by yourself. Sometimes the answers are apparent. If you sell high-priced cars, you will try to reach a select group of people who can afford them. Other products or services demand that you determine what market you wish to solicit. For instance, if you are an interior designer, you may prefer to work with business offices rather than residential design.

It is a matter of knowing your potential clients and customers and determining how to reach them. The markets should be selected very specifically. Some of the typical groups might be:

Teenagers
Senior citizens
Sports-oriented women
Fashion-conscious men
Business persons
Upper-income families
Suburban housewives
Corporate executives
Apartment dwellers

Your product or service need not be limited to only one market. However, your selling approach for each market should be changed to suit the needs and habits of each target. Certain health foods may be offered to senior citizens as life- and health-extending products. The same product might be sold to a younger group by emphasizing the increased activity benefits or sexual drive the product provides.

Once you've analyzed your market, you should determine whether it is large enough to make your business worthwhile. Can the market you have selected afford your product or service? Can you reach and influence potential customers?

There is a wealth of information available to anyone, if you know where to look. Most public libraries have business research material. A nearby university may have a business research department. Your local chamber of commerce can give you valuable information to help determine local markets. Census data are available from the government. If you are planning to open a store, you will be able to identify your market by personal observation. Stand on the street near your intended location and watch the people. Are the streets more crowded at certain times of the day? What economic class do the shoppers represent? What stores seem to get the most business? Go to other areas and ask future competitors about their business (they don't know you plan to compete). Talk to sales clerks, stop customers and ask questions. That's market research.

A student of mine wanted to open a bridal shop and asked how to know if she had chosen a good location. I suggested she find out if there were a lot of churches and synagogues in the area. How many weddings took place in the last year? Were there catering halls in the county?

What was the median age in the area? Were there several high schools nearby? In essence, I wanted her to do market research to see if there was enough potential for weddings to take place and bridal gowns to be purchased. Once she had all the facts, she could then make an educated decision.

The local Yellow Pages are also a good place to begin market research. You can quickly determine that many companies competing for a limited market spells disaster for all but one or two who survive. If there is not a lot of competition, before you get too excited, ask yourself, "Why not?" Perhaps there's no need for what you want to do. Check local records or neighborhood store owners to find out if anyone opened a similar store in the past. Learn from the mistakes of others.

In a service business it may pay for you to do telephone research. Call up potential clients and ask directly if they would consider using a service like yours. Do they use one now? Do they need the service? What would make them consider using you or a similar service? If you receive enough positive responses, you may then feel there is a better prospect of successfully launching the business.

Pricing

One of the most difficult matters that new businesses face is how to determine pricing. Keep in mind that you go into business to make money, not to merely exchange dollars. This means there must be more income than outgo. How much you sell and at what price, determines income. What you must spend to produce the service sold determines outgo. If, with a given price structure, the income is not more than the outgo—that is, if you do not make a profit—one or both of the two are wrong. Your prices are too low or your costs are too high.

It seems basic, doesn't it? Yet these facts of business operations are often ignored by many business persons. Sometimes it's merely the fault of poor record keeping. Often, it's not understanding the nature of your own business.

The pricing of an item or service should also convey the image of what you are selling. People are skeptical about low prices for luxury items. They resist high prices on low-quality products. There is a much-told story that, while obviously not based on fact, illustrates this point.

A man saw an advertisement in the local newspaper that read, "Brand-new Cadillac for sale—$50." It was obviously a misprint, so he ignored it. However, after several weeks he noticed the ad was still running, so he decided to followup. He called the number listed, and the woman who answered invited him to come over.

Much to his pleasure, there really was a beautiful car. He test-drove it and could hardly pay the woman fast enough, ever fearful it was a gag. After the papers were signed and the car was legally his, he asked why she had sold it so inexpensively.

"My husband ran off with his secretary," she said, bitterly. "He asked me to sell his car and send him the money. Why should I sell it for any more?"

The part of the story (which has been around for decades) that I find illustrative is that the ad went unanswered for a long time. No one believed that the car could sell for $50. Don't undervalue your service or product either. If your prices are too low, the customer will ask, "What's wrong with it?"

Although there is no fixed format for establishing prices, there are some guidelines you can follow:

1. You can charge *the same* as your competition—assuming they know what they're doing.
2. You can charge *less* than the competition if you don't make the customers skeptical. They might think they are getting less if they are paying less.
3. You can charge *more* than the competition if you have something better or present it in a unique way.

An excellent way to figure prices is to take into account all your costs—materials, overhead, profit. You will see, in this process, why I suggested you budget for overhead, even if you did not incur most of the costs.

Let us suppose, for this exercise, that you were producing and selling chocolate chip cookies. How much should you charge per pound? Using the three items listed above, you can calculate the price.

Materials:	Flour, milk, eggs, chips, nuts, raisins, butter, and sugar.
Overhead:	Time and labor costs. Although you have calculated an actual dollar total, most businesses establish a percentage that represents overhead. Industry sources can give you that number, and eventually you will be able to develop your own. I've selected an arbitrary percentage of 40 percent of costs.
Profit:	After all costs are allocated, whatever remains is profit. When estimating, you can select whatever percentage appears reasonable as long as it does not throw your prices out of line with the market.

Let's put this into an actual budget.

Materials: $1.50 (cost of ingredients)
Overhead
(Includes
advertising):   .60 (40% of materials cost)
                $2.10
Profit (100%): 2.10 (100% of materials and overhead)
                $4.20 Selling price per pound

Does this seem a reasonable and competitive price for a pound of chocolate chip cookies? If the price is too low, you can merely raise the price, thus increasing your profit. If your price is too high, you can cut your profit to bring the selling price into a more competitive area. You might also consider cutting your costs. Eliminate the raisins or the nuts. Take advantage of volume purchasing. Suppose you did cut costs; let's run through it again.

Materials $1.14 (lower costs)
Overhead   .46 (still 40%)
             $1.60
Profit (100%) 1.60 (100% of materials and overhead)
             $3.20 Selling price per pound

That's what you must sell the pound of cookies for in order to cover costs and still make 100 percent profit. If you still sold the cookies for $4.20, while cutting costs, your profit increases to:

$ 4.20 Selling price
− 1.60 Materials and overhead
$ 2.60 Profit

$2.60 ÷ 1.60 = 1.625 or 163% profit

What this really means is that for every pound of cookies you sell, it costs $1.14 for the ingredients, 46¢ for overhead (lights, rent, salaries, etc.), and $2.60 is profit.

How Much to Sell

Even though you've shown a very nice profit, you must be able to calculate how much you have to sell to stay in business by paying costs, covering overhead, and making a profit.

In Chapter 2, we made a sample overhead expense estimate. The total monthly overhead was $3,575. The question you must then ask is, "How much must I sell in order to cover my actual cost, pay for my overhead, and still make my profit?" It's a simple algebraic formula.

$$40\% = \text{Hypothetical overhead (yours can vary)}$$
$$\times = \text{Total gross sales}$$
$$\$3,575 = \text{Overhead expense}$$
$$.40(\times) = \$3,575$$
(40% of what total sales amount will equal my overhead?)
$$\times = \$3,575 \div .40$$
$$\times = \$8,937.50$$

You must sell $8,938 worth of chocolate chip cookies to cover your costs and make a profit. If you sell less, you eat into your profit. If you sell too much less, you won't be able to cover your overhead. If you've done adequate cash planning, you can survive the lower sales for a while. It also means that at $4.20 per pound, you must sell 2,128 pounds to succeed. Once you know how many cookies in a pound, you'll see how many dozen you have to sell. If there are eighteen cookies in a pound, 1.5 dozen cookies, there are 3,192 dozen cookies in 2,128 pounds (2,128 × 1.5).

You should, however, also have an idea of how much to sell in order to break even—cover costs and overhead and make no profit. In other words, just keep the doors open.

To calculate this, you must know the difference between fixed costs and variable costs. Variable expenses are those that change in direct proportion to the volume sold. Instead of getting too complicated, there is a very simple formula that requires you to find S, which means units to be sold to break even.

Fixed expenses—overhead $3,575
Unit sales price—$4.20 per lb.
Unit variable expense—$1.14 cost of ingredients per lb.

$$S = \frac{\text{Fixed expenses}}{\text{Unit sales price} - \text{Unit Variable Expense}}$$

$$S = \frac{\$3,575}{4.20 - 1.14} = \frac{\$3,575}{\$3.06}$$

$$S = 1,168 \text{ lbs. @ } \$4.20 = \$4,906$$

These are rough numbers, but they translate into the number of pounds you have to sell at $4.20 to give you $4,906, which will cover overhead and pay for cost of ingredients with nothing left over. Also, since we learned that there are 1.5 dozen cookies in a pound, 1,168 lbs. × 1.5 = 1,752 dozen.

It is a lot easier to calculate required sales when you are in a service business. Since you do not have to calculate cost of goods to be sold, you have only to estimate how much you would like to earn. If, for example, you would like to earn $35,000 a year, figure your annual costs, start-up costs, add your salary, and you're at the number.

Start-up (from Chapter 2)—$3,600		$ 3,600
Overhead (less salary)—$2,575 × 12		30,900
Desired salary		35,000
	Total required earnings	$69,500
	Monthly earnings	$ 5,792

If you can average $5,792 income a month, you will be able to realize that salary and cover your costs.

7. Advertising

It is important, when running any type of business, to be familiar with all kinds of advertising methods and procedures. You must consider advertising as an integral part of your business and a necessary element of business expense. It is an investment in the future sales of your company.

Advertising is a method of communicating information to the public and can develop attitudes as well as induce favorable action for the advertiser. Very often, this action may merely be a sale. It may be listening to a sales message. Or it may induce a customer to examine the products in a store. The measure of advertising success is how many readers or listeners received the message.

Normally, advertising is supposed to influence, not actually sell—except for mail-order sales. The advertisement brings the advertiser the potential customer, and it is the advertiser's responsibility to make the sale. Even when no apparent selling seems to take place, such as in a self-service store, other factors enter into the purchasing decision. Among those are the product itself, the reputation of the manufacturer, the price, and the display. Your awareness of these factors may all be the result of advertising, but you cannot substitute advertising for the quality of the product or service. No amount of advertising will get back dissatisfied customers. If they tried your product or service once and they were disappointed, you've lost potential sales.

That is the name of the game—developing customers for repeat business. Most things we buy in a lifetime are not one-time purchases. If you buy a certain brand of shoes, you'll keep coming back to the same store. Do you trust Mattel toys? Eat Heinz ketchup or Campbell's soup? Shop at K-Mart? Order from Sears, Roebuck? Drive a Chevy? Most of us develop tastes and stick to those brands that make us happy. In terms of dollars and cents, once you've got the customers, it's cheaper to hold onto them.

A constant problem is competition. If you don't keep reminding a customer you're still around, he may be swayed to a new company's name now in the picture. "What have you done for me lately?" is the consumer's query. It's your obligation to keep reminding him.

No matter how much you advertise, there will always be a percentage of customers whose needs or tastes change. You will lose them. So you must always try to replace these losses with new customers, while adding more at the same time. This is true no matter what products or services you sell.

In addition, advertising must continually tell the products' story to new generations of customers. Children grow up, get married, have children —and all the while their tastes, habits, and needs keep changing. The products or services they once needed no longer are a part of their lives. New items replace the old, and your advertising should try to influence—even if it's for future customers.

Advertising has three functions: to inform, to persuade, to remind. The customer must be told of your product or available service. Once interest is expressed, you have to inform him of the merits, price, etc. Then you try to persuade the customer to purchase your products or hire you to perform your service. If you're successful in selling, your responsibility is to remind customers of the availability of more service or product and where they bought it, and urge them to come back again.

What to Expect from Advertising

Different responses can be anticipated from different types of advertising, which is related to the type of business you own. The result may be direct and immediate action or it may be indirect and delayed.

In store advertising, you may hope for immediate action—the customer comes in to purchase the advertised items. Sometimes, the customer or client may contact you, but not purchase immediately. Here are some of the results you might aim for:

1. Bring people to your store.
2. Attract buyers—old and new customers—to examine special offerings.
3. Receive requests for estimates for services or products.
4. Receive telephone and mail orders.
5. Keep the public informed about your service for future use.
6. Develop new prospects for the sales staff.
7. Thank customers for continued patronage.

When you begin an advertising plan, you must make four decisions about your advertising: *what* to tell in the advertisement, *to whom* to tell it, *how* to tell it, and *where* to tell it. An ad run at the wrong time in the wrong place is useless. If it's missing important facts, you've wasted your money. Placing an ad in the wrong publication or selling through the inappropriate medium will have limited effect.

What to Tell

Be direct! Tell the customer exactly what you're selling. Be precise and not too wordy.

Although teaching what to say in an advertisement would be a book—or series unto itself, I'll try to give you some of the basics. Even so, unless you have a background in advertising, it may be more profitable in the long run to hire someone to do the advertising for you. There are thousands of free-lance copywriters and designers looking for a little extra income. A well-worked ad in the "Help Wanted" section will bring you enough responses from which to choose an advertising person.

Ask what the person has done. Look at a portfolio. What kind of accounts are this person's specialty? Before you discuss price, determine the price range you want to pay. If the person quotes you a high figure, you merely say, "I'm sorry, I was thinking in a much different range. I'll have to get someone else." If the person wants the work, he'll negotiate lower. If not, get someone else. If the original quote is lower than you budget, you're ahead. Never demean a person or argue about what you think he or she is worth. Professionals should be treated as such, and you should both be honest about your needs and budget.

In most advertising, the first principle is to capture the reader's attention. Since there is so much to read and look at in a magazine or newspaper, it's important to "grab the customer." Think of big, bold, and catchy headlines. (We'll talk about some additional principles in the section about mail order.)

Next, tell what the product or service is. Describe it with words that paint a picture and convince the reader that life would be pointless without it. If you are trying to make a direct sale, as in mail order or classified selling, don't forget the price. Or you may discuss discounts or bargain rates.

Then there should be a "take action" line, whether it's "Send today," or "Give us a call," or "Come visit our shop." Finally, don't forget to tell the customer where you are.

The best way to learn how to write advertisements is to see what everyone else is doing. Read everything you can, check approaches in different media to see how the advertiser reaches his target market. Take notes on the competition. Then copy the best of the ads, adding your own unique touches. Try it to see what happens. If it doesn't work, try again, until you get it right.

To Whom

You should, by now, have determined your target market. Once you have begun to develop a product or service, you must immediately do

'I CAN GET IT FOR YOU WOOLSALE.''
—W. Moomjy

Let's face it.

Nothing keeps its looks as well as wool. Or its colors.

But lately the price of woollies has gone wild, causing you to say "baaaa."

Now with the cooperation of mills the world over and sheep the world over, we think you'll say "buy" instead.

I'm Walter Moomjy. For purposes of this sale, you can call me Woolter Moomjy. From now thru November 29th, I can get you wool carpets at woolsale prices. Wool carpets from all over the world. For all over your world. (I can even get you padding and installation included.)

How?

Wool power. The kind of wool power that comes from knowing how to buy and what to buy. And from not being sheepish about buying large quantities.

For example, I can get you a wool from a nation of sheep, New Zealand. There's a Berber at $33.99 a sq. yd. that's 32% down under. And a Saxony that looks like chenille. It's a really big deal at $58.99. Was $82.99.

I can get you a Swiss Berber you'll be anything but neutral about at $58.99 Was $81.99. And a haute couture French velour in lilacs, mauves and roses for a not too haute $69.99. Was $88.99.

Irish snowflakes are falling to $49.99. While criss-crossed London loops are falling down, falling down to $51.99. And the industrial look revolution has hit the floor at $39.99. Speaking of revolutions, I can get you a revolutionary German velour with no seams in the middle of the floor. (It's 15'5" wide.) So understated, you wouldn't believe how underpriced it is. $63.99. Was $76.99.

I could go on and on. But I don't want you to fall asleep counting wool.

The Wools In Our Area Rug Area Come Tumbling Down.

I can get you area rugs from all areas. In all sizes. Wonderful, wonderful Copenhagen rugs, Dhurries, Oriental designs from Belgium, France, Germany, Italy and England.

And if you'd like to go Dutch, now hear these. Our thick, cabled top selling Dutch Berber is a

real dutch treat at its new bottom line. $999 for the 8'3"x11'2" size.

And here's another cable from Holland. Stop. In thick and thin yarns. And natural colors. It's cut pile and cut to save you piles. $599 for the 8'2"x11'2" size.

Last but least our madras from Spain is anything but plain. In blue chi chi and ivory Oushak, it falls main from $875 to $499 for the room size. And it falls equally in other sizes.

Ever Feel Like a Wool in a China Shop?

I can get you the great wools of China at great prices. As wool as the great Orientals of Pakistan and Persia, Romania and India.

I can get you wool flowers, wool hangings for your wall and runners for your hall.

So run over to Einstein Moomjy. In New York or New Jersey before November 29th.

Tell 'em Woolter sent you.

After all, if the price of wool has been making you sick, now's the time to get wool fast.

EM Einstein Moomjy
The Carpet Department Store®

Newspaper advertisement for a carpet store appeared in the daily *New York Times*. It combines humor and fact to make a strong impact on the reader.

your market research. This is the "whom" I am talking about. Who will buy your product or use your service? If you have not, as yet, decided upon the appropriate market, stop here and go back to the chapter about marketing. You will not know how to approach your customer unless you know who the customer will be. Then you can adequately prepare your message and determine the best ways to reach the consumer or client. If you already know who the customer will be, you should determine the best way to reach him or her.

How

Are you going to sell your product in a retail store? Is it a personal service that demands direct selling? Will mail order give you the correct access to the customer? Will regular advertising give you adequate exposure for your product? How you present your message to the customer is most important.

You can begin by determining what your competition does. Obviously, if the retail store is your answer, you have selected where the customer will obtain the merchandise. There are, however, many ways to reach your market. Mail-order advertising can reach the customer in several different ways: direct mail, mail-order space advertisement, or classified advertising.

Again, how you tell your story relates directly to who your customer will be and what it is you are selling. Expensive items will not sell well in classified advertising. If you are offering a service, you may do better with direct-mail response pieces, so you can contact your customer directly. A product designed for the mass consumer market would be more appropriately advertised in a national magazine.

I think you can see that you will have to make several determinations about how to tell your story, and then you can decide where you should advertise.

Where

Because the ultimate success of your advertising will depend on where you advertise, it is important that you make your choice correctly. It is even more important because ultimately most of the money spent for advertising will go to pay for the space or time in the medium you select.

The choice you will have to make, after determining all the other factors we've discussed—what, to whom, and how—is where to sell your product. It is not always obvious. You cannot casually allocate a specific amount of money for your budget and assume it will go into local newspapers. There may be other important support media which will increase the effectiveness of your campaign.

Each medium has special characteristics that must be studied before a decision is reached. For example, newspapers usually reach a limited geographical area, but are read by people of both sexes and most age groups. They may, however, be geared to different income groups and educational interests. Some, because of the level of writing, may be read only by an isolated group. Radio is also a selective medium. Each station has developed its own identity, based on its programming. Classical music, pop, rock, news, etc.—all determine the types of market that listen. Business and trade magazines and papers are selective by industry and profession, and most of these (*Wall Street Journal, Women's Wear Daily*) have a national market.

In print media, where you buy space by the line or page, you can tell your story in as many words as you want and can afford. The more ads you run, the more you increase your chance for success. In radio and television, the method of reaching the customer is slightly different. Commercials usually fit a prearranged time length, and repetitive advertising is more effective than a one-shot deal. Direct mail or mail order must feature a different type of message, and although you can be extremely selective in your marketing (high school mathematics teachers in Rhode Island or photography magazine subscribers in Zip Code 10104), the cost may be higher.

The type of advertising most familiar to us appears in newspapers. Newspapers may be daily, weekly, biweekly, or monthly. Because of large readership and frequency of appearance, they are especially suitable for retail or service advertising.

Newspapers usually have something for everybody. They are read by people of all ages and both sexes. They can appeal to a broad spectrum of educational and income levels and recreational and cultural interests. In addition, most people read newspapers for their advertising as well as for news. The overwhelming intrusion of television into our homes has made the national and local news readily available. Thus, the nature of the need for newspapers has changed.

The advantage of newspaper advertising is that it brings fast response. Also, because you can usually place an advertisement with only a few days' notice before publication date, you have more flexibility. If you have a special sale or want to sell electric heaters during a cold spell, you can rush an ad into publication. In retail sales, this is especially valuable, because you are also reaching a well-defined geographical area. It would be foolish, naturally, to choose a national publication to sell an item available in your store. Would someone travel from Vermont to Utah for a special sale on electric heaters, or snow tires, or fresh leg of lamb?

In a small community, your choice of newspaper will probably be simple. You may not even have a choice. It may be a daily or weekly publication. If you are in a densely populated locality, in a medium to large city, you will find dailies, weeklies, shoppers, morning, evening, and Sunday editions. Which one should you choose?

Statistics indicate that evening (or afternoon) newspapers outnumber morning dailies about five to one. The morning paper usually follows the readers to work, and the paper is skimmed and then discarded. The afternoon paper often comes home from work with the purchaser or is delivered to the home and is geared more for the family.

The Sunday paper is usually a selective publication, and the large newspapers are divided into specific interest sections. Thus, you can easily target your advertising for the right market in the appropriate section. Similar to the Sunday paper is the weekly. It is usually the only edition of the paper that is published but is delivered to the customer when there is more leisure time to read.

Suburban newspapers are usually weeklies, although some are published more often. In medium-sized communities, these papers are read along with the available dailies, since they usually feature local news and features. They also stay in the home for a longer period than a daily; thus your advertisement will get a longer exposure.

Special-interest newspapers are primarily black or foreign language. There are others, however, that are religious, fraternal, labor, and neighborhood publications.

Shoppers are getting more popular, and although they are not strictly newspapers, they usually compete with newspapers for advertising space. Some of them are quite effective for presenting your message. They often consist almost entirely of advertising, and even non-advertising space is basic filler—recipes, household tips, or personal care suggestions.

How to Make Your Selection

Newspapers, as well as magazines, charge advertising rates based on the estimated number of readers they have. Radio rates are set by the number of listeners, and quite naturally, television rates are based on the estimated number of viewers. All of these media publish rate cards.

To determine how much an ad will cost and how big a market you are going to reach, you must obtain rate cards. If you are going the route of newspaper advertising, you must accept the fact that only continual, repetitive advertising in newspapers is effective. So your first commitment must be to frequency. From there you can determine the other components that will make up your costs:

1. Circulation of publication
2. Size of ad
3. Color advertising or black-and-white
4. Display or classified
5. Edition of publication

You will notice, if you read the publication on a regular basis, that some issues are thicker than others. They carry different types of ads on different days. In larger newspapers, each day may bring a specific feature section (home, food, sports, etc.), and you, as advertiser, will be wise to place your ad in that section that best attracts your desired customer. Shoppers are familiar with the schedules of advertising, so don't be intimidated by the quantity of advertising. It's unlikely that your ad will be lost among the others.

The rates the newspapers charge are usually quoted by the column inch. If line rates are quoted, you should know there are fourteen lines to an inch. There are discounts offered if you advertise frequently, and there are additional rates charged if you wish specific placement in the publication. Standard advertising is called R.O.P., Run of Press, which means that the ad will be put wherever there is room, with some attempt made to place it in an appropriate section. If you knew there was to be a feature article about computers and you had a computer consulting service, you would request your ad to be presented on the same page as the article. It would cost extra, but would be well worth the additional expense.

If you need help in preparing your advertisement, you should be aware that if you sell products manufactured by major companies, they can provide you with ready-made advertising "mats." All you have to do is have the newspaper insert your name and address and the prices. These layouts are prepared by leading professionals. You can also work directly with a newspaper in preparing your ad. You supply the photos or artwork and write your own copy. The newspaper people will clean it up, design it, and prepare it for publication. They need to sell space, and very often they will prepare your advertisements free of charge.

Business Publications

Business and trade publications are published for very specific markets and accept advertising that is geared for people who would read that publication. Products and services are usually not consumer-oriented. Almost every industry in this country has at least one publication designed for its workers or management, or both. Some of the more well-known publications are:

Business Week	*Forbes*
Fortune	*Publishers Weekly*
Advertising Age	*Wall Street Journal*
Women's Wear Daily	*Home Furnishings Daily*
Computer Age	*Inc. Magazine*
Venture	

Business papers and magazines have smaller circulations than most other magazines, but their readership is more specific and may be the backbone of your business. One of these trade publications may be the way to reach those people to whom you want to sell your product or service. You can get a good idea of its value as an advertising medium if it is fat. Some publications are better places for ads than others. *Ayer's Directory of Publications* can help you locate appropriate publications.

It is more difficult to measure response to your ads in business and trade publications. Industrial and trade purchases are usually the result of joint decisions and these may take some time before an order is placed. On the other hand, most of these magazines offer reader-service cards. If the reader is interested in your product or service, he will check off a number on an enclosed mail-back card. This response is eventually passed along to you. You can use this as a partial measure, but since these are not necessarily qualified buyers, many of the names may be worthless. Continuous advertising is the most effective way to present your message, and the long run success of your company can be partially attributed to your advertising.

Consumer Publications

Consumer magazines may be either national or local, but for the small business person, national magazines have limited advertising possibilities. Because of the huge circulations of these publications—often in the millions—the rates are generally too high to fit into the advertising budget of a small company.

If you feel that it is necessary to advertise in a national consumer publication, it is possible to purchase a regional edition. The regional edition presents your ad only to a limited geographical region, at a fraction of the cost for a complete national campaign.

As magazines such as the *Saturday Evening Post*, *Look*, and *Life* began to fade in popularity, special-interest publications became more popular. Today, most consumer magazines are written for readers with specific interests. There are magazines for photographers, gardeners, runners, motorcyclists, bicyclists, boaters, and fishermen. If your interest is in food, home decorating, computers, politics, news, money, solar technology, there's a publication to suit your taste. There may even be more than one. One day at my local magazine store I counted fourteen magazines devoted to motorcycling.

There are also travel magazines that look much like consumer magazines and are usually found in airplanes and motels; some are sent to you by credit-card companies.

The advantage of consumer magazines, both general and special interest, is that they have a long reading life. Because there is usually more in the magazine than can be read in one sitting, it is picked up at

NATIONAL ADVERTISING RATES

SPACE UNITS	BLACK AND WHITE	TWO COLOR (Black and One Process Color*)	FOUR COLOR
1 Page, 429 lines	$17,515	$21,350	$22,425
⅔ Page, 286 lines	11,895	14,500	15,250
⅔ Page Horizontal (285 lines, 95 lines by 3 columns)	11,895	14,500	15,250
½ Page, Horizontal or Vertical	10,310	12,790	13,425
Digest Size Page (Junior Page)	10,310	12,790	13,425
⅓ Page, 143 lines (Vertical or Square)	6,475	8,680	9,045
½ Column, 71 lines	3,310	—	—
Per Agate Line	49.60	—	—

*For two-color, matched color, consult publisher.

(Irregular sizes of space in excess of unit sizes will be billed at the price of the last preceding unit, plus the agate line rate for space in excess of that unit.)

Center Spread	—	—	$47,090
2nd Cover	—	—	24,615
3rd Cover	—	—	22,425
Back (4th) Cover	—	—	26,750

Magazines and newspapers provide you with Rate Cards, which will enable you to select the appropriate publication, by evaluating size of market, costs, format, etc.

12 GEOGRAPHIC REGIONS

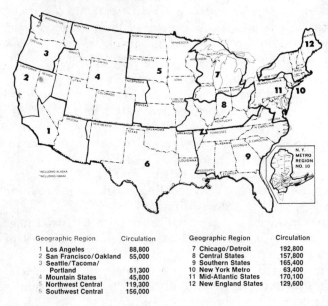

*INCLUDING ALASKA
*INCLUDING HAWAII

N. Y. METRO REGION NO. 10

Geographic Region	Circulation		Geographic Region	Circulation
1 Los Angeles	88,800		7 Chicago/Detroit	192,800
2 San Francisco/Oakland	55,000		8 Central States	157,800
3 Seattle/Tacoma/ Portland	51,300		9 Southern States	165,400
4 Mountain States	45,800		10 New York Metro	63,400
5 Northwest Central	119,300		11 Mid-Atlantic States	170,100
6 Southwest Central	156,000		12 New England States	129,600

intervals, and your advertisement has a better chance of being seen more often.

The disadvantage, besides high costs, is that it usually takes two to three months of lead time to place your ad. You must schedule your ad well in advance not only for placement but for preparation. However, product ads and mail-order-type ads have good exposure in these magazines.

There is another type of consumer magazine that should not be overlooked: city or town, society, or school publications. Also, sports and theater programs can be considered. Hotel visitors' guides are good for local restaurants, theaters, and services.

Rates for magazines are based upon the number of readers and the frequency of your advertising, just like the newspapers. Normally, rates quoted are for pages or fractions of pages for general advertising. Many of these publications also have special line rates for mail order and classified.

Mail Order and Direct Mail

In the chapter that deals specifically with mail order and direct mail as businesses, we have gone into more detail. However, it's important when selecting where to advertise that you be aware of the basic techniques. Although the terms are often used interchangeably, direct-mail advertising is sent through the post office. Mail order (sometimes known as direct advertising) usually is in a publication demanding an immediate response, is handed out by salespeople, distributed house-to-house or in office buildings.

This is the most selective and flexible of all media. It is selective because you can decide who is to receive your advertising. You present your merchandise or service only to those potential customers who will use what you sell. You can be selective in the number of people you sell to or the area in which they live. You are flexible in the presentation of your advertising, which can be elaborate or simple, large, or small. You have complete control of all the elements.

1. *Mail Order*

As a technique, mail order has been discussed in a prior chapter. There we talked about the types of ads, the products, and where to advertise. But since mail order ads usually appear in the publications we have discussed earlier in this chapter, a review of the material on newspapers, magazines, business and trade publications would aid in determining where to place your ads.

2. *Direct Mail*

Again, the techniques were discussed in the chapter about mail order, but you should understand where and how it goes to the customer. A common term for direct mail pieces is "junk mail." If you have any intention of using direct mail, do not think of it as junk mail. It is your livelihood. Well prepared, selectively mailed advertising pieces are not junk mail—certainly not to those people who have made millions of dollars in the business. A U.S. Postal Service survey showed that more than three-quarters of all advertising and promotional material was opened and read. If your service or product is of interest and well presented, your mailing piece can be an effective selling piece.

The major components of direct mail are:

The mailing piece
The mailing list
Postage costs
Follow-up

The mailing piece: This can be as simple as a postage-paid return card with an advertising message on the other side. It can also be a multiple package, including letter, brochure, reply card, return envelope, and outer mailing envelope. A self-mailer can be two-part cards or a larger brochure without envelopes. The brochure can unfold into a giant poster, and the reply card can be a part of the brochure. Because of the costs involved, it is preferable to make your piece a selling attempt. Included with the mailer should be a simple way for the customer to respond, whether it's a business card or a reply card and envelope.

The mailing list: This is your target market, selected for any of the characteristics necessary to purchase your product. Mailing lists can be compiled from directories, phone books, catalogs, prior customers, visitors, etc., or they can be purchased from a mailing list company or broker. However, before you purchase or rent a list, you must ask marketing questions:

1. What is the purpose of your mailing? (Approach)
2. Where do you want your mailings sent? (Geography)
3. Who will receive your mailings? (Market)

When you have the answers to these questions, you can make an intelligent decision. The Approach will determine the style, format, and content of the mailer. The Geography will determine where it will be mailed. You can target an entire country, community, city, Zip Code area. The Market is the who—to whom will this be mailed within the geographical area. This is your determination of sex, age, economic characteristics, occupations, etc. When you order mailing lists from companies and brokers, you will have to decide the specifics. Often, a broker can direct you if you work with him. He can also help develop your product advertisement.

The postage costs: These can be substantial. If you mail first class, which is a more effective way to do a mailing, you will pay the full first class postage rate, which is currently 18¢ per ounce, or $180 per thousand. If you had a bulk mailing permit, you would be able to mail the same material at almost half the amount. In order to send a mailing at the bulk mail rate, you have to sort the mail into Zip Code order and bundle each batch separately. There are, fortunately, mailing services that can do it all for you, for a nominal fee.

Follow-up to an initial mailing is too often overlooked. Like continuous ads in newspapers, regular mailings to potential customers and follow-up letters to those who have expressed interest in your product or service are extremely effective. Since you do not have face-to-face contact with the customer, you have to be able to find another way to persuade him to purchase. Perhaps the first mailing will do the job, perhaps the third. There's no way to tell, except after extensive testing. As you begin to get response to your mailing pieces, you should maintain the names of those who answer and compile your own mailing list. From time to time you send them a reminder, either that it's the season to consider a purchase or that their supply of *gizmos* might be exhausted and should be reordered. If you've ever subscribed to a magazine, I'm sure you are used to receiving reminders that your subscription will expire in a few months.

Costs for direct mail vary with the size of the package, the lists purchased, and the postage rates selected. Before you get into mail order, make sure you've covered all the costs and budgeted adequately. Start with the largest possible market, and then break it into selected smaller markets. You can test a few thousand, or the entire list, depending on your budget.

Remember that one prime advantage of direct mail is the lack of other reading matter that accompanies your brochure or catalog. Unlike mail-order ads in a magazine or newspaper, no one else is competing for attention. It is also the easiest method by which to measure results of the advertising dollar. Not only can you count return of answers but you can quickly evaluate its effectiveness in true dollars.

Broadcast Advertising

Radio and television are carrying an increasing volume of local (small) advertising, especially retail advertising, because small-business owners recognize that more and more of their prospects come from a generation that has been immersed in the broadcast media. We spend far more time today watching television or listening to the radio in the car, for example, than we do reading. You may find it necessary to supplement your regular advertising with broadcast advertising.

Broadcast advertising permits you to be flexible and to appeal to specific types of prospects. It can be as effective as special-interest magazine advertising. Radio and television stations program their material to particular audience segments and thus make it easier for you to select exactly the market you wish to reach.

Another advantage is the immediacy of the medium. Unlike national publication advertising, you have the ability to place an ad within a very short time period. This is more true for local advertising than for national time slots.

Unlike the coldness of print advertising, radio and television introduces the consumer to an individual. The human touch can be more persuasive, more urgent, and possibly more successful. It is very similar to personal selling, since it can combine the best advertising approaches.

The major problem with this type of approach is expense. Broadcast advertising is most effective when the ad is run on a continuous basis. Because you have no absolute guarantee that everyone in your market is listening or watching when your message is broadcast, you must repeat the broadcast at intervals to assure the maximum visibility of your advertisement. That's where the expense comes in. If, however, you have enough money in your budget, you might want to consider broadcast advertising.

In a small town, your choice of local advertising may be limited to one radio and one television station. However, where you have a choice, be sure to consider what your prospective customers would listen to, rather than what you listen to. Consider AM or FM radio, VHF or UHF television. Don't overlook cable TV. It is rapidly becoming a very important broadcast medium, with dozens of new cable stations opening their doors every month. Do you want to use a spot announcement, one that lasts one minute or less? Or can you afford to sponsor an entire program or segment?

You might consider sponsoring a particular feature. If, for example, you are in the business of trimming dogs, you might sponsor a regular three- or five-minute segment dealing with pet care. A hardware store might produce a brief do-it-yourself feature for the handyman. The best advice for broadcast advertising may come from your local radio or television sales representatives. They will know what has succeeded or failed in the past and why. They can help you design an advertising program within your budget and counsel you in making the major decisions as to type of ad, length, number, when, where, how, etc.

A call to your local stations will bring you rate cards, much like those you receive from magazines except that the rates are based on viewers or listeners in different time categories. Your choice of market will determine rates.

Outdoor Advertising

Outdoor advertising might include posters, bulletins, and billboards. It is especially effective for products or services related to travel or outdoor living. Compared to publications and broadcast media, there is a limited audience selection. Outdoor use should be considered for support advertising.

More and more posters are being utilized in the advertising business. Improvements in the printing industry have brought down costs of production. It is important to locate posters in areas with a lot of traffic. You can hire teenagers or local organizations to put the posters up around town.

Transit Advertising

There are two basic types of transit advertising: inside the vehicle (train, cab, or bus) or outside the vehicle or in the station. Rates vary with size and position of display. In large metropolitan areas, the costs and market are larger. In smaller towns, the costs are lower.

Specialties and Premiums

Small and large businesses employ both specialty and premium advertising. You have probably received these types of advertising items, sometimes without realizing it. How many calendars do you receive at the end of every year, whether from a local card shop, hardware store, or bank? The name on the calendar is the advertising message, and it can last for twelve months.

Pens and pencils may have become too popular as an advertising specialty; since many companies give out these items to their customers, yours may end up in a pile with many others and lose its effectiveness.

Premiums are items that are given away free or at minimal costs to encourage the customer to buy, or at least write to inquire about additional information. For years, the oil companies gave out free maps, dish sets, car accessories, and games to entice customers into their gas stations. That era has passed. However, banks today deal in toasters, blenders, and blankets as well as bank accounts. These are premiums and are used as an inducement to open your new account. You might consider both sides of the business. You can offer a free gift to potential customers for purchasing an item or using your service. Or you may produce an item that itself is ideal for premium use.

Advertising is successful if it produces results, whether in sales or in recognition. It involves careful planning and effective use of your budget dollars. There is, unfortunately, no set formula for determining the amount of money to spend on advertising. Some companies allocate a percentage of each item manufactured to advertising; others set an overall percentage based on the prior year's sales. My own recommendation is to establish a budget when you start your business, based on the amount of money you have available or can raise. Commit yourself to spending that money, whether business goes up or down. Unfortunately, when business drops off, many businessmen immediately cut their advertising budget to take up the financial slack. The result is a loss of potential new customers, as well as old customers. It may pay, in those circumstances, to *increase* the budget, to hold on to slipping sales and replace the lost customers with new ones. If your budget relies on prior sales, a poor year will mean less advertising. Less advertising may mean poorer sales. And the chain continues to grow—until there is no business at all.

Determine from the beginning how much you have to spend, being aware that if business increases you may be able to increase your advertising budget. Then decide how you want to spend the money— print, broadcast, or other forms of advertising. Using a percentage method, determine which are the most important media, and then allocate the money for each of them.

It is important for you not to be intimidated by your responsibility for effective advertising. Because you know the product or service better than anyone else, you should determine the various aspects of an advertising program. If you cannot do it yourself, consider hiring someone who has experience in the field. Producing advertising is a talent, and it may become important to find someone to write or produce your ads. Most of all, don't shortchange yourself in this area—it may be the key to success or failure.

8. Management and Record Keeping

The single largest factor contributing toward failure of a new business is poor management technique. Included in that is poor record keeping. The proper organization and record-keeping systems will help your business operations flow easily from day to day. None of the systems is at all complicated. They take some time to set up, but once they are in place, they take very little effort to maintain. Once they are written down, you can use them for constant reference and employee training.

The Organization Chart

Every company has an organization chart. Even small businesses have them, although in the beginning they are tucked away in some drawer. The purpose of the chart is to assist you in the growth of the company and to enable you to plan personnel growth.

When you start, your name may be in all of the blanks—you run every division and every function. Regardless of how small your business is, you should have separate functions. They may not be similar to our illustration, because every business is different and has specific requirements. But once you've done a business proposal and understand all of the functions of your business, you will find it easy to develop your organization chart.

Some of the areas to be included, along with president, are:

Finance
Marketing
Advertising
Production
Sales
Administration
Shipping
Inventory

Sometimes you can combine divisions and functions, and sometimes you may want to break them into more detailed components.

The organization chart is used in planning the growth of your business; whenever you have to add personnel, you consult the chart. Usually, the area that will require someone will be that function in which you have become overworked. If, for example, you are weakest in sales and would prefer to handle all of the administrative functions in the business, sales is the area you will fill in first.

Continually consult the chart, to see where you're being overworked. If, indeed, the sales area is the one that needs relief, start looking for someone to fill that job. Allow several months to find the best possible individual. The amount of time it takes to find a qualified employee gives you the opportunity to reevaluate your needs and to determine if you can actually afford someone else.

Also, small businesses cannot afford to hire incompetent employees. Because everyone works at many jobs in a small business, each employee's function and performance becomes critical. An ineffective worker will drag you down and can put you in jeopardy. The problem is that you may not have time to look constantly over an employee's shoulder to determine effectiveness. It doesn't take long for the bad apple to ruin the entire barrel.

As you progress, you begin to look at other areas of the operation. Where else do you need someone? Now that you've hired a salesperson, you will have reduced the pressure on yourself, and that will give you an enormous emotional lift. You will find that your output and enthusiasm will increase for a while. When another area becomes burdened by overwork, you are once again ready to fill in another space on the organizational chart.

Your job is to supervise each of the people on that chart. To do so most effectively, it is best to determine goals for each employee and set up adequate reporting techniques. Encourage feedback, so that you will be constantly—and consistently—informed. Whatever transpires in your company is ultimately your responsibility. You cannot excuse failures to your customers by blaming them on your employees. Customers are concerned only with results, and these can be achieved only with proper supervision.

Hiring

It may seem a bit premature in the development of this new small business of yours, but you may find that you will need assistance before you've made any plans. The help may be as simple as hiring a part-time typist or bookkeeper, or even someone to help you carry packages to the post office.

There are a number of sources you can explore, the last of which are employment agencies, because they charge a fee that the employer — you — must pay.

If it's only minimal work, you can consider hiring family and friends. The problem with friends is that if they don't work out, it's very difficult and embarrassing to fire them. Your spouse however, as a partner in your business, can provide you with a variety of financial advantages, which will be discussed in the next chapter.

You might consider asking your friends if they know anyone they can recommend. In 1970 I owned a small publishing company that sold books through the mail to public high schools. At that time I had a small staff to pack the books and carry them to the post office. In addition, I had three people working in the billing office, typing orders, answering telephones, and compiling school listings. All of my employees were seniors in high school. Toward the end of every school year, they would introduce me to another half-dozen students who would be seniors the next year and wanted to work for me.

My success with them came from treating them like adults. They were all given goals and told what to do and when things were due. I didn't care when they did it, as long as it got done. Often, they would come in after school and work into the evenings, long after I had gone home. Sometimes they would come in on weekends to work, and if it was busy, they would bring friends to help them. They were always completely reliable and efficient.

There are other places to hire students. If you are near a university, you can try its placement office. You can hire students in different academic majors to help you on specific projects, if you wish. You can also hire people through a variety of organizations such as the Boy Scouts, Girl Scouts, handicapped groups, and assorted other organizations that are interested in making money.

The local state employment agency may provide you with very qualified people. In today's marketplace, where thousands of people are losing jobs through no fault of their own, there are many individuals — professionals included — who are unemployed and might consider working for you for less money in order to guarantee themselves a steady income.

Before you hire anyone, however, make sure you have prepared a complete job description. Go back to the box you wish to fill on your organization chart and write down all of the functions that you require of a new employee. If you have kept good records, you should have little problem detailing the job. Be sure to explain to anyone you interview that his or her responsibilities may go beyond the job description, by the nature of working for a small business. Jobs overlap, and the employee must be willing to do a task that technically doesn't appear in the job description.

When you have hired a new employee, check with your accountant about various benefits and expenses. You will now have to pay a variety of taxes for the employee and possibly supply such benefits as medical coverage, paid vacations, and even some sort of retirement program. You will also find yourself playing the role of psychiatrist and mediator once you have several people on your payroll. Of course, despite the problems, an increase in employees normally means an increase in business.

If you keep in mind that every dollar in and out of your company is really yours, you will be sufficiently motivated to become an effective supervisor. It also requires you to be able to fire someone. Firing an employee is one of the more difficult tasks anyone is faced with—and despite what others say, it doesn't become easier. You should not avoid it, however, since the longer you wait to fire an ineffective employee (regardless of whose fault it may be), the more you hurt your own company. Part of the problem may be your fault, in that you hired the wrong person for the wrong job. Admit your mistake and get on with the unpleasant task.

Keeping Records

Hand in hand with good management techniques go good record-keeping techniques. Many small businesses have slipshod record-keeping systems and fail to plan for long-term growth. By setting up systems that can be consulted and amended, you will always have at your fingertips any information necessary to make proper decisions, to guide the growth of your business.

I find that a system of loose-leaf notebooks for each important function in the business is an effective way to have information immediately available to you and to make it easy for you to add or subtract material when necessary. Each notebook should be labeled on the outside spine by the topic it covers. Some appropriate books may be:

Sales Facts and Figures
Warehouse and Shipping Control
Quality Standards
Production Information
Inventory Control
Purchasing Facts and Figures
Finance and Credit

Although I use a backup filing system, I try to make a copy of all necessary information and include it in my appropriate notebook. Thus, if I want immediate inventory status, I can pull the book and turn easily to the page where I keep those numbers. I also keep backup information and my own notes in the book. Ideas for new projects are kept in a separate notebook, and I try to refer to the book from time to time. Merely writing down information helps it stick in your memory. I keep a separate book for individual job functions, and I continually ask employees to update the descriptions for me.

There are many advantages to using effective systems such as the notebooks. First, it gives you accurate information about the various components of your business when you need it; it's there at your fingertips, instead of searching through files. Second, it improves your time management. Effective systems free you from unnecessary extra work, whether it's locating material or recreating information that has been misplaced or never recorded. Third, you will have an effective method for training new employees. If everything is adequately recorded, you can merely direct an employee to the appropriate file or notebook or system, and he or she can determine the systems and procedures for themselves.

Finally, an effective systems procedure enables your business to grow smoothly. The time and effort you spend with your systems will be far less than if you were forced to recall and recreate material that was not adequately recorded.

Bookkeeping Systems

One of the important parts of record keeping is bookkeeping. There are certain types of records you should maintain for your own information and to assist you in directing the growth of your business. If you are a corporation, the government may require more records from you. Remember, it is not necessary to get upset by the numbers, since they are merely tools to assist you when planning.

There are five basic types of records you should keep:

1. *Original documents:* Any correspondence, orders, sales slips, receiving records, invoices, or checks are considered original documents. They should be filed under the appropriate sections, by customer, operation, or any other system that is consistent with your business.
2. *Journals:* A journal is usually a booklet that is used to record various financial transactions in chronological order. Ordinarily you may have one journal for each function: sales, purchases, cash, etc. In a retail store, a cash register acts as a journal to record sales. You may have a separate book to record purchases, including date, name, and amount of purchase.
3. *Ledger:* In order to make the information in the journal usable, you will need a ledger. The ledger has a separate page or section for each category of expenditure. Your operating budget gives

you the guide for the category breakdowns: rent, utilities, tele-phone, advertising, travel and entertainment, etc.

At the end of the month, go through the journal, pulling out expenses for each of the ledger categories, recording them in the appropriate sections. In this way, you will quickly see how the money has been allocated.

A very simple system involves setting up code numbers or letters for each category: A1 = Rent; A2 = Utilities; B1 = Advertising Space; B2 = Advertising Postage, etc. Affix this code list to the inside of your business checkbook. Every time you write a check, indicate the appropriate code for that expense on the check stub still in the checkbook. At the end of the month, you can easily go through the checkbook, pull out the expenses by category, and enter them into your ledger.

4. *Trial balance:* The trial balance is nothing more than a summary of each of the ledger accounts. You now have a total of each separate account, so you can see where your money is going.
5. *Financial statements:* After all the accounting work has been completed, you will be able to prepare the financial statements we discussed earlier in this section. You can revise your budget, if necessary, after listing the current month's operating expenses next to the budgeted expenses. Prepare a variance budget to have some idea as to your ability to operate within your budget. If the variance is consistently higher or lower, it may be necessary to rebudget.

   This variance can be an effective operating tool. If, for example, you have budgeted $250 a month for photocopying and you consistently are running at $300, does it pay to buy your own copying machine? If your budget for messenger service is consistently high, you might ask if it's more economical to hire your own messenger, or perhaps find a way to cut further and use the mails instead.

   Along with the budget, you can prepare a P&L (profit and loss statement), balance sheet, revised cash-flow statement, and any other financial items you find necessary.

That's all there is to efficient bookkeeping. Some of these items you can record yourself, when you are starting out. If it gets more complicated, you can think about hiring a part-time bookkeeper to do the work.

One effective technique for financial record keeping is the use of standardized purchase orders and invoices. These can be purchased as blank forms in most stationery supply stores. As your business increases, you can then have your own forms printed.

Purchase orders are used to record any purchases or orders you place. These are multipart forms, and you can determine how many parts of the form you will need. One part should go into a permanent record file. At the end of the month, you can add up the amounts on all of those copies and know the total you have spent. You can use that number when preparing a profit and loss statement, if you use the purchase orders for all cost-of-sales purchases. A second and third part can be sent to the company from whom you order the goods or service. One copy they will keep for their records, and another copy will be returned to you with the order, so you can check it against your original. You may want a fourth copy, filed under a dated or supplier file, so you can follow up the purchase at the appropriate time.

An invoice form also comes in many parts and is to be used when selling an item or service. In essence, it is your customer's bill. In retail operations you will have a cash register receipt or an order book, which provides an original copy to the customer and a carbon for your files. If you wish, you can use more than one part for your record keeping.

You must maintain one copy (in numerical order) for a permanent file. In fact, in case you make a mistake while typing it, you must keep that permanent copy in order in the file, and merely mark "VOID" across the face of it.

In addition to the permanent copy, you will need a customer's copy, which is presented or mailed to the customer with the merchandise. Hopefully, the customer will pay his bill from the invoice, if not already paid. If it is paid, you must indicate that on the invoice.

A third copy may be used as a customer file copy, and that is kept in a file set up by the type of accounts. It may be filed by customer name, city, state, number, or any other system that is easy to use. There are also two sections to that customer file: open and closed files.

The open file is for any orders that have not been paid, and the closed file is for paid orders. (Partial payments remain in the open file until fully paid.) Any additional information, such as shipping, is included on that copy. Thus, when a customer calls to check on an order, you can determine its status by locating the copy in the customer file. Merely inquire whether it has been paid or not, and you'll know where to look.

At the end of the month, all of the open files are removed and given to a typist, and statements are sent out to the customers, indicating how much they owe and for what invoices. If they haven't paid from the invoice, they should pay from the statements. If you have a department store charge, or any of the popular charge cards, every month you receive a notice from the company, indicating what you owe. This is a combined invoice and statement.

When a customer responds to the statement with a payment, pull the order from the open file, indicate on it the amount paid and the check number. If the payment was complete, you can then file the customer's order in the closed file.

It should be pretty obvious to you that it is really not an overwhelming proposition. Bookkeeping—in fact any kind of record keeping—is really pretty simple, as long as you get the jump on it.

Set up a system or borrow one from another company. Use mine, if you wish, since I can assure you it works. You may, naturally, have to modify it somewhat for your own needs. If you start early and never let it all get ahead of you, you will have one of the major formulas for successful growth. Then, as you will see in the following chapter, you will have enough money and time to enjoy yourself, along with running a successful business.

9. Personal Pleasures

Why else would you want to own your own business, except to enjoy yourself by being independent and to make a lot of money? I think by now you see how it is possible to make money, using whatever it is that you know and utilizing some of the tools of business that we have spoken about in this book.

The greatest pleasure you can derive from being independent is calling your shots, going and coming whenever and wherever you want. Of course, you've got to be able to afford it, if you want some of the good things in life. Here are some guidelines in order to live like a millionaire, and earn $15,000–$20,000 a year.

In order to prepare yourself and set goals, write down a list for yourself and your family indicating how you would like to live the rest of your life. Do you want a quiet cabin near a fishing stream? Or a cooperative apartment overlooking New York's East River? Does a two-week vacation in the south of France appeal to you? Dinners at five-star restaurants?

There are only two requirements to get everything you want:

1. Have your company earn enough money.
2. Find a business reason for doing all of these things.

Don't forget the first rule about running your own business. Every dollar that goes into the company is yours. The key to financial security is learning how to take as much of it as you can, without having to pay taxes on it.

Let's take a look at how that works. If you earned $30,000 a year and had four dependents, your salary would look something like this:

$30,000 income
− 10,245 taxes
─────────────
$19,755 after taxes

Those are approximate numbers, of course, but close enough to the actual taxes you would have to pay. But what if you took only half the amount in salary?

$15,000 salary
− 3,117 taxes
$11,883 after taxes

Wait, don't get upset, and say, "But now I'm taking home too little to live on." Suppose you took the other $15,000 you used to take in salary as expenses, without having to pay any taxes on the income. Then, here's what you'd have.

$11,883 after-tax salary
+ 15,000 cash as expenses
$26,883 take-home

By taking $15,000 out of the company in expenses, you have increased your annual income by $7,128 over what you would normally take home if you took all of the money out as salary.

Best of all, the more you make, the more you get to take home — within reason. Why do I say that? Uncle Sam (IRS) is generous in its own way, but immediately suspicious of anyone flaunting its rules back in its face. If, for example, your business is earning $250,000 a year, your salary is $5,000, and your expense account is $120,000, the IRS people would immediately jump all over you. They would probably rule that at least half of the expense money is either salary or bonus, and you would be taxed appropriately.

Thus, there's no sense being greedy. If you keep a careful set of records and find a way to justify everything you do, they can have very little disagreement with you. It's what is called "creative accounting."

Travel and Entertainment

Most of these deductions you will be able to justify under the operating budget category of Travel and Entertainment (T&E). Expenses you incur in the conduct of your trade or business, or in an effort to produce or collect income, are expenses that you can ordinarily deduct for tax purposes. The rules issued by the IRS are extremely specific about what you can and cannot deduct. Not only that, you must detail all of your expenses.

It is my belief that once you have read through this chapter, and perhaps other books that discuss the tax laws, you should have no trouble at all in justifying most expenses that can be picked up by your company. Remember, you don't have to take the money out of the company directly either. If, for example, you and your wife want to go to Mexico, and can justify a business reason for going, you can put everything on your American Express Card, including air fare, hotels, meals, even the serape you buy in the market. Then let the company pay the bills when they come in next month. Although you haven't taken the money out as cash, if the entire trip cost you $3,000, it's like getting a present of that money. Normally, it would have come from your earnings, *after taxes*. As you just saw above, we've found a way for you to increase your take-home pay by $7,128. You can use some of it to pay for your vacation/business trip.

Why do I call it a "vacation/business trip"? Because the government doesn't want to pay for your pleasures. Thus, wherever you go, you must find a business justification. If you are in the mail-order business and normally try to develop products, you can write off the Mexican trip as a buying trip. Can you deduct your wife too? I'll show you how to do that.

The two basic types of expenses to consider here are Travel and Entertainment. *Travel expenses* are any ordinary expenses that are incurred while traveling away from home in order to conduct business. Some of these items are:

Meals (to and from business and those at your destination)
Lodging (wherever you stay on the way to your destination and
    while you are conducting your business)
Baggage charges
Air, bus, train fares
Cleaning and laundry expenses
Telephone and telegraph expenses
Transportation charges to and from hotels, airport, meetings, cus-
    tomers, etc.
Operating or renting a car
Tips
Any other reasonable charges involved in the conduct of your busi-
    ness

As long as you can justify any expenses, they are considered legitimate expenses, regardless of where they are incurred. If your trip is partially for pleasure and partially for business, you may deduct only those expenses related to business. If the major reason for the trip is for pleasure, then you cannot deduct the travel expenses, only those directly related to business. However, proper recording of your expenses and planning your trip properly will permit you to make the appropriate deductions.

For example, Peter Smith travels to Los Angeles from Chicago to contact suppliers for his small retail store. While in Los Angeles, he spends several evenings with his cousins who live there. Technically, if most of his trip was planned to conduct business, he can deduct all of the traveling expenses to get to Los Angeles, including the cab to the airport, the airline tickets, rented car at Los Angeles Airport, and all of the other expenses, including his hotel. He may not deduct the meals with his cousins, or any expenses related to seeing them.

Here's the big question: can you take your wife (or husband)? You cannot legitimately deduct your spouse's expenses, unless you can prove that her presence served a legitimate business purpose.

However, you will have no problems, if she is an employee of your company. If she receives a minimal salary from the company, she is indeed, an employee. How about "Director of Special Operations" or "Research Assistant?" Any appropriate title will be sufficient. And you don't have to take any additional money from the company to pay her salary. If you want to take a salary of $15,000, divide it between the two of you, either equally, or $10,000 for you as president and $5,000 for her, for her position. You must be able to show that she has done some work for you. Even though it'll cost a few extra dollars in taxes, the difference between the taxes and the possible deductions is well worth it.

While we're on this topic, what about children? If you can justify a position for them in your company, you can deduct their expenses also; as long as you can prove they're legitimate employees. It's a good way to pay them allowances from pretax dollars. Salaries for children should be in line with what you would pay other employees.

Let's also talk about automobiles here. If you can prove an actual business use for your car, you can deduct all expenses, such as gasoline, maintenance, supplies, garage and parking fees, tolls, chauffeur's salary, and depreciation. In addition, you can deduct the costs of interest on loans to purchase the car. However, it makes sense in some cases for your company to own the car and pay all of the expenses through the company. Then you don't have to worry about deductions. Also, consider leasing your car, with the company paying for it directly. Many executives lease cars through their company, in a method that permits the company to pay a high monthly fee. At the end of a specified period, three or four years, you then can purchase the car for a minimal fee, often as low as $100. At that point, you own the car and can resell it. The cash from the car is yours, although it is considered income and is taxable.

Entertainment expenses include the cost of entertaining guests involved with your business, at places such as nightclubs, movies, theaters, and country clubs. They include such things as sporting events, yacht trips, and other vacations such as hunting, fishing, etc. They may also cover services provided to business customers and their family, such as hotel rooms, cars, and food. The major requirement by the IRS is that your expenses must be ordinary and necessary to the conduct of your trade or business.

You can deduct some expenses if you entertain business clients at home. In addition, if you belong to social or athletic clubs in order to conduct business (solicit new clients, etc.), you can deduct those expenses. Almost anyone who has some business relationship can be entertained. Some of these people may be customers, suppliers, clients, employees, agents, partners, professional advisors, prospective accounts, etc.

Sometimes it takes a little "creativity" to justify those expenses. But as long as you keep accurate records of what you have spent, why you have spent it, and for whom, you have a good chance of being able to make the deduction.

My favorite example of "creative accounting" appears in the book *Kramer Versus Kramer*, by Avery Corman.

> "We're all going out for dinner on Ralph," Harold announced.
>
> "Ralph, I don't want you bankrolling my stay here," Ted said.
>
> "Forget it. I'm writing a lot of it off."
>
> "How are you going to do that?"
>
> "Easy."
>
> Ralph approached one of Dora and Harold's friends, a bony octogenarian sunning himself on a chaise lounge.
>
> "Mr. Schlosser, I meant to ask you. Would you be interested in a liquor delivery route in Chicago?"
>
> "You kidding? I wouldn't be interested in a walk to the grocery."
>
> "Thank you. There, Ted—it goes in a diary. 'Discussed liquor route with S. Schlosser in Florida.' I just made this a business trip."

The key here is the diary. In order to justify any expense, you must keep an expense diary. The diary is a bound book (not a loose-leaf) in which you keep a record of all deductible expenses.

You do not normally need any receipts for expenses under $25; however, any records you have, do make your record keeping more complete, and in case of an IRS audit, they demonstrate your accuracy. Also, the diary entries should be made close to the time the expenses were incurred. The IRS will not permit deductions that are merely approximations.

Receipts are not a problem, since most restaurants, hotels, nightclubs, and other places provide you with some form of documentation. By using one of the major credit cards: American Express, Diners Club, Master Charge, Visa, or any others you might have, you will always have a handy record of your expenses at the end of the month. Whenever you get a check in a restaurant, there is usually a little stub at the bottom that can be removed, filled out, and used for documentation.

Remember, even if you have recorded the expense in your diary, you must have some form of backup.

It is very easy to keep up your diary. Basically, there are four categories that must be recorded in the book.

1. Amount of the expense
2. Date and location of the expense
3. Business purpose
4. Who was entertained or fed

There are only two qualifications about these items: 1) they must not be approximations, and 2) the expenses cannot be too extravagant.

Here's how to record your expenses. The diary is a date book, normally, so you have only to record the amount under the appropriate date. For example:

1. $125.00 (amount)
2. Sept. 15, 1981, Galatoire's, New Orleans, LA (date and location)
3. Discussed potential new business (business purpose)
4. Mr. Harry Johnson, Sales Mgr., Liquid Industries (who was entertained)

As long as you can show that there was a legitimate business intent, you don't actually have to show any specific result of your travel or entertainment. After all, if you are a salesman, the IRS cannot refuse your deductions merely because you aren't a very good salesman and couldn't make the deal.

I had a young entrepreneur in one of my classes who had a novel idea for vacations. He set up a small publishing company as a sole proprietorship. It cost him $33. Then he kept very extensive records for everything he did. He took five or six vacations a year, and each vacation was recorded as "research for prospective title." One was about "Fishing in the Keys." Another was "Cheap European Vacations." A third book was to be titled, "Cooking Cross Country."

None of the books ever got published. He did write some of the manuscripts and had some photographs he took on each of the vacations. The intent, though, was there. They were all legitimate deductions.

One of the best deductions you must know about is the office at home. If you earn your sole income from a business that is located in your home, you may deduct that part of your home that is devoted to the operation of that business. For example, if you are a salesman and use one room of your eight-room home for an office, you may deduct one-eighth of your rent or mortgage payment. Or you can calculate the square footage, and determine what percentage your business uses, and deduct that amount. In addition, you can deduct that portion of your utility bills; of course, the business should have its own telephone, which is entirely deductible. Any furniture or equipment (television, video tape machine, etc.) that is used for your "office" may be deducted.

It's important to understand the concept behind taking deductions. First, and most obviously, before you can deduct expenses, you must spend the money. And to do so, it means that your company has to make money. Even though items are deductible, you must first have the money to make the purchase.

Second, by having the company pay for most of these expenses, including travel and entertainment, you can afford to improve your life-style without increasing your salary or the amount of taxes you will have to pay. If you go back to the first examples in this chapter about how to take less salary but more income, you can adjust the numbers any way you want. Whenever you read about famous athletes or performers earning millions of dollars, they don't normally receive million-dollar paychecks. Instead, some of those millions go to buy houses, make loans, buy stocks, provide limousines and chauffeurs, pay club memberships, provide luxury vacations, and more. Otherwise most of the earnings will be taken in taxes. Instead, perhaps, they receive $100,000 in salary, on which they pay taxes, and the rest they receive in "perks," or perquisites. It is these perks that make having your own business the best investment of time and money that you can make.

Set yourself a base salary that will increase by about 10 percent–15 percent every year, or divide it between you and your spouse. The balance of the available amount (whatever your company can afford) is used to pay expenses. Every year, as your salary increases, your expense account should increase. Thus, if you determine your company can afford to pay you a total income of $60,000 next year, you may divide it as follows:

$12,500	your salary
7,500	your spouse's salary
40,000	expense account
$60,000	

Most of the information in this chapter should be considered merely a guideline to what you can legitimately use as deductions. However, you can obtain a list of rules and regulations from the IRS. The tax people are always willing to work with you and to answer questions you might have.

The only rules you should always follow are: never be greedy and use common sense.

10. Buying a Business

To become the owner of a business, you may decide to buy a going business. If you do, most of the same factors already discussed should be considered. But you must first evaluate some specific advantages against the possible disadvantages.

Advantages:

1. You may be able to buy the business at a bargain price. For personal reasons, an owner may be sufficiently anxious to give you favorable terms.
2. Buying a business will save you time and effort in setting up your establishment with equipment and stock.
3. You may acquire customers who are accustomed to trading with the establishment. Thus you eliminate an initial waiting period for business while you are getting started.
4. The owner should be able to give you the benefit of his experience in the business and in the community.

Disadvantages:

1. You may pay too much for the business because of your inaccurate appraisal or the former owner's misrepresentation.
2. The owner may have had a bad reputation. You would then be battling prejudices of former customers and, perhaps, of merchandise and equipment suppliers.
3. The location may be poor.
4. The former owner's choice of fixtures and equipment may have been poor. Or they may be outmoded or in bad condition.
5. Too much of the merchandise or materials on hand may have been poorly selected.

How Much to Pay?

In deciding how much you should pay for a going business, you should consider its profit potential. Of course, the tangible assets, such as equipment and inventory, are important to you, but only to the extent that they contribute to future profits. If the seller is asking something for the intangible asset of good will, take care in estimating how much it will add to your future profits. Furthermore, you must assess the cost of any liabilities you will be expected to assume.

Profit Potential

What you are concerned with is the *future* possibility of the business. Therefore, you should carefully estimate the sales and profits for the next few years. For how many years depends on your expected return on investment. For example, if you expect a 10 percent return on your initial investment, it will take ten years to recover the investment. So, you would be interested in trying to forecast sales and profits for ten years.

To estimate future profits, you should start by analyzing balance sheets and profit and loss statements of the present owner for at least the last five years. Going back ten years would be even better. Some businesses may have inadequate records, but all should have copies of their income tax returns. What has been the rate of return on investment? Does it compare favorably with the rate you can obtain from other investment opportunities? How does it compare with averages for other businesses of the same kind? Industry trade associations can furnish average standards for that specific business area.

Have sales over the years been increasing or decreasing? What share of the market is the business obtaining within its market area? To find this out requires an analysis of the local market for the particular firm in which you are interested. What is the competition in the area, the population, the purchasing power? What are the trends? What is the outlook for increasing sales?

Are the profits satisfactory? If not, what are the chances of increasing them? Have profits been consistent over a period of years? If the last year's profit was unusually high in comparison with previous years, why was it? What is the profit trend? Have profits been increasing consistently or have they leveled off or started to decrease? What are the reasons for the profit trend, whatever it may be? Such questions should be answered to your satisfaction before you buy.

You will not necessarily be discouraged from buying the business if past profit records are not favorable. Very often the reason a business is for sale is because of recent records of poor earnings. Your examination may reveal that these have been brought about by poor management—and you may be convinced that your management will improve the situation. By the same token, an excellent past earnings' record, in itself, should not cause you to pay a large amount for the business without further investigation.

You should ask the seller to prepare a projected statement of profit and loss for at least the next twelve months. This means he will prepare his estimate of sales along with estimates of cost of goods sold and operating expenses. The seller should follow the same format and approach that you did earlier in this book, when considering a start-up operation. The seller has access to data about the business not available to you. However, this must be compared with your own estimate, recognizing that the seller's estimate of profits is likely to be less conservative than yours. With a detailed estimate of the next twelve months' operation, you can compute working-capital requirements for each month. Then estimate the value of assets and liabilities as of the end of that period. Find the estimated return on investment. Do this by dividing the projected net profit by the price asked for the business. If you believe additional investment will be needed immediately to make the business run profitably, add this to the price. The highest price for the firm that brings you a return with which you are satisfied is the maximum price you will wish to pay. Thus an estimate of future profitability gives you the basis of a logical offer for the business.

If you are not familiar with accounting and income tax records, so that you may verify records of past operations and make a reasonable forecast of future operations, have an experienced accountant do this for you.

Tangible Assets

The most commonly purchased tangible assets are merchandise inventory, equipment and fixtures, and supplies. If the business you plan to purchase sells on credit, you probably will take over accounts receivable.

What is the condition of the inventory you are buying? Is the stock of goods made up of timely, fresh, well-balanced selections of materials or merchandise? How much of it will have to be disposed of at a loss? A careful appraisal of the stock must be made. Each item should be separately priced and given a reasonable value. If at all possible, the inventory should be "aged"; that is, the length of time each group of items has been in stock should be determined. Then, the total dollar value of stock over eighteen months old, one year to eighteen months, six months to one year, and less than six months should be calculated. Usually, the older the inventory, the less value it has.

Equipment and fixtures should be carefully examined. Remember that you are buying secondhand furnishings with only a percentage of their original value. You must be sure equipment is in working order. Find out its age and obtain evaluations of similar equipment from dealers in new or secondhand equipment. Not only do you want to know how much equipment and fixtures have depreciated, but you must know how obsolete they may be. Office equipment may be in working order, but so obsolete that to use it instead of modern devices would be inefficient. Also, it may be difficult to obtain repair parts for old models in case of a breakdown. Many store fixtures quickly become out of date. New, modernized fixtures are necessary to attract customers. Machines used in factories may have been superseded by far more efficient equipment. To pay an exorbitant price for the old machine, no matter how good its condition, would be most unwise.

If you are taking over other assets, such as accounts receivable, credit records, sales records, mailing lists, or leases, investigate them closely. Accounts receivable should be aged to determine how many of them may be so old that collection will be difficult. All have real value, and you should make certain that these are included in the sale.

Good Will

Over and above the total appraisal of inventories, fixtures, equipment, and other assets, there will usually be an amount asked for good will. This is the amount the owner is asking for the favorable public attitude toward his going concern. It is not to be confused with "net worth," which is the difference between the dollar values of the assets and liabilities of the business. Rather it is the ability of the business to realize a higher rate of return on the investment than ordinary in the particular type of business. When good will exists it is a valuable asset.

You should be realistic in determining how much you should pay for good will. No fixed formula can substitute for good judgment. Since it is payment for favorable public attitude, you should make some effort to check this attitude. You might question customers, bankers, and others whom you feel have unbiased opinions. Then you must consider who will have the good will after the business changes hands. Does it belong to the business, or is it personally attached to, and will it go with, the seller?

Perhaps this good will is most important in a service business. Since the success of a service business rests on the capabilities and personal relationships of the owner, it is important to determine what the customers really think of the seller. If the seller has developed a reputation for being unreliable, it may be too difficult for you to revive the original trust customers had for the business. It is possible that the owner did not keep pace with increased technological requirements and lost customer confidence. Are you capable of obtaining that knowledge fast enough to avoid the erosion of the business? It is vital to check the customers and ask them their opinions. Their attitudes will often tell you a lot more than the financials and owner's statements.

A test of the price asked is to compare it with past profits of the business. How many months or years will it take before the price of the "good will" can be paid out of profits? During that period you will, in effect, be working for the seller rather than for yourself. Another way of judging the value of this intangible asset is to estimate how much more income you will receive by buying the going business than by starting a new one.

Compare the price asked for good will with that asked for good will in similar businesses. In other words, if you are "shopping around" for a business, compare not only total prices asked, but the amounts asked over and above the reasonable value of net tangible assets. This will work in reverse, too. If others are interested in buying the business, what they offer may determine what you will have to pay.

Liabilities

You should be sure that the seller pays off accumulated debts before you pay the money agreed upon in the terms of sale. Find out if there are mortgages, back taxes, liens upon the assets, or other creditors' claims. Obtain full information about any undelivered purchases. Although it is generally not desirable to assume any liabilities, it may be necessary in some instances. If liabilities are assumed, their value must be subtracted from the agreed-upon value of the assets to determine the net value.

The Price

After you have determined what you believe to be the net value, this does not mean that you have reached the final price to be paid for the business. Value relates to what the business is worth. Other factors affect the final price. It is determined through negotiation and bargaining.

Try to find out what the seller's reputation has been among employees and suppliers. Poor relationships may require extra effort on your part to establish a smoothly running organization. Make sure that suppliers will deal with you. If a franchise is involved, you should obtain satisfactory assurance from the supplier that it will not be withdrawn.

Why does the owner wish to sell? This should be one of your first questions. Is the reason given (such as a death in the family, poor health, or a needed change in climate) the really decisive factor? Or does the seller know that the neighborhood is changing so that need for his specific type of business will soon cease to exist; or that a new civic development, or zoning law, will affect the business unfavorably? You should search for his true reasons for selling by questioning not only the seller but others whom you know to be reliable.

Some business owners have sold out only to start a new business in competition with the buyer of the old one. Careful consideration should be given to placing limitations upon the seller's right to compete with you for a specific period of time and within a specified area.

Legal Advice

As a safeguard against costly errors, legal advice should be obtained before any agreement is made. The agreement should be drawn up by a lawyer to insure that it covers all essential points and is clearly understood by the parties. Among the items covered in a typical contract covering the sale of a small business are:

1. A description of what is being sold
2. The purchase price
3. The method of payment
4. A statement of how adjustments are to be handled at the time of closing (for example, adjustments for inventory sold, rent, payroll, and insurance premiums)
5. Buyer's assumption of contracts and liabilities
6. Seller's warranties (for example, warranty protection for the buyer against false statements of the seller, inaccurate financial data, and undisclosed liabilities)
7. Seller's obligation and assumption of risk pending closing
8. Covenant of seller not to compete
9. Time, place, and procedures of closing

The seller and buyer must comply with the bulk sales law of the state in which the transaction takes place. The purpose of such a law is to make certain that the seller does not sell out, pocket the proceeds, and disappear, leaving his creditors unpaid. The seller must furnish a sworn list of his creditors, and you, as the buyer, must give notice to the creditors of the pending sale. Otherwise the seller's creditors may be able to claim the personal property you purchased.

As soon as possible after signing the contract, take possession. Otherwise, the seller may deplete the inventory and, in some cases, create ill will for you.

11. Buying a Franchise

Many small business owners have been helped in getting a sound start by investing in a franchise. You may want to consider such an investment. Franchising can minimize your risk. It will enable you to start your business under a name and trademark that have already gained public acceptance. You will have access to training and management assistance from people experienced in your line of business. Sometimes, you can obtain financial assistance that will make it possible to start your business with less cash than you would have needed otherwise.

On the other hand, you must make some sacrifices when entering a franchised operation. You lose a certain amount of control of your business. You will no longer truly be your own boss in some situations. And, of course, you must pay a fee to, or share profits with, the franchiser.

The franchise industry has grown rapidly, and the types of business today range from the old standby, McDonald's, to computerized dating and body-tanning centers. There are franchises for quick printing, maternity clothes like Lady Madonna, business services, tax services like H & R Block, and even Playboy Clubs. There are day-care schools, muffler shops such as Midas, fast Chinese food, Cookie Coach, super hero toys, underground houses, discos, and haircutting shops. If the franchise business is for you, there are hundreds of different types from which to choose.

This section will present some of the advantages and disadvantages of franchising, where to look for a franchise, and how to evaluate one.

First, what is franchising? Essentially, franchising is a plan of distribution under which an individually owned business is operated as though it were a part of a large chain. Services or products are standardized. Uniform trademarks, symbols, design, and equipment are used. A supplier (the franchiser) gives the individual dealer (the franchisee) the right to sell, distribute, or market the franchiser's product or service by using the franchiser's name, reputation, and selling techniques. The franchise agreement (or contract) usually gives the franchisee the exclusive right to sell, or otherwise represent, the franchiser in a specified area. In return for this exclusive right, the franchisee agrees to pay either a sum of money (a franchise fee) or a percentage of gross sales, or to buy equipment or supplies from the franchiser—or some combination of these considerations.

Advantages of Franchising

As a franchisee, you can start a business with:

1. Limited experience. You are taking advantage of the franchiser's experience that you might otherwise have to obtain the hard way— through trial and error.

2. A relatively small amount of capital and a strengthened financial and credit standing. Sometimes the franchiser gives financial assistance, making it possible for you to start with less than the usual amount of cash. For example, the franchiser may accept a down payment with your note for the balance of the needed initial capital. Or he may allow you to delay in making payments for royalties, purchases, or other fees in order to help you over the rough spots. With the name of a well-known successful franchiser behind you, your standing with financial institutions and credit associations will be strengthened.

3. A well-developed consumer image and good will with proven products and services. Your business has instant pulling power. To develop such pulling power on your own might take years of promotion and considerable investment.

4. Competently designed facilities, layout, displays, and fixtures based upon experience with many dealers.

5. Chain buying power. You may receive savings through chain-style purchasing in volume of products, equipment, supplies, advertising materials, and other business needs.

6. The opportunity for business training and continued assistance from experienced management in proven methods of doing business. You can normally expect to be trained in the mechanics of the particular business and guided in its day-to-day operation until you are proficient at the job. Moreover, management consulting service is provided by the franchiser on a continuing basis. This often includes help with record keeping as well as other accounting assistance.

7. National or regional promotion and publicity, which will help business. Also, you will receive help and guidance with local advertising. The franchiser's program of research and development will assist you in keeping up with competition and changing times.

All of these factors can help raise your income and lower your risk of failure.

There is no question that there is a lot of hard work involved in running a franchise, and any prior experience one has had in the field would be very helpful, although not a necessary ingredient for success.

Tom Poby of Lansing, Illinois, was employed by a major commercial printing firm that printed a number of national magazines, including *Time*, *Look*, and *Life*. On the day that Tom was to receive a promotion, *Look* magazine went out of business. Tom was subsequently held back, but at least he had his job.

When *Life* magazine was canceled, Tom and his wife Fran were faced with what many people in the country are now facing—unemployment. Would Tom be lucky again and keep his job this time? The Pobys knew that it was time to make some changes in their lives, so they began to investigate franchise opportunities.

When they came across an ad for "Big Red Q Quickprint Centers," they felt that Tom's experience might be valuable here. They found that the instant printing business fared well in times of economic recession, and that this would increase and protect their job security.

Together, the Pobys have grown into a two-store operation, with eight employees including their son Jerry, who manages one of the stores. They anticipate that their daughter Sharon will eventually join them in the business. Their second store was the first existing franchise to have received financing from a bank-sponsored SBA-guaranteed loan program. This package is unique to franchising, not just to Big Red Q.

Finally, Tom and Fran have also reached the enviable position that many small business owners strive for—being able to let their employees run the business when they go on vacation!

Disadvantages of Franchising

1. Submission to imposed standardized operations. You cannot make all the rules. Contrary to the "be your own boss" lures in franchise advertisements, you may not truly be your own boss. In the first place, you must subjugate your personal identity to that of the name of the franchiser. If an important satisfaction to you is to have your business known by your name, a franchise operation is not for you. The franchiser exerts control and pressure on you (1) to conform to standardized procedure, (2) to handle specific products or services that may not be particularly profitable in your marketing area, and (3) to follow other policies that may benefit others in the chain but not you.

2. Sharing of profits with the franchiser. The franchiser nearly always charges a royalty or a percentage of gross sales. This royalty fee must ultimately come out of the profits of the franchisee—or be paid whether the franchisee makes a profit or not. Sometimes such fees are exorbitant, way out of proportion to the profit. A government-sponsored study revealed that a large number of fast-food franchisers were misleading potential franchisees as to expected profits and that many franchisees who were required to buy a large proportion of supplies from their franchisers were paying higher prices than if they had ob-

tained the merchandise on their own. In some franchising operations, some franchisees pay more than other franchisees for the same services.

3. Lack of freedom to meet local competition. Under a franchise you may be restricted in establishing selling prices, in introducing additional products or services or dropping unprofitable ones, regardless of local competition.

4. Danger of contracts being slanted to the advantage of the franchiser. Clauses in some contracts imposed by the franchiser provide for unreasonably high sales quotas, mandatory working hours, cancellation or termination of the franchise for minor infringements, and/or restrictions on the franchisee in transferring his franchise or recovering his investment. The territory assigned the franchisee may overlap that of another. franchisee or may be otherwise inequitable. In settling disputes of any kind, the bargaining power of the franchiser is usually greater than that of the franchisee.

For example, the same study referred to above showed that fast-food franchisees worked a median amount of 60 hours a week, some as much as 120 hours. Alleged infringement of the franchisee's exclusive territory was a major source of friction between franchisee and franchiser. The power imbalance in favor of the franchiser is due not only to the franchisee's smaller financial resources but to his lack of information, information the franchiser has. For example, the franchiser understands thoroughly the implications of the agreement that he himself has devised, and he has experience in negotiating under this agreement.

5. Time consumed in preparing reports required by the franchiser. On the other hand, you should recognize that, if these reports are helpful to the franchiser, they probably will help you to manage your business more effectively.

6. Sharing the burden of the franchiser's faults. While ordinarily the franchiser's chain will have developed good will among consumers, there may be instances in which there is ill will. For example, if a customer has been served a stale roll or a burnt hamburger, or received poor service in one outlet, he is apt to become disgruntled with the whole chain. As one outlet in the chain, you will suffer regardless of the excellence of your particular unit. Furthermore, the franchiser may fail. You must bear the brunt of the chain's mistakes as well as share the glory of its good performances.

Don't be discouraged, however, since prospective franchisees today are afforded much more protection than they were even a few years ago. The Federal Trade Commission adopted a regulation that requires protection for the investor and full disclosure of all the elements of the franchise offering. There are also individual state laws, and you can easily evaluate the quality of the prospective franchise if it willingly provides any information you request. Honest franchisers have nothing to hide.

Finding Franchise Opportunities

Now that you've looked into what franchising is and considered its advantages and disadvantages, where do you look for a franchise opportunity? Some of the sources are:

Newspapers. Classified sections of most daily metropolitan newspapers carry franchise offers under the "Business Opportunities" section. Sometimes the franchiser runs a blind ad, not giving his name but listing a box number. This enables him to perform a preliminary screening in an effort to eliminate the shoppers from the buyers.

Trade publications. If you are interested in going into business in a particular trade, seek out the publications for that trade. Franchisers advertise in trade publications related to their franchised businesses.

Franchising publications. Publications devoted strictly to franchising are another source of information. Two worthwhile publications are: *Franchising in the Economy 1973–75*, available from the U.S. Department of Commerce, Washington, D.C., and *Investigate Before Investing: Guidance for Prospective Franchisees*, Fels and Rudnick, from the International Franchise Association, Washington, D.C. Another excellent guide is the *Franchise Opportunities Handbook*, available from the Superintendent of Documents, U.S. Government Printing Office, Washington, D.C.

Franchiser exhibitions. Attendance at franchiser exhibitions, held in major cities, will give you the opportunity to meet franchiser representatives face to face and to compare a number of offers at one time. You should be wary of any franchiser who is willing to sign a contract on the spot. Your reason for attending is not to make commitments but to engage in give-and-take discussions directly with franchiser representatives and to obtain brochures and printed materials for further study.

Franchise marketing agencies. Franchise marketing agencies and franchise consultants serve to help prospective investors locate a profitable franchise. They also furnish information on the reputation and profitability of particular franchisers and their franchisees.

Franchising companies. Once you have narrowed your interest down to one or two fields, you can prepare a list of the top franchising companies in each field and write directly to them for details. You should give some background information about yourself and the sincerity of your interest. Hastily and sketchily written inquiries are often ignored by franchisers.

Other sources. While the above are the most important sources of information, there are other direct and indirect leads to franchise opportunities. These include radio, television, direct mail, as well as suggestions from bankers, friends, business brokers, equipment and product suppliers.

Once you have located an opportunity in which you are interested, the next job is to evaluate it.

Evaluating a Franchise Opportunity

A franchise costs money. One can be purchased for as little as a few hundred dollars or as much as a quarter of a million dollars or more. Hence it is vital that you investigate and evaluate carefully any franchise before you invest.

Beware of the fast buck artists. The popularity of franchising has attracted an unsavory group of operators who will take you if they can. Sometimes known as "front money men," they usually offer nothing more than the sale of equipment and a catchy business name. Once they sell you the equipment, they do not care whether you succeed or fail. If you are promised tremendous profits in a short period of time, be wary.

The following checklist will aid you in selecting the right franchise. Check each question when the answer is "yes." Most, if not all, questions should be checked before you sign a franchise contract.

Questions To Answer Affirmatively Before Going Into Franchising

check if
answer
is "yes"

The Franchiser

1. Has the franchiser been in business long enough (five years or more) to have established a good reputation? _____
2. Have you checked Better Business Bureaus, Chambers of Commerce, Dun and Bradstreet, or bankers to find out about the franchiser's business reputation and credit rating? _____
3. Did the above investigations reveal that the franchiser has a good reputation and credit rating? _____
4. Does the franchising firm appear to be financed adequately so that it can carry out its stated plan of financial assistance and expansion? _____
5. Have you found out how many franchisees are now operating? _____
6. Have you found out the "mortality" or failure rate among franchisees? _____
7. Is the failure rate small? _____
8. Have you checked with some franchisees and found that

the franchiser has a reputation for honesty and fair dealing among those who currently hold franchises? _____

9. Has the franchiser shown you certified figures indicating exact net profits of one or more going operations that you have personally checked yourself? _____

10. Has the franchiser given you a specimen contract to study with the advice of your legal counsel? _____

11. Will the franchiser assist you with:
    a. A management-training program? _____
    b. An employee-training program? _____
    c. A public-relations program? _____
    d. Obtaining capital? _____
    e. Good credit terms? _____
    f. Merchandising ideas? _____
    g. Designing store layout and displays? _____
    h. Inventory control methods? _____
    i. Analyzing financial statements? _____

12. Does the franchiser provide continuing assistance for franchisees through supervisors who visit regularly? _____

13. Does the franchising firm have an experienced management trained in depth? _____

14. Will the franchiser assist you in finding a good location for your business? _____

15. Has the franchising company investigated *you* carefully enough to assure itself that you can successfully operate one of its franchises at a profit both to it and to you? _____

16. Have you determined exactly what the franchiser can do for you that you cannot do for yourself? _____

The Product or Service

17. Has the product or service been on the market long enough to gain good consumer acceptance? _____

18. Is it priced competitively? _____

19. Is it the type of item or service that the same consumer customarily buys more than once? _____

20. Is it an all-year seller in contrast to a seasonal one? _____

21. Is it a staple item in contrast to a fad? _____

22. Does it sell well elsewhere? _____

23. Would you buy it on its merits? _____

24. Will it be in greater demand five years from now? _____

25. If it is a product rather than a service:
    a. Is it packaged attractively? _____
    b. Does it stand up well in use? _____
    c. Is it easy and safe to use? _____

d. Is it patented?   _____
e. Does it comply with all applicable laws?   _____
f. Is it manufactured under certain quality standards?   _____
g. Do these standards compare favorably with similar products on the market?   _____
h. If the product must be purchased exclusively from the franchiser or a designated supplier, are the prices to you, as the franchisee, competitive?   _____

The Franchise Contract

26. Does the franchise fee seem reasonable?   _____
27. Do continuing royalties or percent of gross sales payment appear reasonable?   _____
28. Are the total cash investment required and the terms for financing the balance satisfactory?   _____
29. Does the cash investment include payment for fixtures and equipment?   _____
30. If you will be required to participate in company-sponsored promotion and publicity by contributing to an "advertising fund," will you have the right to veto any increase in contributions to the "fund"?   _____
31. if the parent company's product or service is protected by patent or liability insurance, is the same protection extended to you?   _____
32. Are you free to buy the amount of merchandise you believe you need rather than being required to purchase a certain amount?   _____
33. Can you, as the franchisee, return merchandise for credit?   _____
34. Can you engage in other business activities?   _____
35. If there is an annual sales quota, can you retain your franchise if it is not met?   _____
36. Does the contract give you an exclusive territory for the length of the franchise?   _____
37. Is your territory protected?   _____
38. Is the franchise agreement renewable?   _____
39. Can you terminate your agreement if you are not happy for some reason?   _____
40. Is the franchiser prohibited from selling the franchise out from under you?   _____
41. May you sell the business to whomever you please?   _____
42. If you sell your franchise, will you be compensated for the good will you have built into the business?   _____
43. Does the contract obligate the franchiser to give you continuing assistance after you are operating the business?   _____

44. Are you permitted a choice in determining whether you will sell any new product or service introduced by the franchiser after you have opened your business? _____

45. Is there anything with respect to the franchise or its operation that would make you ineligible for special financial assistance or other benefits accorded to small business concerns by federal, state, or local governments? _____

46. Did your lawyer approve the franchise contract after he studied it paragraph by paragraph? _____

47. Is the contract free and clear of requirements that would call upon you to take any steps that are, according to your lawyer, unwise or illegal in your state, county, or city? _____

48. Does the contract cover all aspects of your agreement with the franchiser? _____

49. Does it really benefit both you and the franchiser? _____

Your Market

50. Are the territorial boundaries of your market completely, accurately, and understandably defined? _____

51. Have you made any study to determine whether the product or service you propose to sell has a market in your territory at the prices you will have to charge? _____

52. Does the territory provide an adequate sales potential? _____

53. Will the population in the territory given you increase over the next five years? _____

54. Will the average per capita income in the territory remain the same or increase over the next five years? _____

55. Is existing competition in your territory for the product or service not too well entrenched? _____

YOU — The Franchisee

56. Do you know where you are going to get the equity capital you will need? _____

57. Have you compared what it would take to start your own similar business with the price you must pay for the franchise? _____

58. Have you made a business plan—for example:
    a. Have you worked out what income from sales or services you can reasonably expect in the first six months? The first year? The second year? _____
    b. Have you made a forecast of expenses including a regular salary for yourself? _____

59. Are you prepared to give up some independence of action to

secure the advantages offered by the franchise? _____

60. Are you capable of accepting supervision, even though you will presumably be your own boss? _____
61. Are you prepared to accept rules and regulations with which you may not agree? _____
62. Can you afford the period of training involved? _____
63. Are you ready to spend much or all of the remainder of your business life with this franchiser, offering his product or service to the public? _____

Franchising creates distinct opportunities for the prospective small-business owner. Without franchising it is doubtful that thousands of small-business investors could ever have started. The American consumer might well have been denied ready access to many products and services. The system permits these goods and services to be marketed without the vast sums of money and number of managerial people possessed only by large corporations. Therefore, it opens up economic opportunities for the small business.

But not even the help of a good franchiser can guarantee success. You will still be primarily responsible for the success or failure of your venture. As in any other type of business, your return will be related directly to the amount and effectiveness of your investment in time and money. Because of this, most of the suggestions and information in other chapters of this book are appropriate even though you plan to operate under a franchise.

Appendix A: Venture Capital Sources

Small Business Investment Companies (SBICs)

Following is an up-to-date listing of SBIC's, including the company contacts, and their locations. To understand the codes that accompany each listing, the explanation of codes that follows should be read before trying to contact a company.

Explanation of Codes

Preferred Limit for Loans or Investments

> A — up to $100,000
> B — up to $250,000
> C — up to $500,000
> D — up to $1-million
> E — Above $1-million

Investment Policy

> *   — Will consider either loans or investments
> ** — Prefers to make long-term loans
> *** — Prefers financings with right to acquire stock interest

Industry Preferences

> 1. Communications & Movies
> 2. Construction & Development
> 3. Natural Resources
> 4. Hotels, Motels & Restaurants
> 5. Manufacturing & Processing
> 6. Medical & Other Health Services

7. Recreation & Amusements
8. Research & Technology
9. Retailing, Wholesaling & Distribution
10. Service Trades
11. Transportation
12. Diversified

MESBIC—an SBIC which concentrates in placing its loans and investments with a small businessman who is socially or economically disadvantaged.

ALABAMA

Benson Investment Co., Inc.
Mr. W. T. Benson, Pres.
406 S. Commerce St.
Geneva, AL 36340
(205) 684-2824
A * 9

Coastal Capital Co.
Mr. David C. Delaney, Inv. Mgr.
3201 Dauphin St., Suite B
Mobile, AL 36606
(205) 476-0700
B * 2

First Small Business Investment Co.
    of Alabama
Mr. David C. Delaney, Pres.
3201 Dauphin St., Suite B
Mobile, AL 36606
(205) 476-0700
B * 12

Western Financial Capital Corp.
Mr. Fredric M. Rosemore, Pres.
306 North Temple Ave.
Fayette, AL 35555
(205) 932-3528
A * 12

ARIZONA

American Business Capital Corp.
Mr. Leonard A. Frankel, Pres.
3550 N. Central, Suite 520
Phoenix, AZ 85012
(602) 277-6259
A ** 12

ARKANSAS

First SBIC of Arkansas, Inc.
Mr. Fred C. Burns, Pres.
Room 702, Worthen Bank Bldg.
Little Rock, AR 72201
(501) 378-1876
A *** 12

Kar-Mal Venture Capital, Inc.
Mr. Tommy Karam, Pres.
Suite 917, University Towers Bldg.
Little Rock, AR 72204
(501) 661-0010
MESBIC B *** 9

Small Business Investment Capital,
    Inc.
Mr. C. E. Toland, Pres.
10003 New Benton Highway
Little Rock, AR 72203
(501) 455-2234
B ** 9

Equitable Capital Corp.
Mr. John C. Lee, Pres.
419 Columbus Ave.
San Francisco, CA 94133
(415) 982-4028
MESBIC A *** 12

Florists' Capital Corp.
Mr. Christopher M. Conroy, Pres.
10524 W. Pico Blvd.
Los Angeles, CA 90064
(213) 204-6956
A * 2,7,9,10,12

Grocers Capital Co.
Mr. William O. Christy, Pres.
2601 S. Eastern Ave.
Los Angeles, CA 90040
(213) 728-3322
A ** 4,9

HUB Enterprises, Ltd.
Mr. Richard Magary, Gen. Mgr.
5874 Doyle St.
Emeryville, CA 94608
(415) 653-5707
MESBIC A * 2,5,10,12

Imperial Ventures, Inc.
Mr. Richard D. Robins, VP
P.O. Box 92991
Los Angeles, CA 90009
(213) 649-3886
A *** 2,5,9,12

Krasne Fund for Small Business Inc.
Mr. Clyde A. Krasne, Pres.
432 S. Arnaz Dr., Suite #4
Los Angeles, CA 90048
(213) 274-7007
A * 2,5

Marwit Capital Corp.
Mr. Martin W, Wittee, Pres.
610 Newport Ctr. Dr., Suite 480
Newport Beach, CA 92660
(714) 640-6234
D *** 1,2,4,5,6,10,12

MCA New Ventures, Inc.
Mr. Norbert A. Simmons, Pres.
100 Universal City Plaza
Universal City, CA 91608
(213) 985-4321
MESBIC C *** 1,7

Branch Office:
Nelson Capital Corp.
Mr. Norman Tulchin, Chmn.
1901 Ave. of the Stars, Suite 584
Los Angeles, CA 90067
(213) 556-1944
D ** 12
(Main Office: NY)

Oceanic Capital Corp.
Mr. Robert H. Chappell, Pres.
350 California St., #2090
San Francisco, CA 94104
(415) 398-7677
B * 5,6,8

Opportunity Capital Corp.
Mr. J. Peter Thompson, Pres.
100 California St., Suite 714
San Francisco, CA 94127
(415) 421-5935
MESBIC B *** 1,5,9,11

Roe Financial Corp.
Mr. Martin J. Roe, Pres.
9000 Sunset Blvd., Suite 412
Los Angeles, CA 90069
(213) 275-4723
A * 5,9,10

San Joaquin Capital Corp.
Mr. Richard D. Robins, Pres.
P.O. Box 1555
Bakersfield, CA 93302
(805) 323-7581
B * 2,5,9,12

CALIFORNIA

Associates Venture Capital Corp.
Mr. Walter P. Strycker, Pres.
632 Kearney St.
San Francisco, CA 94108
(415) 981-4915
MESBIC B *** 5,6,9,12

BankAmerica Capital Corp.
Mr. Steven L. Merrill, Pres.
555 California St.
San Francisco, CA 94104
(415) 622-2271
E *** 5, 8

Brantman Capital Corp.
Mr. W. T. Brantman, Pres.
P.O. Box 877
Tiburon, CA 94920
(415) 435-4747
A *** 4,5,6,7,8,9,10,11,12

Brentwood Associates
Mr. Frederick J. Warren, Gen. Ptnr.
11661 San Vicente Blvd., Suite 707
Los Angeles, CA 90049
(213) 826-6581
E *** 1,3,5,6,8,9,10,11,12

Builders Capital Corp.
Mr. Victor Indiek, Pres.
2716 Ocean Park Blvd.
Santa Monica, CA 90406
(213) 450-0779
C * 2

Business Equity & Development
  Corp.
Mr. Ricardo J. Olivarez, Pres.
1411 W. Olympic Blvd.
Los Angeles, CA 90015
(213) 385-0351
MESBIC B *** 1,5,12

California Northwest Fund, Inc.
Mr. Kirk L. Knight, Pres.
Mr. Yung Wong, Sen. VP
Mr. Ken E. Joy, VP
Mr. H. Dubose Montgomery, Jr., VP
3000 Sand Hill Rd.
Menlo Park, CA 94025
(415) 854-2940
D * 12

California Partners
Mr. William H. Draper, III, Gen. Ptnr.
Two Palo Alto Sq., Suite 700
Palo Alto, CA 94304
(415) 493-5600
A *** 1,5,6,8

Branch Office:
Citicorp Venture Capital Ltd.
Mr. William T. Comfort, Chmn.
Mr. Larry J. Lawrence, Pres.
44 Montgomery St., Suite 3950
San Francisco, CA 94104
(415) 954-1155
E *** 1,3,5,6
(Main Office, NY)

Crocker Capital Corp.
Mr. Charles Crocker, Pres.
111 Sutter St., Suite 600
San Francisco, CA 94104
(415) 983-2156
B *** 1,3,4,5,6,8,9

Crocker Ventures, Inc.
Mr. Owen H. Harper, Chmn.
One Montgomery St.
San Francisco, CA 94104
(415) 983-7024
B *** 1,5,8,11

Crosspoint Investment Corp.
Mr. Max S. Simpson, Pres.
1015 Corporation Way
Palo Alto, CA 94303
(415) 964-3545
A *** 1,5,6,7,8,9,12

Developers Equity Capital Corp.
Mr. Larry Sade, Pres.
9201 Wilshire Blvd. #204
Beverly Hills, CA 90210
(213) 278-3611
B * 2,4

San Jose Capital Corp.
Mr. H. Bruce Furchtenicht, Pres.
130 Park Ctr. Plaza, Suite 132
San Jose, CA 95123
(408) 293-8052
A *** 1,5,6,8

Space Ventures, Inc.
Mr. Sidney Nadler, Pres.
3901 MacArthur Blvd., Suite 101
Newport Beach, CA 92660
(714) 851-0855
MESBIC E * 1,2,4,5,7,8,9,10,11,12

TELACU Investment Co., Inc.
Mr. Gus Paladines, Pres.
1330 S. Atlantic Blvd.
Los Angeles, CA 90022
(213) 268-6745
MESBIC C * 3,5,8

Union Venture Corp.
Mr. Brent T. Rider, Pres.
445 S. Figueroa St.
Los Angeles, CA 90017
(213) 687-5797
C *** 12

Unity Capital Corp.
Mr. Frank W. Owens, Pres.
3620 30th St., Suite G
San Diego, CA 92104
(714) 295-6768
MESBIC A *** 12

West Coast Venture Capital
Mr. Gary W. Kalbach, Gen. Ptnr.
10375 Bandley Dr.
Cupertino, CA 95014
(408) 996-2702
C *** 1,5,8,12

Westamco Investment Co.
Mr. Leonard G. Muskin, Pres.
8929 Wilshire Blvd., Suite 400
Beverly Hills, CA 90211
(213) 652-8288
A * 2,6,7,12

Western Bancorp Venture Capital Co.
Mr. David B. Jones, Pres.
707 Wilshire Blvd., Suite 1850
Los Angeles, CA 90017
(213) 614-5903
D *** 12

COLORADO
Branch Office:
Central Investment Corp. of Denver
Mr. Blaine E. D'Arcey, Gen. Mgr.
1108 - 15th St.
Central Bank Bldg. West
Denver, CO 80202
(303) 825-3351
D *** 12
(Main Office Northwest Growth
   Fund, MN)

The Davis-Whittle Co.
Mr. Paul D. Whittle, Pres.
950 17th St., Suite 1630
Denver, CO 80202
(303) 629-0205
B *** 1,3,5,6,8,12

Denver Ventures, Inc.
Mr. Stanley Perea, Acting Pres.
4142 Tejon St.
Denver, CO 80211
(303) 433-8636
A * 12

Enervest, Inc.
MR. Mark Kimmel, Pres.
5500 S. Syracuse St.
Englewood, CO 80111
(303) 771-9650
B *** 1,3,5,6,7,8,12

CONNECTICUT
Branch Office:
Activest Capital Corp.
Mr. William N. Vitalis, Pres.
P.O. Box 76
Cornwall Bridge, CT 06754
(203) 672-6651
A * 2,12

APCO Capital Corp.
Mr. S. David Leibowitt, Pres.
63 Broad St.
Milford, CT 06460
(203) 877-5101
A * 2,5,8,11,12

Asset Capital & Management Corp.
Mr. Robert Nolting, VP
608 Ferry Blvd.
Stratford, CT 06497
(203) 375-0299
A ** 2,5

Capital Resource Co. of Connecticut
Mr. I. Martin Fierberg, Pres.
345 N. Main St., Suite 304
West Hartford, CT 06117
(203) 232-1769
A * 12

The First Connecticut SBIC
Mr. David Engelson, Pres.
Mr. James Breiner, Chmn.
177 State St.
Bridgeport, CT 06604
(203) 366-4726
D * 1,2,5,10,12
(Branch Office: NY)

Branch Office:
First Miami SBIC
Mr. Irve L. Libby, Pres.
P.O. Box P
Orange, CT 06477
(203) 799-2056
A * 1,7,10,12
(Main Office: FL)

Foster Management Co.
Mr. John H. Foster, Pres.
1010 Summer Street
Stamford CT 06905
(203) 348-4385
C *** 1,3,5,6,8,11

Hartford Community Capital Corp.
Mr. Roger E. Bunker, Pres.
777 Main St.
Hartford, CT 06115
(203) 728-2361
MESBIC A * 12

Manufacturers SBIC, Inc.
Mr. Louis W. Mingione, Exec. Dir.
310 Main St.
East Haven, CT 06512
(203) 469-7901
A * 12

Marcon Capital Corp.
Mr. Martin Cohen, Chmn.
49 Riverside Ave.
Westport, CT 06880
(203) 266-7751
B ** 12

Northern Business Capital Corp.
Mr. Joseph Kavanewsky, Pres.
P.O. Box 711
South Norwalk, CT 06856
(203) 866-1000
A * 5,9,12

Nutmeg Capital Corp.
Mr. Leigh B. Raymond, Exec. VP
35 Elm St.
New Haven, CT 06510
(203) 776-0643
A * 1,2,5,12

SBIC of Connecticut
Mr. Kenneth F. Zarilli, Pres.
1115 Main St.
Bridgeport, Ct 06604
(203) 367-3282
B ** 12

DISTRICT OF COLUMBIA

Allied Capital Corp.
Mr. George C. Williams, Pres.
Mr. David Gladstone, Exec. VP
1625 1 St. NW
Washington, DC 20006
(202) 331-1112
C * 1,2,4,5,6,7,9,10,11,12
(Branch: FL)

Amistad DOT Venture Capital, Inc.
Mr. Percy E. Sutton, Pres., Chmn.
1125 15th St., NW
Washington, DC 20005
(202) 466-4323
MESBIC C * 11,12
(Branch Office: NY)

Branch Office:
Broad Arrow Investment Corp.
Mr. Hugh Mulligan
1701 Pennsylvania Ave., NW
Washington, DC 20006
(202) 452-6680
MESBIC A * 4,5,6,9,10,11,12
(Main Office: NJ)

Capital Investment Co. of
    Washington
Mr. Jay Goldberg, Acting Pres.
1010 Wisconsin Ave. NW #900
Washington, DC 20007
(202) 298-3229
A *** 6,12

Columbia Ventures, Inc.
Mr. Richard Whitney, Pres.
1835 K St. NW
Washington, Dc 20006
(202) 659-0033
FULLY INVESTED
(Branch Office: MS)

D.C. Investment Co.
Mr. Joseph D. Jackson, Pres.
1420 New York Ave., NW
Washington,DC 20005
(202) 628-0303
MESBIC C * 1,2,4,5,6,9,10

Fulcrum Venture Capital Corp.
Mr. Steven L. Lilly, Pres.
Suite 714, 2021 K St., NW
Washington, DC 20006
(202) 833-9580
MESBIC B * 12

Greater Washington Investors, Inc.
Mr. Don A. Christensen, Pres.
1015–18th St., NW
Washington, DC 20036
(202) 466-2210
B *** 5,8,12

FLORIDA

Branch Office:
Allied Capital Corp.
Mr. George C. Williams, Pres.
1614 One Financial Plaza
Ft. Lauderdale, FL 33394
(305) 763-8484
C *** 1,2,4,5,6,9,10,11,12
(Main Office: DC)

Biscayne Capital Corp.
Mr. Ruy R. Sanches, Chmn.
100 N. Biscayne Blvd., Suite 2803
Miami, FL 33132
(305) 371-3500
MESBIC A *** 12

Corporate Capital Inc.
Mr. Jerry Thomas, Pres.
2001 Broadway
First Marine Bank Bldg.
Riviera Beach, FL 33404
(305) 844-6070
B * 12

Cuban Investment Capital Co.
Mr. Anthony G. Marina, Pres.
7425 NW 79th St.
Miami, FL 33166
(305) 855-8881
MESBIC A * 12

The First American Lending Corp.
Mr. G. M. Caughlin, Pres.
1200 N. Dixie Hwy.
Lake Worth, FL 33460
(305) 586-0146
MESBIC B * 2,4,5

First Miami SBIC
Mr. Irve L. Libby, Pres.
1195 NE 125th St.
North Miami, Fl 33161
(305) 893-5537
A * 1,7,10,12
(Branch Office: CT)

Gulf Coast Capital Corp.
Mr. Oscar M. Tharp. Pres.
70 N. Baylen St.
P.O. Box 12790
Pensacola, FL 32575
(904) 434-1361
B * 12

LeBaron Capital Corp.
Mr. Roy Hess. Pres.
4900 Bayou Blvd. Suite 106
Pensacola, FL 32503
(904) 447-9733
A * 12

Market Capital Corp.
Mr. E. E. Eads, Pres.
1102 N. 28th St.
Tampa, FL 33605
(813) 247-1357
A * 9

The M.E.S.B.I.C., Inc.
Mr. LeBon B. Walker, Mg. Dir.
3830 W. Flagler St.
Coral Gables, FL 33134
(305) 448-9770
MESBIC B *** 5,6,12

The Quiet SBIC
Mr. Ed Gray, III, VP
105 E. Garden St.
Pensacola, FL 32501
(904) 434-5090
A * 12

Safeco Capital, Inc.
Dr. Rene J. Leonard,Pres.
8770 SW 8th St.
Miami, FL 33174
(305) 551-0809
MESBIC B * 12

Small Business Assistance Corp.
Mr. Charles S. Smith, Pres.
2615 W. 15th St.
P.O. Box 1627
Panama City, FL 32401
(904) 785-9577
C * 4

Southeast SBIC, Inc.
Mr. Clement L. Hofmann, Pres.
100 S. Biscayne Blvd.
Miami, FL 33131
(305) 577-3174
C *** 12

Universal Financial Services, Inc.
Mr. Norman W. Zipkin, CEO
225 NE 35th St.
Miami, FL 33137
(305) 573-6326
MESBIC A *** 1,2,10,12

GEORGIA

Affiliated Investment Fund, Ltd.
Mr. Sameul Weissman, Pres.
2225 Shurfine Dr.
College Park, GA 30337
(404) 766-0221
A ** 9

CSRA Capital Corp.
Mr. Allen F. Caldwell, Jr., Pres.
1058 Claussen Road, Suite 102
P.O. Box 11045
Augusta, GA 30907
(404) 736-2236
B *** 2

Branch Office:
CSRA Capital Corp.
1401 West Paces Ferry Road, NW,
    Suite #E-116
Atlanta, GA 30327
(404) 231-1313

Enterprises NOW, Inc.
Mr. Hugh Dash, Pres.
898 Beckwith St., SW
Atlanta, GA 30314
(404) 753-1163
MESBIC B * 12

Fidelty Capital Corp.
Mr. Alfred F. Skiba, Pres.
180 Interstate North Pkwy. Suite
    400
Atlanta, GA 30339
(404) 955-4313
C *** 2,12

Investor's Equity, Inc.
Mr. Robert W. Fisher, Dir.
2902 1st Nat'l Bank Tower
Atlanta, GA 30303
(404) 658-1002
A *** 2,5,12

Mome Capital Corp.
Mr. J. A. Hutchinson, Pres.
234 Main - P.O. Box 960
Thomson, GA 30824
(404) 595-1507
A *** 12

Rio Investment Corp.
Mr. John Mock, Pres.
1415 Industry Ave.
Albany, GA 31702
(912) 435-3575
A * 9

Southeastern Capital SBIC
Mr. J. Ray Efird, Pres.
100 Northcreek, 3715 Northside
    Pkwy, NW, Suite 505
Atlanta, GA 30327
(404) 237-1567
B *** 12

Southern Investment and Funding
    Corp.
Mr. George Eng, Pres.
300 W. Peachtree St.
Atlanta, GA 30308
(404) 522-9151
MESBIC A * 12

HAWAII
Pacific Venture Capital, Ltd.
Mr. Michael J. Coy, Pres.
1505 Dillingham Blvd.
Honolulu, HI 96734
(808) 847-6502
MESBIC B * 12

SBIC of Hawaii, Inc.
Mr. James W. Y. Wong, Chmn.
1575 S. Beretania St.
Honolulu, HI 96826
(808) 946-1171
A *** 2,12

IDAHO
First Idaho Venture Capital Corp.
Mr. Dick B. Miller, VP
One Capitol Ctr., Suite 1102
Boise, ID 83702
(203) 345-3460
A * 5,9,10,12

ILLINOIS
Abbott Capital Corp.
Mr. Richard E. Lassar, Pres.
120 S. LaSalle St., Suite 1100
Chicago, IL 60603
(312) 726-3803
B *** 5,6,10,12

Agribusiness Capital Co.
Mr. James W. Erickson, Pres.
1401 N. Western Ave.
Lake Forest, IL 60045
(312) 295-6300
C *** 3

Amoco Venture Capital Co.
Mr. L. E. Schaffer, Pres.
200 E. Randolph
Chicago, IL 60601
(312) 856-6523
MESBIC B *** 12

Chicago Community Ventures, Inc.
Ms. Phyllis George, Pres.
19 S. LaSalle St., Suite 1114
Chicago, IL 60603
(312) 726-6984
MESBIC B *** 12

Chicago Equity Corp.
Mr. Morris Weiser, Pres.
One IBM Plaza
Chicago, IL 60611
(312) 321-9662
A *** 12

Combined Opportunities, Inc.
Mr. Peter H. Ross, VP
300 N. State St.
Chicago, IL 60610
(312) 266-3091
MESBIC B * 5,9,12

CEDCO Capital Corp.
Mr. Frank B. Brooks, Pres.
Mr. Joseph W. Miller, VP
180 N. Michigan, Suite 333
Chicago, IL 60601
(312) 984-5971
MESBIC A *** 1,4,5,6,7,9,10.11,12

Continental Illinois Venture Corp.
Mr. John L. Hines, Pres.
Suite 1617 - 231 S. LaSalle St.
Chicago, IL 60693
(312) 828-8023
D *** 12

Branch Office:
Evergreen Capital Corp.
Mr. Jeffery C. Garvey, Exec. VP
208 S. LaSalle St., Suite 1990
Chicago, IL 60604
C *** 12
(Main Office: Houston, TX)

First Capital Corp. of Chicago
Mr. Carl Thoma, Acting Pres.
One First National Plaza, Suite
   2628
Chicago, IL 60670
(312) 732-8060
E *** 12

Frontenac Capital Corp.
Mr. Martin J. Koldyke, Pres.
208 S. LaSalle St.
Chicago, IL 60604
(312) 368-0047
D *** 12

Heizer Capital Corp.
Mr. E. F. Heizer, Jr., Chmn.
20 N. Wacker Dr.
Chicago, IL 60606
(312) 641-2200
E *** 1,3,5,6,7,8,11,12

Branch Office:
Nelson Capital Corp.
Mr. Irwin B. Nelson, Pres.
8550 W. Bryn Mawr Ave., Suite 515
Chicago, IL 60631
(312) 693-5990
D ** 12
(Main Office: NY)

Tower Ventures Inc.
Mr. Ray J. Graham, Pres.
Sears Tower
Chicago, IL 60684
(312) 875-0564
MESBIC B * 12

United Capital Corp. of Illinois
Mr. Jack K. Ahrens, VP
United Ctr., State and Wyman
Rockford, IL 61101
(815) 987-2179
C * 1,5,6,8

The Urban Fund of Illinois, Inc.
Mr. Peter H. Ross, Pres.
300 N. State St.
Chicago, IL 60610
(312) 266-3050
MESBIC B * 5,9,12

INDIANA
Tyler Refrigeration Capital Corp.
Mr. J. R. Widner, VP
2222 E. Michigan Blvd.
Michigan City, IN 46360
(219) 874-3181
A * 9

IOWA
MorAmerica Capital Corp.
Mr. Robert W. Alisop, Pres.
200 American Bldg.
Cedar Rapids, IA 52401
(319) 363-8249
C *** 12
(Branch Offices: MO, WI)

KANSAS
Kansas Venture Capital, Inc.
Mr. George L. Doak, Pres.
First National Bank Towers
One Townsite Plaza, Suite 1030
Topeka, KS 66603
(913) 233-1368
A *** 5

KENTUCKY
Equal Opportunity Finance Inc.
Mr. Frank P. Justice, Jr., Pres.
P.O. Box 1915
Louisville, KY 40201
(502) 583-0601
MESBIC A * 12

Financial Opportunities, Inc.
Mr. Anthony W. Foellger, Pres.
981 S. Third St.
Louisville, KY 40203
(502) 584-1281
A * 9

Mountain Ventures, Inc.
Mr. Frederick J. Beste, III, Pres.
911 N. Main St., Box 628
London, KY 40741
(606) 878-6635
(606) 864-5175
D * 1,2,3,5,6,7,10,11,12

LOUISIANA

Business Capital Corp.
Mr. David R. Burrus, Pres.
1732 Canal St.
New Orleans, LA 70112
(504) 581-4002
MESBIC E * 12

CADDO Capital Corp.
Mr. Thomas L. Young, Jr., Pres.
2924 Knight, Suite 335
Shreveport, LA 71105
(318) 865-4629
A *** 12

Capital for Terrebonne, Inc.
Mr. Hartwell A. Lewis, Pres.
1613 Barrow St.
P.O. Box 1868
Houma, LA 70361
(504) 868-3933
A ** 12

Commercial Capital, Inc.
Mr. Wes Pierce, Pres.
P.O. Box 939
Covington, LA 70433
(504) 892-4921
A ** 12

Commercial Venture Capital Corp.
Mr. William H. Jackson, Pres.
P.O. Box 21119
Shreveport, LA 71152
(318) 226-4602
A *** 12

Dixie Business Investment Co., Inc.
Mr. Steve K. Cheek, Pres.
P.O. Box 588
Lake Providence, LA 71254
(318) 559-1558
A ** 9

EDICT Investment Corp.
Mr. Clay V. Bland, Chief
   Operating Officer
2908 S. Carrollton Ave.
New Orleans, La 70115
(504) 861-2364
MESBIC A ** 12

The First SBIC of Louisiana
Mrs. Alma O. Galle, Pres.
133 S. Dongenois St.
New Orleans, LA 70119
(504) 523-6705
A * 12

First Southern Capital Corp.
Mr. John Crabtree, Chmn.
Mr. Dennis Cross, Pres.
6161 Perkins Rd., Suite 2-C
Baton Rouge, LA 70808
(504) 769-3004
B *** 12

Louisiana Equity Capital Corp.
Mr. N. L. Phillips, Exec. VP
Mr. W. W. Scheffy
451 Florida
Baton Rouge, LA 70801
(504) 389-4421
B ** 12

Royal Street Investment Corp.
Mr. William D. Humphries, Pres.
4646 One Shell Square
New Orleans, LA 70319
(504) 588-9271
B *** 12

Savings Venture Capital Corp.
Mr. David R. Dixon, Exec. VP
6001 Financial Plaza
Shreveport, LA 71130
(318) 687-8996
B * 12

Venturtech Capital, Inc.
Mr. E. M. Charlet, Pres.
Suite 706, Republic Tower
5700 Florida Blvd.
Baton Rouge, LA 70806
(504) 926-5482
B *** 12

MARYLAND

Albright Venture Capital, Inc.
Mr. William A. Albright, Pres.
8005 Rappahannock Ave.
Jessup, MD 20794
(301) 799-7935
MESBIC A * 2,4,9,10,11,12

Minority Investments, Inc.
Mr. Frederick L. Sims, Pres.
8121 Georgia Ave.
Silver Spring, MD 20910
(301) 589-6626
MESBIC A ** 2,6,9,10,11,12

MASSACHUSETTS

Advent Capital Corp.
David B. Croll, Chmn.
Mr. E. Roe Stamps, Pres.
111 Devonshire St.
Boston, MA 02109
(617) 725-2300
D * 1,3,5,6,8,12

Atlas Capital Corp.
Mr. Herbert Carver, Pres.
55 Court St., Suite 200
Boston, MA 02108
(617) 482-1218
B ** 12

Boston Hambro Capital Corp.
Mr. James F. Stone, Pres.
One Boston Pl.
Boston, MA 02106
(617) 722-7055
C *** 1,2,5,6,8,12
(Branch Office: NY)

Charles River Resources, Inc.
Mr. Richard M. Burnes, Jr., Pres.
133 Federal St., Suite 602
Boston, MA 02110
(617) 482-9370
B *** 1,5,6,8,12

Devonshire Capital Corp.
Mr. David D. Croll, Chmn.
111 Devonshire St.
Boston, MA 02109
(617) 725-2300
C * 1,3,5,6,8,12

First Capital Corp. of Boston
Mr. Richard A. Farrell, Pres.
100 Federal St.
Boston, MA 02110
(617) 434-2442
D *** 12

Hellman, Gal Capital Corp.
Mr. Joseph J. Gal, Pres.
One Federal St.
Boston, MA 02110
(617) 482-7735
C * 1,6,8,10,11

Massachusetts Capital Corp.
Mr. David V. Harkins, Pres.
1 Federal St.
Boston, MA 01945
(617) 426-2488
C * 1,3,5,6,10,11,12

Massachusetts Venture Capital Corp.
Mr. Charles T. Grigsby, Pres.
141 Milk St.
Boston, MA 02109
(617) 426-0208
MESBIC A *** 12

New England Enterprise Capital
  Corp.
Mr. Z. David Patterson, VP
28 State St.
Boston, MA 02109
(617) 742-0285
C *** 1,5,8,9,10,12

Schooner Capital Corp.
Mr. Vincent J. Ryan, Jr., Pres.
141 Milk St.
Boston, MA 02109
(617) 357-9031
C *** 1,5,8,10,12

Transatlantic Capital Corp.
Mr. Bayard Henry, Pres.
60 Batterymarch St., Rm 728
Boston, MA 02110
(617) 482-0015
C * 1,5,6,8

UST Capital Corp.
Mr. Stephen R. Lewinstein, Pres.
40 Court St.
Boston, MA 02108
(617) 726-7260
E * 1,2,3,5,6,8,12

WCCI Capital Corp.
Ms. Robin L. Chenarack, VP
791 Main St.
Worcester, MA 01610
(617) 791-0941
MESBIC A * 12

Worcester Capital Corp.
Mr. Robert L. Whitmore, Mgr.
446 Main St.
Worcester, MA 01608
(617) 853-7298
A * 5,6,8

MICHIGAN
Doan Resources Corp.
Mr. Ian R. N. Bund, VP
110 E. Grove St.
Midland, MI 48640
(517) 631-2623
C *** 3,5,6,8

Federated Capital Corp.
Mr. Louis P. Ferris, Jr., Pres.
20000 W. 12 Mile Rd.
Southfield, MI 48076
(313) 559-0554
A ** 12

Independence Capital Formation, Inc.
Mr. Walter M. McMurtry, Jr., Pres.
3049 E. Grand Blvd.
Detroit, MI 48202
(313) 875-7669
MESBIC B *** 2,5,8,9,11

Metro-Detroit Investment Co.
Mr. William J. Fowler, Pres.
18481 W. Ten Mile Rd., Suite 202
Southfield, MI 48075
(313) 557-3818
MESBIC B ** 9

Michigan Capital & Service, Inc.
Mr. Joseph F. Conway, VP
580 City Center Bldg.
Ann Arbor, MI 48104
(313) 663-0702
B *** 12

Motor Enterprises, Inc.
Mr. James Kobus, Mgr.
3044 W. Grand Blvd.
6-248 General Motors Bldg.
Detroit, MI 48202
(313) 556-4273
MESBIC A ** 5,9,10

PRIME, Inc.
Mr. Jimmy N. Hill, Pres.
1845 David Whitney Bldg.
Detroit, MI 48226
(313) 964-3380
MESBIC B * 12

MINNESOTA
Consumer Growth Capital
Mr. John T. Gerlach, Pres.
430 Oak Grove
Minneapolis, MN 55403
(612) 874-0694
B *** 1,4,5,10,12

Control Data Capital Corp.
Mr. Richard C. Pflager, Pres.
8100 34th Ave. South
P.O. Box 0
Minneapolis,MN 55440
(612) 853-5421
C *** 1,3,5,6,8,12

Control Data Community Ventures
    Fund, Inc.
Mr. Timothy J. O'Connor, Pres.
8100 34th Ave., South
Bloomington, MN 55420
(612) 853-8100
MESBIC C * 1,2,5,6,8,11

Eagle Ventures, Inc.
Mr. Thomas M. Neitge, VP
700 Soo Line Bldg.
Minneapolis, MN 55422
(612) 339-9693
C *** 1,5,6,7,8

First Midwest Capital Corp.
Mr. Alan K. Ruvelson, Pres.
15 S. Fifth St., Suite 700
Minneapolis, MN 55402
(612) 339-9391
B *** 12

Northland Capital Corp.
Mr. George G. Barnum, Jr., Pres.
613 Missabe Bldg.
227 W. First St.
Duluth, MN 55802
(218) 722-0545
A *** 12

North Star Ventures, Inc
Mr. Terrence W. Glarner, Exec, VP
Northwestern Financial Center,
    Suite 2301
7900 Xerxes Ave., South
Minneapolis, MN 55431
(612) 830-4550
B *** 1,5,6,7,8,11,12

Northwest Growth Fund, Inc.
Mr. Daniel J. Haggerty, Pres.
960 Northwestern Bank Bldg.
Minneapolis, MN 55402
(612) 372-8770
D *** 12
(Branch Offices: CO, OR)

Retailers Growth Fund, Inc.
Mr. Cornell L. Moore, Pres.
380 Gamble Bldg.,
    5100 Gamble Dr.
Minneapolis, MN 55416
(612) 546-8989
A * 9

Sagera Venture Corp.
Mr. Gerald Stone, Pres.
2850 Metro Dr.
Bloomington, MN 55420
(612) 854-2258
MESBIC A * 2,5,9,11

Westland Capital Corp.
Mr. James B. Goetz, Pres.
Suite 115, Hennepin Sq. Bldg.
2021 E. Hennepin Ave.
Minneapolis, MN 55413
(612) 331-9210
B * 1,5,6,9,10

MISSISSIPPI

Branch Office:
Columbia Ventures, Inc.
P.O Box 1066
Jackson, MS 39205
FULLY INVESTED
(Main Office: DC)

DeSoto Capital Corp.
Mr. William B. Rudner, Pres.
8885 E. Goodman
Olive Branch, MS 38654
(601) 895-4145
A *** 12

Invesat Corp.
Mr. J. Thomas Noojin, Chmn.
162 E. Amite St., Suite 204
Jackson, MS 39201
(601) 969-3242
C * 12

Sun Delta Capital Access Center, Inc.
Mr. Chalres Bannerman, Chmn.
819 Main St. - P.O. Box 588
Greenville, MS 08701
(601) 335-5291
MESBIC B *** 1,5,12

Vicksburg SBIC
Mr. David L. May, Treas.
P.O. Box 852
Vicksburg, MS 39180
(601) 636-4762
A * 5,9,12

MISSOURI

Bankers Capital Corp.
Mr. Raymond E. Glasnapp, Pres.
4049 Pennsylvania
Kansas City, MO 64111
(816) 531-1600
A * 12

Intercapco West, Inc.
Mr. Thomas E. Phelps, Pres.
7800 Bonhomme
St. Louis, MO 63105
(314) 863-0600
C * 1,2,3,5,11

Branch Office:
MorAmerica Capital Corp.
Mr. Robert L. Kuk, Reg. VP
Suite 600, 111 W. Port Plaza
St Louis, MO 63141
(314) 434-1822
C *** 12
(Main Office: IA)

Branch Office:
MorAmerica Capital Corp.
Mr. Larry C. Maddox, Reg. VP
Suite 2724A - Commerce Tower
911 Main St.
Kansas City, MO 64105
(816) 842-0114
C *** 12
(Main Office: IA)

NEBRASKA

Community Equity Corp. of Nebraska
Mr. Herbert M. Patten, Mgr.
5620 Ames Ave., Suite 109
Omaha, NE 68104
(402) 455-7722
MESBIC A * 12

NEW JERSEY

Broad Arrow Investment Corp.
Mr. C. N. Bellm, Pres.
P.O. Box 2231-R
Morristown, NJ 07960
(201) 452-6680
MESBIC A * 4,5,6,9,10,11,12
(Branch Office: DC)

Engle Investment Co.
Mr. Murray Hendel, Pres.
35 Essex St.
Hackensack, NJ 07601
(201) 489-3583
B * 12
(Branch Office: NY)

ESLO Capital Corp.
Mr. Leo Katz, Pres.
163 Washington St.
Morristown, NJ 07960
(201) 267-3152
A ** 12

Lloyd Capital Corp.
Mr. Solomon T. Scharf, Pres.
77 State Highway 5
Edgewater, NJ 07020
(201) 947-1717
D *** 12

Main Capital Investment Corp.
Mr. S. Sam Klotz, Pres.
818 Main St.
Hackensack, NJ 07601
(201) 489-2080
A *** 1,2,3,4,7,10,12

Monmouth Capital Corp.
Mr. Charles P. Kaempffer, VP
125 Wyckoff Rd.
P.O. Box 335
Eatontown, NJ 07724
(201) 542-4927
C * 12

Quidnet Capital Corp.
Mr. Stephen W. Fillo, Pres.
909 State Rd.
Princeton, NJ 08540
(609) 924-7665
B *** 12

Rutgers Minority Investment Co.
Mr. Louis T. German, Pres.
92 New St.
Newark, NJ 07102
(201) 648-5287
MESBIC A * 12

NEW MEXICO

Albuquerque SBIC
Mr. Albert T. Ussery, Pres.
P.O. Box 487
Albuquerque, NM 87103
(505) 247-4089
A *** 2,3,10,12

Associated Southwest Investors, Inc.
Mr. John R. Rice
2425 Alamo SE
Albuquerque, NM 87106
(505) 842-5955
MESBIC B * 1,5,8,12

Roger Cox SBIC
Mr. Roger S. Cox, Pres.
4121 Wyoming Blvd., NE
Albuquerque, NM 87111
(505) 293-3080
A * 2,12

First Capital Corp. of New Mexico
Ms. Shirley A. Williams, Pres.
8425 Osuna Rd., NE
Albuquerque, NM 87111
(505) 293-5057
A * 12

Fluid Capital Corp.
Mr. George T. Slaughter, Pres.
200 Lomas Blvd., NW, Suite 527
Albuquerque, NM 87102
(505) 243-2279
B * 2,12

Branch Office:
The Franklin Corp.
Mr. Herman E. Goodman, Pres.
200 Lomas Blvd., NW, Suite 818
Albuquerque, NM 87102
(505) 243-9680
D *** 1,5,7,8,12
(Main Office: NY)

New Mexico Capital Corp.
Mr. William R. Christy, Exec. VP
2900 Louisiana, NE, Suite 201
Albuquerque, NM 87110
(505) 293-7600
D * 2,10

Southwest Capital Investments, Inc.
Mr. Roger L. Ford, Pres.
8000 Pennsylvania Circle, NE
Albuquerque, NM 87110
(505) 265-9564
A ** 2,5,9

Venture Capital Corp. of New Mexico
Mr. Ben Bronstein, Pres.
5301 Central Avenue, NE, Suite 1600
Albuquerque, NM 87108
(505) 266-0066
B *** 4,5,12

NEW YORK

AMEV Capital Corp.
Mr. Martin S. Orland, Exec. VP
Two World Trade Center
Suite 9766
New York, NY 10048
(212) 775-1912
C *** 1,4,5,6,7,9,12

Branch Office:
Amistad DOT Venture Capital, Inc.
Mr. Percy E. Sutton, Chmn.
211 E. 43rd St., Suite 805
New York, NY 10017
(212) 490-3970
MESBIC C * 11,12
(Main Office: DC)

BanCap Corp.
Mr. William L. Whitely, Pres.
155 E. 42nd St.
New York, NY 10017
(212) 687-6470
MESBIC B *** 12

Basic Capital Corp.
Mr. Paul W. Kates, Pres.
40 W. 37th St.
New York, NY 10018
(212) 868-9645
A * 4,5,7,12

Beneficial Capital Corp.
Mr. John J. Hoey, Pres.
645 Fifth Ave.
New York, NY 10022
(212) 752-1291
A * 3,12

Bohlen Capital Corp.
Mr. Harvey Wertheim, Pres.
230 Park Ave., Suite 1260
New York, NY 10017
(212) 867-9535
D *** 3,5,6,8,12

Branch Office:
Boston Hambro Capital Corp.
17 E. 71st St.
New York, NY 10021
C *** 1,2,5,6,8,12
(Main Office: MA)

BT Capital Corp.
Mr. James G. Hellmuth, VP
600 Third Ave.
New York, NY 10016
(212) 692-4840
D *** 12

Capital for Future, Inc.
Mr. Jay M. Schwamm, Pres.
635 Madison Ave.
New York, NY 10022
(212) 759-8060
B *** 2,12

CEDC-MESBIC, Inc.
Mr. John L. Kearse, CEO
106 Main St.
Hempstead, NY 11550
(516) 292-9710
MESBIC B * 2,5,8,9,10,11,12

Central New York SBIC, Inc.
Mr. Robert E. Romig, Pres.
5900 South Salina
Syracuse, NY 13205
(315) 475-7201
FULLY INVESTED

Citicorp Venture Capital, Ltd.
Mr. William T. Comfort, Chmn.
Mr. Larry J. Lawrence, Pres.
399 Park Ave., 20th Fl.
New York, NY 10043
(212) 559-1113
E *** 1,3,5,6
(Branch Office: CA)

CMNY Capital Co., Inc.
Mr. Robert Davidoff, VP
77 Water St.
New York, NY 10005
(212) 437-7080
B *** 1,5,9,12

Cornell Capital Corp.
Mr. Barry M. Bloom, Pres.
405 Lexington Ave.
New York, NY 10017
(212) 490-9198
C * 12

Edwards Capital Corp.
Mr. Edward H. Teitlebaum, Pres.
1 Park Ave.
New York, NY 10016
(212) 686-2568
A ** 11

Branch Office:
Engle Investment Co.
Mr. Murray Henoel, Pres.
135 W. 50th St.
New York, NY 10020
(212) 757-9580
B * 12
(Main Office: NJ)

Equico Capital Corp.
Mr. Terrance G. Blount, Pres.
1270 Ave. of the Americas
New York, NY 10020
(212) 489-7033
MESBIC C *** 12

Equitable Small Business
    Investment Corp.
Mr. David Goldberg, Pres.
350 Fifth Ave., Suite 5805
New York, NY 10001
(212) 564-5420
A * 6

ESIC Capital, Inc.
Mr. George H. Bookbinder, Pres.
110 E. 59th St., Suite 1008
New York, NY 10022
(212) 421-1605
D ** 12

European Development Capital Corp.
Mr. Harvey Wertheim, Pres.
230 Park Ave., Suite 1260
New York, NY 10017
(212) 867-9535
D *** 3,5,6,8,12

Exim Capital Corp.
Mr. Victor Chun, Pres.
290 Madison Ave.
New York, NY 10017
(212) 683-3200
MESBIC A * 12

Fairfield Equity Corp.
Mr. Matthew A. Berdon, Pres.
200 E. 42nd St.
New York, NY 10017
(212) 867-0150
B *** 1,5,9

Fifty-Third St. Ventures, Inc.
Mr. Edwin A. Goodman, Pres.
One E. 53rd St.
New York, NY 10022
(212) 753-6300
D *** 1,4,5,6,12

Branch Office:
The First Connecticut SBIC
Mr. David Engelson, Pres.
Mr. James Breiner, Chmn.
680 Fifth Ave.
New York, NY 10019
(212) 541-6222
D * 1,2,5,10,12
(Main Office: CT)

First Wall Street SBIC, Inc.
Mr. John W. Chappell, Pres.
767 Fifth Ave., Suite 4403
New York, NY 10022
(212) 355-6540
A *** 3,8

The Franklin Corp.
Mr. Herman E. Goodman, Pres.
1 Rockefeller Plaza
New York, NY 10020
(212) 581-4900
D *** 1,5,7,8,12
(Branch Office: NM)

Fundex Capital Corp.
Mr. Howard Sommer, Pres.
525 Northern Blvd.
Great Neck, NY 11021
(516) 466-8550
C ** 12

Hanover Capital Corp.
Mr. Daniel J. Sullivan, Pres.
223 E. 62nd St.
New York, NY 10021
(212) 752-5173
B * 12

Intercoastal Capital Corp.
Mr. Herbert Krasnow, Pres.
380 Madison Ave., 18th Fl.
New York, NY 10017
(212) 986-0482
B * 2,4,5,6,7,9,11,12

Intergroup Venture Capital Corp.
Mr. Ben Hauben, Pres.
230 Park Ave.
New York, NY 10017
(212) 661-5420
A * 12

International Film Investors, Inc.
Mr. Josiah H. Child, Jr., Pres.
595 Madison Ave.
New York, NY 10022
(212) 832-1920
E *** 7

Irving Capital Corp.
Mr. J. Andrew McWethy, Exec. VP
One Wall St.
New York, NY 10015
(212) 487-6424
D *** 1,3,5,9,12

Japanese American Capital Corp.
Mr. Stephen Huang, Pres.
120 Broadway
New York NY, 10005
(212) 964-4077
MESBIC B * 2,4,5,9,10

Lake Success Capital Corp.
Mr. Herman H. Schneider, Pres.
5000 Brush Hollow Rd.
Westbury, NY 11590
(516) 997-4300
A *** 2

M & T Capital Corp.
Mr. Harold M. Small, Pres.
One M & T Plaza
Buffalo, NY 14240
(716) 842-4881
C *** 12

Midland Capital Corp.
Mr. Thomas B. Healy Jr., Pres.
110 William St.
New York, NY 10038
(212) 577-0750
D *** 12

Minority Equity Capital Co., Inc.
Mr. Patrick Owen Burns, Pres.
275 Madison Ave., Suite 1901
New York NY 10016
(212) 686-9710
MESBC C *** 1,5,6,8,9,12

Multi-Purpose Capital Corp.
Mr. Eli B. Fine, Pres.
31 South Broadway
Yonkers, NY 10701
(914) 963-2733
A ** 12

Nelson Capital Corp.
Mr. Irwin B. Nelson, Pres.
591 Stewart Ave.
Garden City, NY 11530
(516) 222-2555
D ** 12
(Branch Officees: IL, CA)

North Street Capital Corp.
Mr. Ralph L. McNeal, Pres.
250 North St., TA-2
White Plains, NY 10625
(914) 683-6306
MESBIC A *** 12

NYBDC Capital Corp.
Mr. Marshall R. Lustig, Pres.
41 State St.
Albany, NY 12207
(518) 463-2268
A *** 5

Percival Capital Corp.
Mr. George Simpson, Pres.
300 E. 42nd St. 2nd Fl.
New York, NY 10017
(212) 953-1474
B * 12

Pines Venture Capital Corp.
Mr. Robert H. Pines, Pres.
Suite 7929,
    One World Trade Center
New York, NY 10048
(212) 432-1660
A * 2,4,7,12

Pioneer Investors Corp.
Mr. James G. Niven, Pres.
One Battery Park Plaza
New York, NY 10004
(212) 248-2759
C *** 3,5,6,8

R & R Financial Corp.
Mr. Imre J. Rosenthal, Pres.
1451 Broadway
New York, NY 10036
(212) 790-1400
A * 12

Rand Capital Corp.
Mr. Donald A. Ross, Pres.
2600 Rand Bldg.
Buffalo, NY 14203
(716) 853-0802
B * 1,8,12

Realty Growth Capital Corp.
Mr. Lawrence A. Benenson, Pres.
575 Lexington Ave.
New York, NY 10022
(212) 755-9044
A ** 11

Royal Business Funds Corp.
Mr. Seon Pierre Bonan, Pres.
60 E 42nd St.
New York, NY 10017
(212) 986-8463
D * 2,7

Peter J. Schmitt SBIC, Inc.
Mr. Denis G. Riley, Mgr
678 Bailey Ave.
Buffalo, NY 14206
(716) 825-1111
A * 1,5,8,9,10,12

Sherwood Business Capital Corp.
Mr. Lewis R. Eisner, Pres.
230 Park Ave.
New York, NY 10017
(212) 661-2424
B ** 12

Small Business Electronics
  Investment Corp.
60 Broad St.
New York, NY 10004
(212) 952-7531
A * 12

Southern Tier Capital Corp.
Mr. Irving Brizel, Pres.
55 S. Main St.
Liberty, NY 12754
(914) 292-5508
A * 4,9

Sprout Capital Corp.
Mr. L. Robert Johnson, Pres.
140 Broadway
New York, NY 10005
(212) 943-0300
D * 1,3,4,5,6,8,9,10,12

Tappan Zee Capital Corp.
Mr. Jack Birnberg, Exec. VP
120 N. Main St.
New City, NY 10956
(914) 634-8890
(212) 562-9333
A *** 12

Taroco Capital Corp.
Mr. David Chang, Pres.
120 Broadway
New York, NY 10005
(212) 964-4210
MESBIC B * 12

Telesciences Capital Corp.
Mr. George Carmody, Pres.
135 E. 54th St.
New York NY 10022
(212) 935-2550
B *** 1

TLC Funding Corp.
Mr. Philip G. Kass, Pres.
200 E. 42nd St.
New York, NY 10017
(212) 682-0790
B *** 12

Van Rietschoten Capital Corp.
Mr. Harvey Wertheim, Pres.
230 Park Ave., Suite 1260
New York, NY 10017
(212) 867-9535
D *** 3,5,6,8,12

Vega Capital Corp.
Mr. Victor Harz, Pres.
10 E. 40th St., Suite 4010
New York, NY 10016
(212) 685-8222
D * 12

Winfield Capital Corp.
Mr. Stanley Pechman, Pres.
237 Mamaroneck Ave.
White Plains, NY 10605
(914) 949-2600
C * 12

Wood River Capital Corp.
Mr. Edward B. Ory, Pres.
645 Madison Ave.
New York, NY 10022
(212) 355-3860
D * 12

NORTH CAROLINA

Delta Capital, Inc.
Mr. A. B. Wilkins, Jr., Pres.
Mr. Walter H. Wilkinson, Jr., VP
202 Latta Arcade
Charlotte, NC 28202
(704) 372-1410
B *** 1,2,3,4,5,6,9,11

Heritage Capital Corp.
Mr. Randy Gregory, Pres.
2290 First Union Plaza
Charlotte, NC 28282
(704) 334-2867
D *** 12

Vanguard Investment Co., Inc.
Mr. James F. Hansley, Pres.
309 Pepper Bldg.
Winston Salem, NC 27101
(919) 724-3676
MESBIC B *** 1,4,5,6,12

NORTH DAKOTA

First Dakota Capital Corp.
Mr. James S. Lindsay, Pres.
317 S. University Dr.
Fargo, ND 58103
(701) 237-0450
A * 2,4,5,9,10,12

OHIO

Clarion Capital Corp.
Mr. Peter D. Van Oosterhout, Chmn.
Union Commerce Bldg. Arcade—
   Room 1000
Cleveland, OH 44115
(216) 687-1096
D *** 1,2,5,12

Community Venture Corp.
Mr. Si Sokol, Pres.
88 E. Broad St., Suite 1520
Columbus, OH 43215
(614) 228-2800
A ** 12

Dayton MESBIC, Inc.
Mr. L. A. Lucas, Pres.
Miami Valley Tower, Suite 1820
40 W. Fourth St.
Dayton, OH 45402
(513) 223-9405
MESBIC B * 12

Dycap, Inc.
Mr. A. Gordon Imhoff, Pres.
88 E. Broad St., Suite 1980
Columbus, OH 43215
(614) 228-6641
A * 12

Branch Office:
Evergreen Capital Corp.
Mr. Jeffery C. Garvey, Exec. VP
3733 Park East Drive
Cleveland, OH 44122
C *** 12
(Main Office: Houston, TX)

Fourth Street Capital Corp.
Mr. Robert H. Leshner, Pres.
508 Dixie Terminal Bldg.
Cincinnati, OH 45202
(513) 579-0414
B *** 2,5,9,10

Glenco Enterprises, Inc.
Dr. Lewis F. Wright, Jr., VP
1464 E. 105th St.
Cleveland, OH 44106
(216) 721-1200
MESBIC B *** 12

Greater Miami Investment Service,
   Inc.
Mr. Emmett Lewis, Pres.
3131 S. Dixie Dr., Suite 505
Dayton, OH 45439
(513) 294-6124
B * 5,12

Gries Investment Co.
Mr. Robert D. Gries, Pres.
2310 Terminal Tower
Cleveland, OH 44113
(216) 861-1146
B *** 12

Intercapco, Inc.
Mr. Ronald E. Weinberg, Pres.
Mr. Robert Haas, Exec. VP
One Erieview Plaza
Cleveland, OH 44114
(216) 241-7170
C *** 1,3,5,9

National City Capital Corp.
Mr. Michael Sherwin, pres.
623 Euclid Ave.
Cleveland, OH 44114
(216) 861-4900 ext. 121
C * 1,3,5,6,8,10,11,12

Tamco Investors, Inc.
Mr. Nathan H. Monus, Pres.
375 Victoria Rd.
Youngstown, OH 44515
(216) 792-0805
A ** 5,9

Tomlinson Capital Corp.
Mr. John A. Chernak, VP
13700 Broadway
Cleveland, OH 44125
(216) 663-3363
A ** 5,9

OKLAHOMA
Activest Capital Corp.
Mr. Willim N. Vitalis, Pres.
6212 N. Western
Oklahoma City, OK 73118
(405) 840-5597
A * 2,12
(Branch Office: CT)

Alliance Business Investment Co.
Mr. Barry M. Davis, Pres.
Suite 500, Mcfarlin Bldg.
11 E. Fifth St.
Tulsa, OK 74103
(918) 584-3581
B *** 3,5,12
(Branch Office: TX)

Bartlesville Investment Corp.
Mr. J. L. Diamond, Pres.
P.O. Box 548
Bartlesville, OK 74003
(918) 333-3022
A *** 2,3,12

Investment Capital, Inc.
Mr. James J. Wasson, Pres.
101 W. Broadway
Cushing, OK 74023
(918) 225-5850
A * 2,5,6,9,11

Oklahoma Capital Corp.
Mr. William T. Daniel, Pres.
2200 Classen Blvd., Suite 540
Oklahoma City, OK 73106
(405) 525-5544
A * 6

Southwest Venture Capital, Inc.
Mr. D. J. Rubottom, Pres.
1920 First Pl.
Tulsa, OK 74103
(918) 584-4201
A *** 5,6,9,10

OREGON
Branch Office:
Cascade Capital Corp.
Mr. Wayne B. Kingsley, VP
1300 SW Fifth Ave., Suite 3018
Portland, OR 97201
(503) 223-6622
D *** 12
(Main Office: Northwest Growth
    Fund, MN)

Northern Pacific Capital Corp.
Mr. John J. Tennant, Jr., Pres.
P.O. Box 1530
Portland, OR 97207
(503) 245-3147
B *** 1,3,5,10,11

PENNSYLVANIA

Alliance Enterprise Corp.
Mr. Richard H. Cummings, Jr., Pres.
1616 Walnut St., Suite 802
Philadelphia, PA 19103
(215) 972-4230
MESBIC B *** 1,5,9

American Venture Capital Co.
Mr. Knute C. Albrecht, Exec. VP
Suite 200, Axe Wood West
Skippack Pike & Butler Pike
Ambler, PA 19002
(215) 643-5955
B *** 12

Capital Corp. of America
Mr. Martin M. Newman, Pres.
1521 Walnut St.
Philadelphia, PA 19102
(215) 563-7423
B *** 2,3,4,5,6,8,10

Central Capital Corp.
Mr. John G. Schofer, VP
1097 Commercial Ave.
P.O. Box 3595
Lancaster, PA 17604
(717) 569-9650
B *** 12

Greater Philadelphia Venture
  Capital Corp., Inc.
Mr. Wilson E. DeWald, VP
225 S. 15th St., Suite 920
Philadelphia, PA 19130
(215) 732-3415
MESBIC B *** 12

Osher Capital Corp.
Mr. L. Cantor, Pres.
Wyncote House
Township Line Road & Washington
  Lane
Wyncote, PA 19095
(215) 624-4800
B *** 5,6,9,10,12

Sharon SBIC
Mr. H. David Rosenblum, Pres.
385 Shenango Ave.
Sharon, PA 16146
(412) 981-1500
A * 9

TDH Capital Corp.
Mr. J. Mahlon Buck, Jr., Pres.
P.O. Box 234
Two Radnor Corporate Ctr.
Radnor, PA 19087
(215) 293-9787
C *** 12

PUERTO RICO

North American Investment Corp.
Mr. Santiago Ruiz-Bentancourt,
  Pres.
G.P.O. Box 6066
San Juan, PR 00936
(809) 759-7860
MESBIC A * 5,9,10,12

RHODE ISLAND

Industrial Capital Corp.
Mr. A.A.T. Wickersham, Pres.
111 Westminster St.
Providence, RI 02903
(401) 278-6770
C *** 12

Narragansett Capital Corp.
Mr. Arthur D. Little, Pres.
40 Westminster St.
Providence, RI 02903
(401) 751-1000
E * 1,5,9,10,12

SOUTH CAROLINA
Charleston Capital Corp.
Mr. Henry Yaschik, Pres.
134 Meeting St.
Charleston, SC 29402
(803) 723-6464
A * 2,4,12

TENNESSEE
C & C Capital Corp.
Mr. Don L. Jones, Pres.
P.O. Box 90
1 Regency Sq.
Knoxville, TN 37901
(615) 637-9220
B *** 12

Chickasaw Capital Corp.
Mr. Wayne J. Haskins, Pres.
67 Madison P.O. Box 387
Memphis, TN 38147
(901) 523-6404
MESBIC A *** 12

Financial Resources, Inc.
Mr. Milton C. Picard, Chmn.
2800 Sterick Bldg.
Memphis, TN 38103
(901) 527-9411
A *** 4,5,12

Tennessee Equity Capital Corp.
Mr. Richard Kantor, Pres.
4515 Poplar Ave., Suite 222
Memphis, TN 38117
(901) 761-3410
MESBIC B * 12

TEXAS
Branch Office:
Alliance Business Investment Co.
Mr. Barry M. Davis, Pres.
2660 S. Tower
Pennzoil Pl.
Houston, TX 77002
(713) 224-8224
B *** 3,5,12
(Main Office, OK)

Allied Bancshares Capital Corp.
Mr. D. Kent Anderson, Pres.
P.O. Box 3326
Houston, TX 77001
(713) 224-6611
D * 1,2,3,4,5,6,7,8,9,10,11

Brittany Capital Corp.
Mr. Robert E. Clements, Pres.
2424 LTV Tower
1525 Elm St.
Dallas, TX 75201
(214) 742-5810
D *** 12

Capital Marketing Corp.
Mr. John King Myrick, Pres.
9001 Ambassador Row
Dallas, TX 75247
(214) 638-1913
C ** 9

CSC Capital Corp.
Mr. William R. Thomas, Pres.
12900 Preston Rd., Suite 700
Dallas, TX 75230
(214) 233-8242
C *** 1,3,5,6,7,8,9,11,12

Diman Financial Corp.
Mr. Don Mann, CEO
13601 Preston Rd., Suite 717E
Dallas, TX 75240
(214) 233-7610
A *** 2,3

Energy Assets, Inc.
Mr. L. E. Simmons, VP
1800 S. Tower, Pennzoil Pl.
Houston, TX 77001
(713) 236-9999
B *** 3

Evergreen Capital Corp.
Mr. Jeffery C. Garvey, Exec. VP
7700 San Felipe, Suite 180
Houston, TX 77063
(713) 783-5003
C *** 12
(Branch Offices: TX, OH, IL)

Branch Office:
Evergreen Capital Corp.
Mr. Jeffery C. Garvey, Exec. VP
1500 City National Bank Bldg.
Austin, TX 78701
C *** 12
(Main Office: Houston, TX)

First Bancorp Capital, Inc.
Mr. George F. Baum, Jr., Pres.
100 N. Main St.
Corsicana, TX 75110
(214) 874-4711
A *** 2,3,5,9,10

First Dallas Capital Corp.
Mr. Eric C. Neuman, Pres.
P.O. Box 83385
Dallas, TX 75283
(214) 744-8050
D *** 12

Great American Capital Investors,
   Inc.
Mr. Albert S. Dillard, Pres.
P.O. Box 449, 1006 Holiday
Wichita Falls, TX 76307
(817) 322-4448
A *** 9

Grocers SBIC
Mr. Milton Levit, Pres.
3131 E. Holcombe Blvd.
Houston, TX 77021
(713) 747-7913
A ** 9

Livingston Capital Ltd.
Mr. J. Livingston Kosberg, Pres.
5701 Woodway, Suite 336
Houston, TX 77057
(713) 977-4040
B * 12

Mercantile Dallas Corp.
Mr. James B. Gardner, Pres.
P.O. Box 222090
Dallas, TX 75222
(214) 741-1469
E ** 12

MESBIC Financial Corp. of Dallas
Mr. Walter W. Durham, Pres.
Empire Central Bldg., Suite 850
7701 N. Stemmons Freeway
Dallas, TX 75247
(214) 637-0445
MESBIC B * 12

MESBIC Financial Corp. of Houston
Mr. Richard Rothfeld, Pres.
717 Travis, Suite 600
Houston, TX 77002
(713) 228-8321
MESBIC A * 12

MESBIC of San Antonio
Mr. A. John Yoggerst, VP
2300 West Commerce
San Antonio, TX 78207
(512) 224-0909
MESBIC B *** 3,5,9

Permian Basin Capital Corp.
Mr. Douglas B. Henson, Pres.
303 W. Wall
Midland, TX 79701
(915) 685-2000
A * 12

Red River Ventures, Inc.
Mr. T. H. Schnitzius, Pres.
535 Houston Natural Gas Bldg.
Houston, TX 77002
(713) 658-9806
B *** 12

Republic Venture Group, Inc.
Mr. William R. Cain, Pres.
P.O. Box 225961
Dallas, TX 75265
(214) 653-6933
C *** 12

Rice Country Capital, Inc.
Mr. William H. Harrison, Jr., Pres.
100 Commerce—P.O. Box 215
Eagle Lake, TX 77434
(713) 234-2506
A * 12

San Antonio Venture Group, Inc.
Mr. William A. Fagan, Jr., Pres.
2300 Commerce
San Antonio, TX 78207
(512) 223-3633
B *** 1,3,4,5,6,7,8,9,11

The SBIC of Houston
Mr. William E. Ladin, Pres.
1510 Esperson Bldg.
Houston, TX 77002
(713) 223-5337
B *** 2,5,9,11,12

Texas Capital Corp.
Mr. W. Grogan Lord, Chmn.
2424 Houston Natural Gas Bldg.
Houston, TX 77002
(713) 658-9961
C *** 1,5,6,9,10,12

Trammell Crow Investment Corp.
Mr. George Swanson, Pres.
2001 Bryan, Suite 3200
Dallas, TX 75201
(214) 651-0346
E * 2

TSM Corp.
Mr. L. Joe Justice
4171 N. Mesa, Suite A203
El Paso, TX 79902
(915) 533-6375
A * 12

West Central Capital Corp.
Mr. Howard W. Jacob, Pres.
440 Northlake Ctr., Suite 206
Dallas, TX 75238
(214) 348-3969
A *** 2,4,5,6,12

VERMONT
Mansfield Capital Corp.
Mr. Stehen H. Farrington, Pres.
Mountain Rd.
Stowe, VT 05672
(802) 253-9400
A * 2,9,11,12

Vermont Investment Capital, Inc.
Mr. Harold Jacobs, Pres.
Box 84
South Royalton, VT 05068
(802) 763-8878
A * 12

VIRGINIA
East West United Investment Co.
Mr. Bui Dung, Pres.
6723 Whittier Ave., Suite #206B
McLean, VA 22101
(703) 821-6616
MESBIC A * 4,9,12

Inverness Capital Corp.
Mr. Harry Flemming, Pres.
424 N. Washington St.
Alexandria, VA 22314
(703) 549-5730
C *** 12

Metropolitan Capital Corp.
Mr. P. W. Scoville, Pres.
2550 Huntington Ave.
Alexandria, VA 22303
(703) 960-4698
B * 12

Norfolk Investment Co., Inc.
Mr. Kirk W. Saunders, Pres.
201 Granby St., Suite 515
Norfolk, VA 23510
(804) 622-0013
MESBIC B * 5,9,10,12

Virginia Capital Corp.
Mr. Robert H. Pratt, Pres.
P.O. Box 1493
Richmond, VA 23212
(804) 644-5496
B *** 1,3,4,5,8,12

WASHINGTON
Market Acceptance Corp.
Mr. Archie E. Iverson, Pres.
1718 NW 56th, Suite B
Seattle, WA 98107
(206) 782-7600
A * 2,6

Northwest Business Investment
   Corp.
Mr. C. Paul Sandifur, Chmn.
W. 929 Sprague Ave.
Spokane, WA 99204
(509) 838-3111
A * 7

Northwest Capital Investment Corp.
Mr. Dale H. Zeigler, Pres.
1940 — 116th Ave., NE
P.O. Box 3500
Bellevue, WA 98009
(206) 455-3049
B *** 12

Trans-Am Bancorp, Inc.
Mr. Harold T. Wosepka, Pres.
3211 NE 78th St.
Vancouver, WA 98665
(206) 574-4749
A *** 2

Washington Capital Corp.
Mr. G. A. Scherzinger, Mgr.
1417 Fourth Ave.
Seattle, WA 98101
(206) 682-5400
D ** 12

Washington Trust Equity Corp.
Mr. Alan Bradley, Pres.
P.O. Box 2127
Spokane, WA 98210
(509) 455-4206
C *** 12

WISCONSIN
CERTCO Capital Corp.
Mr. Howard E. Hill, Pres.
6150 McKee Rd.
Madison, WI 53711
(608) 271-4500
A ** 9

Branch Office:
Moramerica Capital Corp.
Mr. Gregory B. Bultman, Reg. VP
Suite 333, 710 N. Plankington Ave.
Milwaukee, WI 53203
(414) 276-3839
C *** 12
(Main Office: IA)

SC Opportunities, Inc.
Mr. Robert L. Ableman, Sec'y
1112 7th Ave.
Monroe, WI 53566
(608) 328-8400
MESBIC A *** 9

Venture Capital Publications

Guide to Venture Capital Sources (5th ed.), 1981
Capital Publishing Corporation
P.O. Box 348, Two Laurel Ave.
Wellesley Hills, MA 02181

Small Business Administration (SBA) Field Offices

Agana, GU	Knoxville, TN
Albany, NY	Las Vegas, NV
Albuquerque, NM	Little Rock, AR
Anchorage, AK	Los Angeles, CA
Atlanta, GA	Louisville, KY
Augusta, ME	Lubbock, TX
Baltimore, MD	Madison, WI
Biloxi, MS	Marquette, MI
Birmingham, AL	Marshall, TX
Boise, ID	Melville, NY
Boston, MA	Memphis, TN
Buffalo, NY	Milwaukee, WI
Camden, NJ	Minneapolis, MN
Casper, WY	Montpelier, VT
Charleston, WV	Nashville, TN
Charlotte, NC	Newark, NJ
Chicago, IL	New Orleans, LA
Cincinnati, OH	New York, NY
Clarksburg, WV	Oklahoma City, OK
Cleveland, OH	Omaha, NB
Columbia, SC	Philadelphia, PA
Columbus, OH	Phoenix, AZ
Concord, NH	Pittsburgh, PA
Coral Gables, FL	Portland, OR
Corpus Christi, TX	Providence, RI
Dallas, TX	Rapid City, SD
Denver, CO	Reno, NV
Des Moines, IA	Richmond, VA
Detroit, MI	Rochester, NY
Eau Claire, WI	St. Louis, MO
Elmira, NY	St. Thomas, VI
El Paso, TX	Sacramento, CA
Fairbanks, AK	Salt Lake City, UT
Fargo, ND	San Antonio, TX
Fresno, CA	San Diego, CA

Greenville, NC
Harlingen, TX
Harrisburg, PA
Hartford, CT
Hato Rey, PR
Helena, MT
Holyoke, MA
Honolulu, HI
Houston, TX
Indianapolis, IN
Jackson, MS
Jacksonville, FL
Kansas City, MO

San Francisco, CA
Seattle, WA
Shreveport, LA
Sioux Falls, SD
Spokane, WA
Springfield, IL
Syracuse, NY
Tampa, FL
Washington, DC
West Palm Beach, FL
Wichita, KS
Wilkes-Barre, PA
Wilmington, DE

Appendix B: Small Business Financial Status Checklist

What an Owner-Manager Should Know

Daily

1. Cash on hand.
2. Bank balance (keep business and personal funds separate).
3. Daily Summary of sales and cash receipts
4. All errors in recording collections on accounts are corrected.
5. A record of all monies paid out, by cash or check, is maintained.

Weekly

1. Accounts Receivable (take action on slow payers).
2. Accounts Payable (take advantage of discounts).
3. Payroll (records should include name and address of employee, social security number, number of exemptions, date ending the pay period, hours worked, rate of pay, total wages, deductions, net pay, check number).
4. Taxes and reports to State and Federal Government (sales, withholding, social security, etc.).

Monthly

1. All Journal entries are classified according to like elements (these should be generally accepted and standardized for both income and expense) and posted to General Ledger.
2. A Profit and Loss Statement for the month is available within a reasonable time, usually 10 to 15 days following the close of the month. This shows the income of the business for the month, the expense incurred in obtaining the income, and the profit or loss resulting. From this, take action to eliminate loss (adjust markup? reduce overhead expense? pilferage? incorrect tax reporting? incorrect buying procedures? failure to take advantage of cash discounts?).

3. A Balance Sheet accompanies the Profit and Loss Statement. This shows assets (what the business has), liabilities (what the business owes), and the investment of the owner.
4. The Bank Statement is reconciled. (That is, the owner's books are in agreement with the bank's record of the cash balance.)
5. The Petty Cash Account is in balance. (The actual cash in the Petty Cash Box plus the total of the paid-out slips that have not been charged to expense total the amount set aside as petty cash.)
6. All Federal Tax Deposits, Withheld Income and FICA Taxes (Form 501) and State Taxes are paid.
7. Accounts Receivable are aged, i.e., 30, 60, 90 days, etc., past due. (Work all bad and slow accounts.)
8. Inventory Control is worked to remove dead stock and order new stock. (What moves slowly? Reduce. What moves fast? Increase.)

Appendix C: Advertising and Marketing Sources

Associations

Media associations will emphasize the benefits of the media they represent, of course. Nevertheless, much of their promotional literature is helpful.

American Business Press, 205 East 42nd Street, New York, N.Y. 10017.

Direct Mail/Marketing Association, 6 East 43rd Street, New York, N.Y. 10017.

Institute of Outdoor Advertising, 485 Lexington Avenue, New York, N.Y. 10017.

Junior Panel Outdoor Advertising Association, 130 Union Street, Springfield, Mass. 01101.

Magazine Publishers Association, Magazine Advertising Bureau, 575 Lexington Avenue, New York, N.Y. 10022.

National Association of Advertising Publishers, 315 Price Place, Madison, Wis. 53705.

National Retail Merchants Association, 100 West 31st Street, New York, N.Y. 10001.

Newspaper Advertising Bureau, 750 Third Avenue, New York, N.Y. 10017.

Rario Advertising Bureau, 555 Madison Avenue, New York, N.Y. 10022.

Television Bureau of Advertising, 1345 Avenue of the Americas, New York, N.Y. 10019.

Transit Advertising Association, 1725 K Street, N.W., Washington, D.C. 20006.

Your own trade association, may publish advertising aids and information. Find out what is available there.

Media Directories

Standard Rate and Data Services, Inc., 5201 Old Orchard Road, Skokie, Ill. 60076, supplies basic information for approximately 14,000 media in a number of directories, many of them monthly. These publications, which are available in many public libraries, include the following:

> *Business Publication Rates and Data*
> *Consumer Magazine and Farm Publication Rates and Data*
> *Direct Mail Lists Rates and Data*
> *Network Rates and Data*
> *Newspaper Circulation Analyses*
> *Newspaper Rates and Data*
> *Spot Radio Rates and Data*
> *Spot Television Rates and Data*
> *Transit Advertising Rates and Data*
> *Weekly Newspaper and Shopping Guide Rates and Data*

Another helpful guide available in public libraries or from the publisher, is:

> *Ayers Directory of Publications*, One Bala Ave., Bala Cynwyd, Pa. 19004

Index

Lee, Byron: mail order business, 82
Legal advice for buying a business, 180
Life insurance agent: as a business, 56
Literary Market Place, 11

Mailing list, 154
Mailing piece, 154
Mail order: as a business, 72–85; in advertising, 153–155
Management assistance, 129–134
Management of a business, 159–166; organization chart, 159–160; hiring, 160–162; record keeping, 162–166
Market price, determining, 135–142
Market research, 136–138
Minority Enterprise Small Business Investment Companies (MESBICs), 125, 192–217
Model dressers: as a business, 47–48
Modeling: as a business, 51–53
Money: how to raise, 119–121; where to find, 123–127; 191–218
Moneysworth, 81

National Science Foundation, 127
Newspaper advertising, 148–150

Off-set printing, 21–22
Operating costs, 99–106
Organization chart, 159–160
Original documents: bookkeeping, 163
Outdoor advertising, 157
Overhead, 99–104

Partnership, 92–95
Partners: management assistance, 129–131
Party service: as a business, 38
Patent: application for, 19
Patent and Trademark Office, 19
Personal bookkeeping: as a business, 32
Photographic modeling: as a business, 52–53
Photography: as a business, 9–10
Plan for advertising, 144–148
Postage costs: mail order, 155

Price, determining the, of a business, 179–180
Prices, guidelines for establishing, 138–140
Printing broker: as a business, 62–64
Printing Industries of America, Inc., 62
Profit and Loss (P&L), 108–109
Profit potential, 176–177
Profit trend, 176
Proprietorship, single or sole, 90–92
Public relations: as a business, 41–43
Publisher's Weekly, 69
Purchase orders and invoices, 164–165

Real estate, agent or broker: as a business, 57–59
Record keeping, techniques of, 162–166
Remaindered books, 68
Return on investment, estimated, 177
Return on Investment (ROI) formula, 123
Roby, Tom: franchise business, 183
Run of Press (R.O.P.), 150

Sales businesses, 55–69
Sales, calculating, 140–142
Sales projections, 110–111
Sales representative: as a business, 59–62
Self businesses, 9–85; hobbies, 9–19; technical, 21–29; services, 31–43; creative, 45–53; sales, 55–69; mail-order, 72–85
Self-Employment Individual Tax Retirement Act, 103
Selling, direct: as a business, 64–67
Service businesses, 31–43
Shopping service: as a business, 36–37
Showcase trimmers: as a business, 47–48
Single or sole proprietorship, 90–92
Small Business Administration (SBA), 125, 126, 127, 183; field offices, 218–219